RADICAL SECTS OF
REVOLUTIONARY NEW ENGLAND

STEPHEN A. MARINI

Radical Sects
of Revolutionary
New England

Harvard University Press

Cambridge, Massachusetts
&
London, England

1982

Publication of this book has been aided by a grant from the
Andrew W. Mellon Foundation

Library of Congress Cataloging in Publication Data
Marini, Stephen A., 1946-
Radical sects of revolutionary New England.
Bibliography: p.
Includes index.
1. Christian sects—New England. 2. New England—Church history. I. Title.
BR520.M36   289   81-6913
AACR2
ISBN 0-674-74625-2

TO SHARON

Love is the sweetest bud that blows,
Its beauty never dies;
On earth among the saints it grows,
And ripens in the skies.
— *The Christian Harmony,* 1866

Acknowledgments

Scholarship is a collective enterprise. Many people have contributed in signal ways to the shaping of this book. Among my teachers and colleagues, Clarke Garrett, Giles Gunn, Martin Marty, Richard Bushman, Daniel Patterson, Charles Long, and Donald Mathews each provided valuable insights on the problem of sectarianism in America. George Huntston Williams and Stephen Botein read and offered helpful criticism of an earlier version. Conrad Wright generously shared with me his immense knowledge of New England church history through every stage of the book's evolution.

During the lengthy preparation of the manuscript, Patricia O'Brien, Karin Knudsen, Patricia Renzi, and Claire Minty translated my inchoate drafts into accurate typescript. At Harvard University Press, Aida Donald's confidence brought this book to fruition, while the editorial staff patiently corrected errors and efficiently directed the manuscript in press.

This work is based on widely scattered and fugitive manuscripts and rare imprints. I wish to thank the librarians and staffs of the following institutions for their unstinting and expert assistance: American Antiquarian Society; American Baptist Historical Society; Andover-Newton Theological Library; Berkshire Atheneum; Congregationalist Library; Emma B. King Memorial Library; Andover-Harvard Theological Library, Houghton Library, and Widener Library of Harvard University; Henry Francis Du Pont Winterthur Museum; Library of the United Society of Shakers; Maine Historical Society; Massachusetts State Archives; New Durham, New Hampshire, Public Library; New Hampshire Historical Society; New Hampshire State Library; Universalist Historical Society; Vermont Historical Society; and Western Reserve Historical Society.

While conducting this research I have been privileged to meet the United Society of Shakers at Sabbathday Lake, Maine. The society and its leaders, Sister R. Mildred Barker, Sister Frances Carr, and Brother Theodore E. Johnson, kindly welcomed me, provided free access to their library, cheerfully answered my many questions, and lovingly gave of their time and substance, minds and hearts. In them a vigorous Maine tradition yet bears witness to the power of Mother Ann Lee's message.

Finally, I wish to give special thanks to William R. Hutchison, Charles Warren Professor of the History of Religion in America at Harvard Divinity School. Since the inception of this work, he has been a constant source of gentle encouragement and perceptive criticism. His probing commentary on successive drafts instilled in me the historian's disciplines of clarity, rigor, and comprehensiveness. Beyond this, his personal integrity, breadth of mind, and exacting standards of scholarship have established for me the criteria of humane learning.

None of these people are in any way responsible for the shortcomings of this book. What pleasure they take in it is but a small return on the debt I owe them.

Contents

Introduction

This book is a study of religious change as manifested in sectarianism. Specifically, it is an examination of the development of religious sects in rural New England during the era of the American Revolution. The most important sects of that time and place called themselves by names scarcely remembered in the twentieth century: Believers in Christ's Second Appearing; Independent Christians; the Church of Christ at New Durham, New Hampshire. They came to be known as the Shakers, the Universalists, and the Freewill Baptists.

These new religious sects of the 1780s challenged the basic tenets of orthodox New England Calvinism, developed successful alternative ecclesiastical organizations, and created innovative forms of ritual expression. They represented the first large-scale popular rejection of Calvinist beliefs and practices in New England's history. This mass movement of dissent flourished in the subsistence farm society of central, western, and northern New England. The zenith of Shaker, Universalist, and Freewill Baptist influence occurred between 1790 and 1820. By the latter date these three sects had established more than three hundred congregations and claimed over fifteen thousand members. They represented more than one fourth of all church organizations and membership in Maine, Vermont, New Hampshire, and western Massachusetts. How this phenomenon came about and what it means are the principal questions addressed in this book.

A sect may be defined as a new form of religious culture that emerges from and in opposition to an antecedent tradition. Sectarian movements are often initiated by charismatic leaders, prophets who break away from the familiar religiousness of their societies by means of intense and lasting spiritual experiences and doctrinal insights. The genesis of new religious groups like the Shakers, Universalists, and Freewill Baptists is to be found in the complex biographies of such leaders, but sects are far more than the lengthened shadows of their founders. The move from idiosyncrasy to a permanent constituency requires both an effective strategy of evangelism and a pool of potential converts. Once a social constituency is discovered, however, the sectarian leaders face the crucial task of differentiating themselves from other faiths. This is accomplished through a gradual process of improvisation and experiment that, if successful, eventuates in the creation of distinctive social organizations, ideologies, and liturgical symbols. The combination of all these elements into a coherent style of religious life constitutes a new religious culture. It is this process of religious change resulting in the creation of a substantively innovative religious culture that I call sectarianism.

Sectarian movements have been of enormous importance in the history of American religions. Sectarianism is a principal source of religious pluralism in America. The characteristic conflict and diversity of American Protestantism have been manifested most clearly in the rise of literally hundreds of sectarian groups. Sects have also been a major consequence of revivalism, another central trait of American religion. Revivals have stimulated and facilitated the emergence of new religions since the Great Awakening. Sectarianism has also been associated with the American frontier experience. The constant reconstruction of society necessitated by the wilderness brought with it an incessant demand for new religious forms.

In response to such a complex and significant phenomenon scholars, primarily historians and sociologists, have offered diverse explanations and analyses. The classic sociological studies of Max Weber and Ernst Troeltsch examined the economic assumptions and social teachings of sectarian movements. The next generation, represented by R. H. Tawney, Elie Halévy, and H. Richard Niebuhr, sought the causes of sectarianism in class antagonism and economic dispossession. In the 1940s and 1950s sociologists like Milton Yinger applied structural-functional analysis to discover the rationale of sectarian institutions. And more recently the work of Bryan Wilson has inspired a typological approach to sects based on psychological response to the secular world.

American historians have also pursued different kinds of inquiry into sectarian movements. Church historians have supplied detailed descriptive accounts mixed with theological advocacy. This enterprise continues today with results of increasing sophistication and objectivity. Among academic historians, the need for dispassionate descriptions of American sects was first supplied by Elmer T. Clark and Charles Braden in the 1930s and 1940s. The landmark interpretations, however, were Alice Felt Tyler's *Freedom's Ferment* and Whitney Cross's *The Burned-Over District*. The former depicted sects as products of an exuberant democratic national character, while the latter argued that "enthusiastic religion" was a consequence of the impact of rapid economic development on traditional society. A new line of interpretation opened in 1962 with C. C. Goen's exploration of religious dissent as a function of revivalism. Since then, there has appeared a wide range of new studies investigating the political and intellectual dimensions of sectarian movements. A fair measure of the new historical awareness of sects is the prominent place they occupy in the general histories of American religion written by Sydney Ahlstrom, Winthrop Hudson, and Robert T. Handy.

Despite the contributions of these works, important lacunae exist in American sectarian studies. With the significant exception of Cross's *Burned-Over District,* written in 1950, no study has examined patterns of sectarianism on a regional scale over several decades. Since most sects acquire regional geographical distribution and constituency, this lack is a serious one. A second weakness is the lack of comparative studies of American sects. Edwin Gaustad's *Dissent in American Religion* is a fine example of intersectarian analysis based on general theological orientation, and John M. Whitworth's *God's Blueprints* and Lawrence Foster's *Religion and Sexuality* make important sociological analyses of sectarian life. But aside from this work, little has been done to compare sects across time or space or to interpret them as parts of larger movements of religious change. Yet a third issue is the problem of sects as new religions. Sectarian scholars have not paid close attention to the processes of religious development revealed by sectarian movements. Their efforts have been directed mainly toward finding causes for sectarianism in nonreligious historical or sociological factors. The crucial matter of how new religions emerge and achieve coherent form remains largely unassayed.

Many questions of sectarian studies can be addressed through an examination of rural New England in the late eighteenth and early nineteenth centuries. The New England case is important because it contains all the elements requisite for the analysis of the sectarian process and also because it is the earliest example of that process in American history. It is also virtually unstudied. The rise of three major and a host of minor sects in Revolutionary New England is noted only by church historians of Shakerism, Universalism, and the Freewill Baptists. Aside from nineteenth-century works by sectarian clergy, few modern critical studies of these three movements have appeared. Universalism has been well served by George Huntston Williams's *American Universalism: A Bicentennial Essay* and Donald Miller's *The Larger Hope: A History of the Universalist Churches in America, 1770–1870;* Shakerism has been chronicled in Edward D. Andrews's *The People Called Shakers* and Marguerite Melcher's *The Shaker Adventure;* the only modern monograph on the Freewill Baptists is Norman Baxter's *History of the Freewill Baptists.* All these works, however, are general treatments or denominational works that do not focus on the questions of sectarianism as a historical process and the comparative analysis of the three groups. William McLoughlin's *New England Dissent, 1630–1833* and C. C. Goen's *Revivalism and Separatism in New England, 1740–1800* come closest to presenting a comprehensive view of New England sectarianism, but both these works concentrate primarily on the Baptists.

To understand the meaning of these movements it is necessary to begin with a historical overview. What has been termed sectarianism — the appearance of indigenous new religious cultures — did not occur in New England in the century after settlement. Rather, the region was thoroughly dominated by the Puritan tradition of British Calvinism. Aside from a scattering of Baptist and Quaker congregations, New England before 1740 was solidly Congregationalist. Congregationalism was the established religion, resting on state maintenance and taxation, a powerful organization of geographical parishes, a learned clergy trained at Harvard and Yale, and a clear standard of orthodoxy articulated in the Cambridge and Saybrook Platforms. Though Congregationalism admitted a certain degree of theological diversity, it was solidly and irrevocably rooted in the doctrines of Calvinism classically expressed in the Westminster Confession of Faith.

The first major outbreak of religious dissent in New England was the result of America's first mass revival, the Great Awakening of 1736–1745. Sparked by the itinerant preaching of George Whitefield and the theological explication of Jonathan Edwards, the revival swept New England with radical demands for spiritual rebirth, moral purity, and emotional engagement with religion. Whitefield went as far as to instruct revived saints to shun the preaching of "unconverted" ministers; and when Whitefield's disciple James Davenport called on the regenerate to come out and be a separate people, many responded.

The Separate, or Strict, Congregationalists were New England's first native sectarian movement, but they failed to consolidate their innovations into distinctive form. Though they incorporated many of Whitefield's revivalistic standards, the Separates did not take issue with the basic theological tenets of Calvinism. Their major contribution was in the area of ecclesiology. Separates endorsed itinerancy and experiential standards for membership and ministerial calling, and attacked the union of church and state. But no decisively new theological standard or liturgical reform or principle of polity distinguished Separates from revivalistic but nonseparating New Light Congregationalists. And the Separate movement proved transient. The speedy accumulation of nearly one hundred Separate congregations in New England during the 1740s and 1750s was followed by an equally quick decline as many churches reunited with the Congregationalist establishment and others joined the Baptist denomination.

The Baptists were the major beneficiaries of the religious dissent generated by the Great Awakening. The Calvinistic, or Particular, Baptists organized their first association in America at Philadelphia in 1707. After the Great Awakening in New England the appeal of Baptist associational polity and of adult baptism as a model of apostolic imitation made the Baptists attractive to restive Separates. By the mid-1750s Separates and Baptists had become roughly equal in size and influence, and thereafter the Baptists became the leading party of dissent within New England Calvinism. In 1767 the Warren, Rhode Island, Baptist Association was organized, providing the first stable institutional structure for Calvinist dissenters.

This first episode of sectarian process generated by the Great Awakening has ambiguous results. Though the revival produced dissent, it did not cause new converts to break with their Calvinist traditions. New ecclesiastical lines were formed, but these groupings occurred for political and ecclesiological reasons, and not from any thoroughgoing rejection or critique of Calvinism. Established Congregationalism had proven able to withstand the shock of revival. As many New Lights had remained in the state church as had left it. The most serious divisions between pro- and antirevival forces had gradually healed. Congregationalism by 1770 could still claim to represent the full amplitude of the New England tradition, and by the Revolution no direct challenge to the Westminster, Cambridge, and Saybrook standards had yet appeared. Dissent existed in the form of the Baptists and remaining Separates, groups that did reject the New England way of church and state but that also continued to endorse the corpus of Calvinist religion. Indeed the Separates claimed that their polity was the true Cambridge norm, while the Baptists embraced the Savoy Confession of 1688, a virtually verbatim version of the Westminster Confession with changes in the mode of baptism and the definition of ecclesiastical organization. Organized dissent remained Calvinist before the Revolution. Sectarianism had appeared in New England but had yet to reach full fruition.

The moment of radical religious change came quickly, however. The Revolution threw New England's cultural institutions into turmoil. The Congregationalist churches suffered severe damage to the parish system as war took a physical, financial, and clerical toll that took until 1790 to recover. During the 1770s and especially immediately after the war, New England experienced yet another societal shock in the form of mass migration to the hill country of the northern and western frontier. Thousands of emigrants from southeastern and coastal New England flocked to newly opened lands in Maine, Vermont, New Hampshire, and the Berkshire Hills of Massachusetts. Many, perhaps most, of these settlers were prorevival New Lights of some kind: Separate, Baptist, or Congregationalist. This massive encounter with the frontier was unprecedented in New England and American history, and it introduced grave problems of social and cultural fragmentation to a generation already bent on establishing national and regional autonomy. The combination of frontier experience, revolution, and a strongly Evangelical Calvinist cohort of settlers resulted, not surprisingly, in the largest revival in New England since the Great Awakening. From 1778 to 1782 a massive frontier revival raged across the hill country spreading millennial expectation and renewal of the Whitefieldian demand for the New Birth.

It was in this turbulent paroxysm of religious, political, social, and economic unrest that radical sectarian movements took their origin in New England. Sectarian prophets—Ann Lee, Caleb Rich, and Benjamin Randel—converged on the northern frontier from Britain and coastal New England. They proclaimed new gospels that pressed far beyond the protests of Separates and Baptists to fundamental critiques of Calvinism and its religious culture. The Shaker Ann Lee proclaimed that the original sin was sexual intercourse, that its only remedy was a celibate life, and that Christ had already made a second appearing in the form of the perfecting action of the Holy Spirit on her and her followers. Universalist Caleb Rich announced that Calvinism's basic tenets of limited atonement and double predestination were false. Instead, he claimed to have received visionary evidence that all human beings would be saved by a benevolent God whose good intentions toward his creatures could not fail to be accomplished. The Freewill Baptist prophet Benjamin Randel also challenged the predestinarian scheme from another perspective. He, too, appealed to visionary experience in proclaiming that God did not damn or save souls, that humans were free to decide their eternal destiny for themselves. Christ's atonement was universal, he said, and was delivered to our minds by the Holy Spirit for our independent judgment to consider; having freely chosen grace, humans could gain the ability to live free of sin.

These radical new gospels and the charismatically gifted prophets who promulgated them were the catalysts of New England sectarianism. In the heat of the New Light revival of 1778–1782 the founders gathered large followings among the Evangelical Calvinists of the hill country. By the mid-1780s these adherents had begun to form distinct sectarian movements, experimenting with new forms of polity, discipline, doctrine, and liturgy. Around 1790 all these nascent sects experienced severe crises of leadership and discipline that propelled them to develop new and systematic plans of church order, theology, and worship. By the mid-1790s the elements of these new religious cultures had cohered, membership had consolidated and expanded, and the first permanent indigenous religious alternatives to Calvinism had been born.

With the appearance of the Shakers, Universalists, and Freewill Baptists, a new stage in the religious history of New England opened. To be sure, Calvinistic Baptists also continued to grow in the last decades of the eighteenth century, and the Second Great Awakening of 1798–1808 consolidated those gains while introducing the Arminian theology of Methodism to rural New England. Out of the Second Awakening also came other indigenous New England sects, the most important being Elias Smith's

Christian Connection and Joseph Smith's Church of Latter-Day Saints, which repeated the growth and cultural development processes of the earlier rural movements. In the first decades of the nineteenth century Unitarianism emerged as yet another indigenous New England movement proposing a liberal anti-Calvinist gospel. But all these developments followed rather than preceded the pluralization of New England religion by the rural Shakers, Universalists, and Freewill Baptists. These were the first native religious movements to attack the Calvinist tradition directly and radically; the first to encounter the archetypal social realities of frontier, revolution, and revival in their most potent combination; the first to construct complete and countervailing religious cultures out of the raw materials of rural New England society.

Each of these sects was unique in its religious culture. The Shakers, Universalists, and Freewill Baptists represented the explosion and fragmentation of Calvinism into many sectarian groups in the hill country. But at the same time these three sects were indissolubly linked by time, space, constituency, and tradition. Together they represented the rejection and transformation of Calvinism by the Revolutionary generation in the New England hills. The sectarians remained a minority movement. At their peak around 1815 they collectively embodied less than a third of hill country religion; Congregationalists and Baptists divided the other two thirds equally. And the sectarians would soon reach steady state, ceasing to grow with vigor or to continue their furious religious creativity after 1840. Yet the pluralization and radicalization they brought to New England religion persisted long afterward in the successes of Methodists, Christians, and Mormons in the nineteenth century. And beyond these direct historical conquences lies the larger importance of these apparently obscure New England sects: In their emergence and maturation the grip of colonial religious culture was broken and a new American style of religious diversity came into being.

One

The
Sectarian
Impulse

1

Radical Evangelicalism

On 30 September 1770 George Whitefield, the Grand Itinerant of the Great Awakening, died of asthma at Newburyport, Massachusetts. His death was mourned by thousands in New England for whom he had become the embodiment of charismatic religion, a prophetic voice blessed by the power of God. In the 1740s the young Whitefield and other "sons of thunder"—James Davenport, Gilbert Tennent, Eleazar Wheelock, David Ferriss—had awakened multitudes by preaching the necessity of the New Birth. Their dramatic message created a generation of seekers who followed the dictates of their own spiritual gifts into schismatic dissent from normative New England Congregationalism.

Many at first organized independent Strict Congregationalist churches. A number of these in turn embraced Calvinist Baptist principles in the 1750s and 1760s. Some, like Wheelock and Ferriss, ranged farther afield to find solace in Presbyterianism and Quakerism. Still others withdrew from church institutions altogether, "standing separate" in informal family and neighborhood conventicles. This diffuse religious movement was Radical Evangelicalism.[1] Ill-organized yet numerically significant, even preponderant, in southeastern New England and the Connecticut Valley, this extreme wing of the Great Awakening was shaped and lastingly influenced by Whitefield's leadership.

Not only in the halcyon days of the Awakening but also in thirty years of subsequent evangelistic tours, Whitefield provided a model and a style for the radical piety he introduced to New England. In a 1757 letter, Eleazar Wheelock spoke for all Whitefieldians in describing the itinerant's visits in the 1740s and 1750s. "Every journey you have taken through New

England, has been eminently serviceable . . . [the] first, for awakening and rousing the stupid and secure. After that, to discredit and beat down a false religion. Your last to remove prejudices from the minds of many against you, and the work of God."[2] Whitefield returned in 1764–65 and again in 1769–70, bringing hopes that somehow revival could reverse the political tide drawing Britain and America apart. These expectations were crushed by his death at the age of fifty-eight, and the movement he had spawned faced a darkening future bereft of its most powerful unifying force. A local poet in the *New Hampshire Gazette* expressed the dismay of Radical Evangelicals at Whitefield's passing:

> His joys are full — while miserable we
> Are left behind to mourn the heavy loss,
> Both to ourselves, and all AMERICA —
> No Whitefield now with tears to plead our cause![3]

In the autumn of 1770 the Radical Evangelicals embarked on a new and curious history of migration, revival, and sectarianism. Part of that history has been ably told, namely that of the Separate Congregationalists and Baptists. But there were other more fugitive branches of their movement that blossomed into the first indigenous religious sects of independent America: Shakers, Freewill Baptists, and Universalists. This is their story, and it begins with the religious milieu generated in the first instance by George Whitefield.

The Whitefieldian gospel was comprehensive but not systematic. It was Calvinist, but it neither dilated on theological problems nor spoke the language of doctrine and hermeneutic. It was more a matter of style and emphasis, drama and rhetoric designed to move emotions and change hearts. The center of Whitefield's message was a new metaphysic of experience that located the crucial transaction between God and humans in an instantaneous conversion of the soul. New England Puritans had understood salvation to depend on covenants made between the Trinity and the human race. Persons included in Christ's covenant of grace returned faith to God and received sanctification in this world and heaven after death. But the inscrutability of God's electing will made certainty of sainthood unattainable. Regeneration was therefore always couched in terms of "reasonable hope" and "evidence of grace" rather than experiential surety. Puritans from William Perkins to Solomon Stoddard elaborated a "morphology of conversion," successive states of consciousness through which the hopeful saint could evaluate the evidence of divine election. Every step in this lifelong process of growth in grace was carefully defined by appropriate attitudes and behavior. In principle, the Puritans never knew they were saved; they could only trust that their minds were enabled by grace to penetrate beyond the veil and dimly discern the hand of God leading them to glory.[4]

Whitefield shortened the morphology of conversion, swept away the casuistry of covenantalism, and focused the issue of salvation on the moment of conversion itself. His God, though still demanding just punishment for sin, actively sought the salvation of sinners, requiring them only to reach out for the "free grace" available through faith in Christ. Divine grace for Whitefield did not operate through slow-moving "legal" stages of growth. It produced its own evidence in the unique and transforming effect it wrought upon the soul. Whitefield called this experience "the New Birth" and cited it as the sine qua non of true religion. The New Birth was a self-validating sacred event in which the Holy Spirit implanted itself directly in the soul as indubitable evidence of divine grace. It was experienced as an act of comprehension between the faithful soul and an electing God, a discrete, punctiliar event that occurred in the twinkling of an eye.

Whitefield's New Birth was not merely an intellectual or psychological phenomenon. He described it as a total renovation of mind and body — the making of a new creature: "The new life imparts new principles, a new understanding, a new will, and new affections, a new conscience, a renewed memory, nay, a renewed body."[5] Other Evangelical interpreters of conversion, particularly Jonathan Edwards, relied on the psychological theory of British empiricism to account for the New Birth through a "spiritual sense" bestowed on the saint by the Holy Spirit. Whitefield postulated no such agency, arguing that the Spirit itself united with the human organism at the moment of conversion. It was not through a new spiritual faculty but precisely through the natural sensory and intellectual capacities of human beings that the Spirit performed its sanctifying work.[6]

This concept opened Calvinism to the acceptance of a whole range of physical, sensory, emotional, and visionary experiences hitherto excluded as enthusiasm by the Puritan morphology of conversion. By the logic of the New Birth, hysterical spasms, glossolalia, trances, and the like became symptoms of spiritual transformation. In principle the transforming effects of the New Birth could even induce Christian perfection and new revelation as the Spirit opened body and soul to divine control. Whitefield's New Birth was an unqualified sacred experience — instantaneous, sensuous, and self-conscious. And wherever Whitefield and his colleagues preached, the people grasped the Pentecostal implications of their message, unleashing their response in a burst of ecstatic behavior.

The anarchic implications of the New Birth were mitigated by Whitefield's concept of the church. Though ordained an Anglican priest, Whitefield was sympathetic with Presbyterians, Congregationalists, and Baptists through his Calvinism. His irenic and nonconformist temperament fostered interdenominational ties, while the primacy he assigned to conversion downgraded the intrinsic importance of church allegiance and ritual performance. The evangelist consistently resisted equating conversion with membership in any particular church. "I don't care whether you go to church or meeting," he declared. "Don't tell me you are a Baptist, an Independent, a Presbyterian, a Dissenter; tell me you are a Christian, that is all I want."[7]

If denominational identity was a matter of indifference to Whitefield, the character of the church's members was not. Whitefield regarded any church as acceptable so long as its minister and people had experienced true conversion. His emphasis on the possession of saving grace enjoined upon him the Calvinist doctrine of visible sainthood, the tenet that church membership be restricted to certifiable converts. His model for the church, derived from his interpretation of apostolic community in the New Testament, was a pure communion of regenerate saints gathered out of the world and exercising mutual discipline among themselves by inspiration of the Holy Ghost. Ministers were subject to particular scrutiny. Here Whitefield himself provided the example for gospel ministers — spirit filled, prophetic, intent on saving souls. Through such leadership the communion of saints would blossom into a "gospel church," an apostolic community exhibiting the gifts of grace. Empowered by the Holy Spirit, these gathered churches were to exhibit consensus in discipline and unity in belief and practice while maintaining the freedom of each member to speak out against weakness and error.[8]

This vision of the gospel church had important social and political implications. The saints were responsible for forming communities that fostered collective sacred experience and protected members from profanation. For Whitefield, this task outweighed all other social, political, or economic considerations. And if government, or business, or ecclesiastical institutions interfered with God's mission for His people, they were to be resisted.

Whitefield's view of New England's Congregational establishment was unambiguous in this regard. As custodians of the Calvinist heritage, Congregationalist ministers had no excuse for falling prey to intellectual fashion and political influence. All true ministers had to be saints; if they did not exhibit the requisite spiritual gifts of the New Birth he denounced them as "ungodly, dead, and unconverted." If such leaders could not be converted or dismissed, it was the duty of the people to separate from them and gather new churches of Christ.[9] Whitefield rejected the century-old New England principle of theological diversity within ecclesiastical unity, demanding the indwelling Spirit rather than the all-too-human workings of Puritan tradition. Whitefield thus did not simply preach the New Birth; he also outlined a social and cultural structure for the saints to adopt and urged them to do so regardless of the consequences to themselves or to worldly institutions.

But perhaps Whitefield's greatest contribution was a new rhetoric and oral style through which his message was articulated. The essential element in his own ministry was preaching. He was uniquely endowed with a "bell-like" voice that could reach a crowd of thirty thousand people by Benjamin

Franklin's estimate. His voice possessed "an orphic tone, a rare timbre and sonority, and a range which enabled him to give expression to almost every human emotion." He also exhibited "a protean face, a penchant for the histrionic, and an almost perfect sense of timing in both word and gesture" that gave every utterance a theatricality that made even David Garrick marvel.[10]

Whitefield turned these powerful qualities into effective mass evangelism by the invention of itinerant field preaching. While evangelizing among colliers at Bristol in early 1739, "he stood upon a mound in a place called Rose Green . . . and preached to as many as came to hear, attracted by the novelty of such an address." Two hundred gathered the first day, but by the third day of field preaching the congregation numbered twenty thousand "at a moderate computation." Whitefield "took the field" partly to reach the miners in their own environment and partly to compensate for the growing number of pulpits closed to his extreme revivalism. But Whitefield's own explanation of the practice was characteristically cast in the prophetic mode: "I thought it might be doing the service of my Creator, who had a mountain for his pulpit, and the heavens for a sounding board; and who . . . sent his servants into the highways and hedges."[11]

In any case, his field preaching became a sensation. It became the principal tool in Whitefield's triumphant American tours that sparked the Great Awakening. The itinerant's extemporaneous sermons skillfully exploited the emotional dynamics of mass meetings to create an atmosphere conducive to conversion. By the 1740s Whitefield was already hailed as the greatest orator of his age.[12] His Radical Evangelical converts called it preaching in the Spirit.

Through his preaching Whitefield became the principal architect of a new oral culture for Radical Evangelicalism. He provided a common vocabulary that mediated the religious experience of converts. That vocabulary combined the languages of the Bible, the marketplace, and the human emotions. Whitefield grounded all his thought and utterance in the Word of God. But unlike the Puritans, he did not interpret it as a text for proof of carefully delineated doctrine. His was not a Bible analyzed, it was a Bible dramatized. Whitefield jettisoned the scholastic hermeneutic of Puritanism and substituted a denotative interpretation that cast the biblical narrative into a coherent dramatic scenario.

Whitefield's homiletic strategy placed his hearers within the cosmic drama of creation, fall, and redemption. His purpose was to have the unconverted redefine themselves as sinners in need of salvation. To that end it was necessary to depict the nature and effects of sin as manifested in the Fall. The perfections of the Creator, the abuse of creation by Adam and Eve, and the just curse pronounced on them and their posterity were essential episodes revealing the situation in which all humans stood. Their need for salvation from eternal pain and death was illustrated by the sacred history of the Old Testament, and the great remedy was provided by Christ through his incarnation, atoning sacrifice, and free offer of mercy to the faithful.[13]

These simple accounts of creation, fall, and redemption — always presented in the most dramatic and vivid language — framed Whitefield's appeal to sinners to choose salvation or damnation. Faithful acceptance of Christ would help bring the New Birth; rejection left sinners vulnerable to death unprotected by divine mercy. The Whitefieldian scenario was a drastic simplification of Reformed theology, a gospel reduced to simplest terms: the divine, the human, the enmity between them, and the Mediator's way of salvation. Whitefield's sermons employed the entire biblical narrative, but it was interpreted in light of this cosmic history of redemption and thereby brought to bear on the sinner's existential dilemma. The dramatic categories of creation, sin, redemption, and conversion became the constituting categories of Whitefield's biblical rhetoric. Through this spiritual hermeneutic he circumvented complex theological problems of Calvinism while articulating in a vibrant and compelling way its vision of divine sovereignty, human depravity, and justification by grace through faith.

The biblical drama, however, was not always sufficient to move an unlettered and unconverted audience. Whitefield normally drove his message home with another sort of rhetoric, what he called "marketplace language." The preacher employed an inexhaustible store of "personal reminiscences, anecdotes, and at times confessions," drawn from his youth as an innkeeper's son and his many travels.[14] If scripture did not convince, this kind of everyday verisimilitude did. By playing the role of his hearers and addressing himself to their world, Whitefield created a bond of identification and trust that he could turn to powerful emotional effect when delivering his gospel appeal.

The culminating element of Whitefield's rhetoric, however, was his direct address to sinners. No longer the dramatist of scripture or the representative of the common man, the Grand Itinerant assumed the very voice of the Spirit pleading with souls to seek free grace: "You are not your own; give Christ then your bodies and souls which are his! Come then, do not send me sorrowful away . . . Do not let me go weeping into my closet and say 'Lord, I have called them, and they will not answer.' "[15] When not tearfully crying for sinners to come to Christ, Whitefield spoke directly to individuals in "the language of the soul," expressing the horrors of hell or the joys of heaven that their souls would experience depending on their response to the gospel. By these devices Whitefield and his imitators drove home the existential impact of their message. A direct assault on hearers by a preacher acting as mediator between them and Christ was accomplished in language as emotionally charged as any in the eighteenth century.

The effect of such preaching was literally to suspend the disbelief of the audience and to bring them into a moment of sacred time when the ulti-mate act of human life—faith in Christ and receipt of the Holy Spirit—was real and available. The psychology of individual appeal combined with the intrinsic emotional power of Whitefieldian rhetoric and the amplifying capacity of collective behavior to remove intellectual doubt and social conformity in certain persons who were thereby opened to potent ex-periences of conversion.

The languages of biblical drama, marketplace, and personal emotion were fused by Whitefield into a popular rhetoric of religion. Through these linguistic formulas he expressed the imperatives of the New Birth and sanctified community with a power and persuasiveness unprecedented in New England experience. These elements of belief, social norms, and language became for his followers the framework of a new religious move-ment. Whitefield was hardly the first to discourse on conversion, gathered church, or biblical drama in New England. But the popular impact of his preaching during the Awakening and later was greater than that of any Congregationalist minister. He brought charisma, international sophistica-tion, and critical perspective to awakened Yankees, and though much of the Congregationalist establishment eventually turned against his message and manner, many of his hearers grasped and held the radical implications of his gospel and vowed to make them into living social reality.

The Great Awakening caused a complex division among the regenerate saints. A substantial number of them sought the spiritual renewal of Congregationalism from within. Following the leadership of Jonathan Ed-wards, these "New Lights" did not renounce the established church as cor-rupt but rather regarded its traditional structure as redeemable and conformable to the new Reformation. Edwards, Joseph Bellamy, and other revival leaders carried out a vigorous intellectual and evangelistic offensive against antirevival "Old Lights" that, although not finally successful, encouraged many New Lights to remain within the ecclesiastical establish-ment. The New Lights were most concentrated in the Connecticut Valley and central New England. From this bastion they fashioned a powerful Evangelical culture—based on the thought of Edwards, the sociopolitical influence of the valley, and the educational leadership of Yale—that flour-ished for a century.

Elsewhere the Evangelical movement took a more radical turn. In south-eastern New England Whitefield was accompanied by other exhorters who preached the need for separation from an unregenerate church. Of these the most extreme was James Davenport, the man who "infused the Great Awakening with an emotional extravagance that eventually dissolved it in countless controversies among the churches."[16] A Congregationalist min-ister of distinguished Connecticut lineage, Davenport settled at Southold, Long Island, in 1738. He experienced the New Birth in 1739 and soon "claimed a commission to preach abroad the things the Holy Spirit had revealed to him." After accompanying Whitefield and Presbyterian itinerant Gilbert Tennent in 1740, Davenport toured independently in eastern Connecticut beginning in 1741. Preaching a radical conversionism informed by his personal experience, Davenport dramatized his message by haranguing individual sinners and unconverted ministers by name. For three years he brought his gospel to many congregations first awakened by Whitefield.[17]

The heart of Davenport's evangel was a demand for exhibition of spiritual gifts in conversion and an insistence that the saints separate themselves utterly from all profane associations. His was Whitefieldian revivalism driven to new heights of frenzy. His visitations lasted several days and featured protracted meetings conducted with frenetic zeal. One eyewitness reported that at Groton, Connecticut, Davenport "preached . . . 4 or 5 days & mighty works followed. Near 1000 hearers from all quarters held the meeting till 2 o'clock at night & some stayed all night under the oak tree & in the meeting house."[18]

Whereas Whitefield relied primarily on the persuasive power of well-wrought sermons to wring conviction from sinners, Davenport exhausted them emotionally and physically, then demanded conversion. His sermons, sometimes lasting as long as twelve hours, lost even the most tenuous coherence and became rambling pronouncements of terror upon the unconverted. To place further pressure on congregations, Davenport exploited even the time after his meetings to confront the most affected listeners in an unguarded moment. His use of extempore prayer and song also had the effect of disorienting traditional congregations and stimulating unexpected spiritual gifts. The result of the whole technique was the conjuring of an intense, spontaneous, and intimate spiritual context that projected participants toward the experience of a new sacred reality.[19]

Davenport's unorthodox tactics worked. He soon gathered converts and lay exhorters who promoted his increasingly ecstatic and lurid exhortations. His field preaching degenerated into near riots and in May 1742 he was arrested in Hartford for disruption of the public peace, a police action that further alienated his followers from church and state. Davenport's odyssey reached its climax on 6 March 1743 at New London, the town "regarded abroad as the focus of enthusiasm, discord, and confusion." In obedience to a personal revelation, Davenport instructed his adherents to "gather the symbols of worldliness — wigs, cloaks, hoods, gowns, rings, necklaces — into a heap and burn them."[20] The Radicals also consigned to the flames theological works written by unregenerate authors, denouncing both books and writers as agents of Satan.

Following this incident, Davenport was formally censured by New Light Congregationalist ministers, and about a year later he ceased itinerating and published his "confession and retractions."[21] But no public repentance could obviate the effects of Davenport's incendiary ministry. His converts still saw visions and dreamed dreams. Despite his retirement and the cooling of the Great Awakening, many of the awakened followed the logic of revival into schism.

Whitefield had supplied the impulse, and Davenport the consummating energy to precipitate widespread disorder in the Congregationalist churches of New England. Between 1745 and 1770 nearly one hundred congregations separated from the established church, about one quarter of all organized parishes. These Separate or Strict Congregationalist churches were concentrated in the rapidly developing agrarian areas of eastern Connecticut and southeastern Massachusetts and were scattered as well throughout the subsistence towns of central Massachusetts and New Hampshire.[22] By the 1750s Radical Evangelicalism in the form of Separate Congregationalism had spread through rural New England society, converting churches en bloc or dividing them into warring factions.

The religious practices developed by the Separates were an amalgam of Whitefieldian radicalism and traditional New England Congregationalism. Early Separates claimed strict adherence to the Cambridge Platform of 1648, precisely to press their claim that gathered churches of reborn saints retained the pure ideals and rigor of Puritanism while contemporary Congregationalism had degenerated into corrupt formalism. Separate churches rested their polity on mutual covenants for discipline and uniformity. After profession of "experimental Acquaintance with Jesus Christ" the saints "enter into covenant with each other, promising that by the grace of God assisting them, they will maintain the publick worship of God, and carefully attend all the institutions of the Gospel, walking as becomes the followers of the Lamb of God."[23] Separate churches also appointed, "tested," and ordained their own members to the traditional offices of elder and deacon. Their polity was absolutely congregational: Each church was completely autonomous, free to make all decisions unhindered by consociational arbitration.

But the crucial element of Separate communal polity was collective discernment of truth in matters of membership and discipline. "A saint of God," wrote Separate leader Ebenezer Frothingham in 1750, "having Divine light shining into the Understanding and the Love of God ruling in the soul, is also to know certainly that such and such persons are true converts or the saints of God."[24] By simply "judging and knowing the Fruits of special sanctifying grace" in the everyday activities of a candidate for admission, Separate saints could infallibly identify a peer. Similarly, accusations of ungodly behavior by members were brought before the whole body. After appropriate testimony was heard, the issue was judged with unanimous agreement in the Spirit necessary to determine the proper course of discipline.

Within this elementary social structure the Separates practiced an emotional and sometimes ecstatic faith. They sought, so to speak, to make the revival permanent. Separate sermons were extemporaneous utterances based on texts "shown" to the preacher by the Spirit. These were delivered in a rich biblical idiom, often with a peculiar "holy whine," a tonality adopted from Whitefield. And as in the Grand Itinerant's own meetings, the congregation gave witness to the truth of the preaching by exercise of spiritual gifts. Separate meetings often included "crying out, falling down, twitching and convulsive motions, foamings and frothings, trances, visions, and revelations."[25] Spontaneous lay exhortation, hysteria, prayer, singing, dancing, glossolalia, and other classic manifestations of ecstatic religion also were prominent in the Separate movement.

The Separates thrived during the 1740s, but during the next decade they slowly lost the intensity and coherence of their religious commitment. Their self-definition continued to claim visible sainthood and the New Birth, but by the 1760s the impetus of revival had cooled to leave them vulnerable to legalism and formalism. Lacking an intercongregational organization, the Separate movement began a long process of dissolution and transformation on a church-by-church basis.

Many individuals and occasionally whole congregations shifted their affiliation to the Baptist denomination during the 1750s and 1760s. Centered in the old areas of Separate strength—southeastern New England, the Connecticut Valley, and the Worcester hinterland—the Baptists by 1767 had organized an association at Warren, Rhode Island, and emerged as the leaders of Radical Evangelicalism. The Warren Association was modeled on the Philadelphia Baptist Association of 1707, the prototypical Calvinist Baptist organization in America, and it endorsed the Savoy Confession of 1688, a virtual restatement of the Westminster Confession with minor modifications of polity and sacramental definition.[26]

The Warren Association provided a new confessional and ecclesiastical platform from which the Baptists could appeal to Separates and New Lights. In addition the Baptists offered three other major advantages to Radical Evangelicals. First, they applied the logic of the New Birth to liturgical practice, demanding that the ordinance of baptism be administered only to adult believers. Many Separates had become convinced that adult baptism rather than "infant sprinkling" was the proper scriptural mode of Christian initiation, and the practice had the added benefit of providing a dramatic ritual act to certify receipt of the New Birth. Second, though the Baptists strongly supported lay exhortation and preaching in the spirit, they also strove for intellectual excellence by founding Rhode Island College at Providence in 1766 under the presidency of James Manning. Treading a careful line between the improvement of spiritual gifts and a learned ministry, the Baptists gained cultural credibility without giving up the demand for a converted clergy. Finally, the Baptists provided a vigorous legal and political voice for religious toleration. Soon after its organization, the Warren Association employed Isaac Backus to carry forward the struggle against ministerial taxes, certification laws, and other legal harassment of dissenters. Under Backus's leadership, Baptists persistently raised the issue of liberty of conscience before the New England public and skillfully gained influence for Radical Evangelicals in the confusion of Revolutionary politics.[27]

Eventually the Baptists "carried off the greater part" of Radical Evangelicals, but during the Revolution the Whitefieldian milieu was neither a Baptist fiefdom nor a unified movement. The Warren Association did not represent a majority of New England Baptist congregations in the 1770s and 1780s. The others remained unassociated in keeping with their Separate origin or formed organizations of their own including the Stonington, Connecticut, Baptist Association of 1772 and the Groton Union Conference of 1785. The Separates, who still constituted fully one half of Radical Evangelical congregations at the time of the Revolution, finally organized an advisory convention in Connecticut during the 1780s, but elsewhere simply remained independent of all formal connection.[28]

These institutional divisions betokened more fundamental issues that confronted Radical Evangelicalism through the 1770s and 1780s. Three problems were paramount: the terms of communion, the need for a philosophical theology, and the question of cultural legitimacy. In 1753 a convention of Separates and Baptists at Exeter, Rhode Island, had apparently fulfilled the Radical hope for an ecumenical gathered communion by covenanting "that all the churches of this body are one church" and that the mode of baptism would not be "a bar to communion" among them. The hope was short-lived. A dispute between Baptist Isaac Backus and Separate Solomon Paine over the legitimacy of pedobaptism precipitated a second convention at Stonington, Connecticut, in May 1754 at which the experiment in intercommunion was abandoned.[29]

From that time a controversy developed between those who supported "open communion" (granting communion to all who affirmed Christian rebirth, regardless of denomination) and champions of "close communion" (granting communion only to saints who agreed on questions of ordinances, polity, and denominational identity). The issue represented the choice between radical idealism and denominational pragmatism that increasingly faced the Whitefieldian movement after mid-century. In 1754 most Separates advocated close communion, most Baptists open communion; but by 1770 the positions had reversed, adding still more to the divisiveness of the issue. In the 1770s and 1780s Baptists became increasingly intolerant of open communion, arguing that believer's baptism was an explicit Christian duty and that no person, however sincere in faith, should be admitted to communion without it. "Sincerity is not the term of communion," wrote Baptist Thomas Baldwin in 1789, "but being conformed to the apostles' doctrine, and continuing steadfastly therein."[30] Separates and New Light Congregationalists, on the other hand, denounced the Baptist view as an obstacle to the Evangelical project, "wholly inconsistent with Christian character, or that mutual forbearance which the gospel requires." The debate over terms of communion continued past the turn of the nineteenth century, an enduring example of the inherent difficulties in the transition of Radical Evangelicalism from revival movement to institutional church.

A second dimension of the same tension was the Radical Evangelicals' need for a more systematic theological position. Baptist and Separate success brought heightened intellectual challenge, not only from Arminian Old Lights but from Calvinist New Lights as well. By the 1780s the Radicals, particularly the Baptists, were strong and well-organized competitors with Congregationalists in the arena of public religious discourse. Baptists had not embraced Edwardsean theology in the 1750s, and they did not find the New Divinity any more appealing in the 1770s and 1780s. Whitefieldian theology, however, was not able to meet the sophisticated critiques of Boston, Newport, and New Haven. The native work of Isaac Backus, James Manning, and Jonathan Maxcy was serviceable, but decisive aid came from London in the form of John Gill's *A Body of Doctrinal Divinity,* published in 1769. Gill, the preeminent British Baptist divine of the late eighteenth century, was a systematic Calvinist who demanded preservation of the entire Reformed position. His arguments, derived from the principles of Scottish moral faculty psychology, gave his American correligionists both intellectual currency and a badly needed philosophical answer to Edwardsean formulations.

The new theology, however, became popular only in New England urban centers where leaders like Boston's Samuel Stillman and Providence's Jonathan Maxcy were arbiters of intellectual style. Rural Radicals such as John Peak, John Leland, and even Isaac Backus were suspicious of Gill's emphasis on moral and intellectual assent to the gospel at the expense of existential choice and conversion experience. Thomas Baldwin of Canaan, New Hampshire, illustrated the growing split between rural and cosmopolitan styles. Reared in the hill country and ordained there in 1783, Baldwin enjoyed great early success as a revival preacher and exhorter. He was called to the Second Baptist Church of Boston in 1790 where he was initiated into the learned Baptist clergy and soon embraced the Gillite system.[31] By the mid-1790s New England Baptists had become polarized by Gill's theology. The rural majority remained Whitefieldians still seeking revival through spiritual exegesis and dramatic rhetoric. The cosmopolitan minority, while not abandoning its tradition, welcomed its new status of intellectual peerage in the learned clergy of New England.

The controversies over communion and philosophical theology pointed to a still larger question facing Radical Evangelicals in the Revolutionary period, namely the desirability of cultural legitimacy. The Whitefieldian movement from the outset was reactionary and dissenting, pitting its gospel church against the social, economic, and political involvements of the world. By 1770, however, Radical Evangelicals, particularly the Baptists, had entered the mainstream of New England cultural life. As revolution approached they were presented with an acute dilemma: Should they remain neutral on religious grounds or enter the conflict; and if the latter, on which side?

The decision was difficult and by no means unanimous. The chief political demand of Radical Evangelicals was religious toleration. Since the Great Awakening they had received little relief from religious taxation and certification laws designed to support the Congregationalist establishment. For this reason many Radicals believed that the Crown rather than a new revolutionary government was more likely to guarantee freedom of conscience. On the other hand, punitive Crown policies had adverse effects on Baptists as well as their Congregationalist brethren, and Baptist arguments for toleration were drawn from the same intellectual sources as Whig ideology, creating a natural bond with the Revolutionaries. Yet other Radicals were Christian pacifists who refused to countenance violence and stood neutral toward both Loyalist and Patriot persuasions.

The commitment of the Radical Evangelicals was thoroughly in doubt until 1775, when the Warren Association leadership declared for the Revolutionary movement. Isaac Backus and Samuel Stillman—the leading Baptist political thinkers—made it clear, however, that the price of their support was liberty of conscience under the new regime. "In all civil governments some are appointed to judge for others, and have power to compel others to submit to their judgment," Backus wrote in 1773. "But our Lord has most plainly forbidden us either to assume or to submit to any such thing in religion."[32]

The Revolutionary order in New England did not put an end to the Congregationalist establishment, but it did alleviate the worst abuses and award the Baptists a new cultural and political legitimacy. The clearest symbol of the Baptists' new status was the selection in 1779 of Samuel Stillman as the first non-Congregationalist ever to preach the Election Sermon to the Massachusetts General Court. Yet even here the dissenting interest was on the defensive. A year earlier Phillips Payson of Chelsea had delivered a stinging attack on "changes or alterations" in the "established modes and usages of religion" being urged by persons—obviously the Radicals—of "the most foaming zeal."[33] To this polemic Stillman replied that government "can neither have more, nor any other kind of power, than the people had to give." And since human authority cannot extend to the Kingdom of God, the state was powerless to rule in matters of religion. "Our Lord Jesus Christ will not stand by," he warned, "an idle spectator of the many encroachments that have been made on his sacred prerogative by the powers of the world."[34]

It was through such encounters that Baptists attained a paradoxical legitimacy in Revolutionary New England, welcomed and honored in the struggle for independence yet unheeded in the very demands that motivated their political participation. Baptist leaders saw in the Revolution a chance to gain religious reform and a stake in the new order for themselves. Yet their effort to gain full disestablishment failed with the ratification of the Massachusetts Constitution in 1780. Many other Radical Evangelicals took alternative positions, rejecting the drive for legitimation. A number of ministers and lay people declared their neutrality. The most notable of these was Dr. Samuel Shepard, Baptist elder at Brentwood, New Hampshire, who refused to sign a Committee of Safety pledge of armed resistance against the British on 12 April 1776. As late as 1780 the Woodstock, Connecticut, Baptist church articulated a classic neutral position: "We feel but little heart to hold the sword against a British invader while our country men are endeavoring to deprive us of liberty of conscience." Other Radical neutrals took a more drastic course, removing to the frontier or British Canada in an effort to separate from the sins of war. Few Radicals Evangelicals were Tories, but a sizable number found revolutionary action inimicable to Christian duty and sought through various means to hold the difficult stance of neutrality in troubled times.[35]

The Radical Evangelical movement this endured the Revolutionary crisis more divided than at any time since its origin in the Great Awakening. The Whitefieldian imperatives that had seemed so clear and attainable in the 1740s and 1750s encountered increasingly severe institutional, intellectual, and political obstacles after 1760 both within and without the Radical fellowship. The death of the Grand Itinerant in 1770 signaled the rise of a new American generation of his spiritual heirs. Some of them, especially cosmopolitan Baptists, though honoring Whitefield's memory, would strive to carry out his mission within the social and cultural constraints of the Revolutionary order. Others, preserving the experiential and communal essence of his message, would seek and find a revolution of the spirit.

2

The New Settlements

Radical Evangelicalism before 1770 existed within the geographical and intellectual confines of traditional New England society. But after the French and Indian War, many Radicals joined the massive migration to maritime Canada and the northern hill country that continued unabated until after 1800. Removal to the hinterland constituted a decisive environmental change that broke the cultural constraints of Radical Evangelicalism and stimulated in it a new creative potency. From the beginning, the "new settlements" of the north exhibited demographic, social, economic, political, and religious patterns subtly but substantively different from those of colonial New England. This new configuration was bonded into permanent form by a series of crises that assaulted the frontier for more than a decade after 1776. By the 1780s the hill country had begun to coalesce into a "new New England," the first regional society of the Republic to experience the boom-and-bust cycle of frontier development and to fabricate a new democratic culture. It was in this context of swift and permanent change that Radical Evangelicalism itself mutated into new indigenous religions.

The first significant movement of Yankee population northward settled in British Nova Scotia. The fall of Louisbourg in 1758 and the subsequent expulsion of the Acadians offered to New Englanders the rare opportunity to occupy developed land at low cost. On 11 January 1759, Governor Charles Lawrence issued a "Charter of Nova Scotia," promising deferred quitrents, minimal speculation, and land grants "in proportion to the abilities of the planter to settle, cultivate, and enclose the same." Lawrence made the offer even more attractive to prospective New England settlers by guaranteeing local governments and courts "constituted in like manner with those of Massachusetts, Connecticut, and other northern colonies and," most important for dissenters, "full liberty of conscience . . . Papists excluded."[1]

By 1763 large numbers of settlers began to migrate from the Radical Evangelical center in southeastern New England to the Minas Basin region of western Nova Scotia and to the Saint John River valley in New Brunswick. "The vast majority of settlers . . . came from that relatively small corner of New England created when a line is drawn from New London, Connecticut, northward to Brookfield, Massachusetts, and then eastward to Plymouth."[2] During the early 1760s about five thousand moved to Nova Scotia from this area, and by 1776 roughly half of the province's twenty thousand inhabitants were from New England. After the outbreak of revolution thousands more — primarily Anglican and Evangelical Loyalists — poured into the Canadian frontier, "from the coast and interior of Connecticut and Rhode Island, from Cape Cod and Nantucket, from New Hampshire, and from all parts of Massachusetts."[3]

The settlers enjoyed swift economic success. By 1776 they had created a network of towns and a stable agrarian economy much like that of their parent society. But this "new New England" differed in political and religious structure.[4] Despite an abortive attempt by American sympathizers to take Fort Cumberland in the Chignecto region during 1776, the Nova Scotia Yankees remained neutral during the Revolution. Some wartime tensions did exist between the New Englanders and the military government at Halifax, but after 1783 the immigrant population quietly returned to normal political life in a British province. This political conservatism, however, accompanied a strong Radical Evangelical identity in religion. Many — perhaps a majority — of the immigrants were New Light Congregationalists, but they encountered grave difficulties in recruiting and supporting ministers from New England. Into this institutional void stepped the farmer-preachers of Radical Evangelical persuasion. Separates Shubael Dimock of Mansfield, Connecticut, and Daniel Hovey of Norton, Connecticut, along with Baptist Ebenezer Moulton of Yarmouth, Massachusetts, and Presbyterian Jonathan Scott of Middleborough, Massachusetts, were the most influential ministers in Yankee Nova Scotia. The province's religious history during the late eighteenth century was, like rural New England's, turbulent and pluralizing; but through revival and denominational competition the Radical Evangelicals — particularly the Baptists — gained permanent and decisive hegemony by 1800.[5]

The New England outpost in Nova Scotia both resembled and differed from the Puritan commonwealths to the south. Economically and socially, settlers were able simply to take over an already flourishing agricultural system and quickly adapt it to the New England tradition of cropping and town organization. In political and religious affairs, however, they adapted

New England norms to new circumstances and evolved a distinctive pattern of political conservatism with religious radicalism. Nova Scotia illustrated some of the cultural potential of New England tradition transposed to the frontier; it was, however, but a prelude to far greater and more complex transformations that took place in the northern hill country.

Northern and western New England is dominated by the great arc of Appalachian Mountains running east from the Hudson Valley almost to the Atlantic Ocean. The several ranges of this mass (Berkshire Hills, Green Mountains, White Mountains) are penetrated by many major river systems (Connecticut, Merrimack, Piscataqua, Saco, Androscoggin, Kennebec, Penobscot). Early settlers projected great economic potential for the valleys, with their combination of fine bottomland, ample water power, and transportation access to coastal markets. The Connecticut Valley in particular offered the best agricultural land in all New England, but like other fertile valleys it was limited in quantity. More typical of hill country land was a combination of light intervale soils and thin high-elevation soil suitable for pasturage and subsistence farming.[6]

This territory became available for New England settlers after the French and Indian War. With the threat of French invasion removed, royal governors distributed huge acreages to colonial elites through conditional proprietary grants. New Hampshire Governor Benning Wentworth was the greatest of these land magnates. From 1750 to 1764 he issued 124 township grants of dubious title including all the land between the Connecticut and the Hudson rivers.[7] Similar policies were followed by Massachusetts governors in the District of Maine. During and after the Revolution the remaining northern frontier was sold by new state governments or granted by them to military veterans. In the thirty years between 1760 and 1790, virtually the entire hill country was thrown open for settlement and land speculation. A few men like William Bingham, General Henry Knox, and the Allens of Vermont accumulated huge land holdings and speculative profits. But more commonly hill country land was owned by absentee proprietors who held it upon condition that it would be improved within five to seven years by a stipulated number of settlers. Many proprietors owned shares in a number of townships, and modest speculation was not uncommon. Throughout this period, however, land prices remained reasonable as proprietors sought to attract settlers to distant agricultural properties.[8]

Abundant land at cheap prices, an increasing proportion of marginal income population, and the economic and political dislocations of revolution created a massive immigration to the frontier in the 1770s and 1780s. Maine and Vermont both had populations of less than 10,000 in 1770, but by 1776 they had passed 20,000 and by 1790 they numbered 96,540 and 85,416 respectively. The population boom continued through the 1790s and early 1800s, with decennial growth rates above 50 percent. By 1820

Maine numbered 298,335 inhabitants and Vermont 235,754. The growth of northern New Hampshire and western Massachusetts also kept pace with the rest of the hill country. Between the Revolution and the War of 1812 the northern frontier received the largest and most intensive population growth of any region in the new United States. Its roughly thirty thousand square miles of available land supported over one-half million people by 1800, almost double the aggregate population of Ohio, Kentucky, and Tennessee.[9] Thus sheerly in terms of population the decades after independence were a time of uniquely high mobility and growth in the new settlements of the hill country.

The diversity of this population movement was as unprecedented as its size. Wide geographical distribution of proprietors guaranteed that settlers were recruited from many different parts of New England. Absentee proprietorship also meant that congregational or community groups abandoned corporate settlement of towns, the traditional method of occupation. These factors resulted in a mosaic of settlers drawn from each of New England's well-differentiated societies. The interior of Maine was settled primarily by immigrants from Rhode Island and eastern Massachusetts. The New Hampshire Grants towns along the Connecticut received original inhabitants from eastern Connecticut and the lower valley. Thousands of people from Cape Ann and coastal New Hampshire occupied the Winnipesaukee country. These were the most significant population flows; other short-range contiguous movements developed from western Connecticut and the Hudson Valley into western Massachusetts and Vermont, from the Worcester Highlands into the Monadnock-Sunapee region of New Hampshire, and from the New Hampshire coast into the Piscataqua and Merrimack valleys.

These myriad movements of people made cultural homogeneity impossible in the hill country. Grafton County, New Hampshire, centrally located in the Connecticut Valley, exhibited typical migration patterns. Of thirty-four towns organized in Grafton before 1800, only twelve were settled by substantially homogeneous populations: seven from New Hampshire, three from Connecticut, and two from Massachusetts. Another seven towns were divided primarily between settlers from two states, and the other fifteen, almost half the total, were originally settled by immigrants from three or more states.[10] The town of Lyme, population 816 in 1790, illustrated the impact of such diversity at the local level. Among Lyme's original settlers were families from Windham and Tolland counties, Connecticut; Worcester, Bristol, Plymouth, and Middlesex counties, Massachusetts; Providence County, Rhode Island; and Hillsborough County, New Hampshire. The few towns, like those of "New Connecticut" on the east bank of the Connecticut river, that managed to transfer whole populations from older regions remained islands in a stream of cultural pluralism.[11]

The population distribution in the new settlements was remarkably uniform, and town size and structure early took regular form. The terrain and its economy established a clear maximum on community development. Of 600 hill towns reported in the first census, only 7 had populations above 2,000 persons. Again Grafton County was representative. Its total population increased from 7,802 in 1787 to over 30,000 in 1820. Average town size increased from 410 to 927, but in 1820 only one community, Hanover, reported more than 2,000 inhabitants. Although the county tripled its size between 1790 and 1820, its largest town grew by only 62 percent.[12] Population growth was roughly equally distributed in the hill country. Despite natural advantages and early settlement, valley towns did not develop into major population centers whereas more marginal locations gradually increased toward the statistical average.

Hill towns typically were communities of between five hundred and fifteen hundred people, about seventy-five to two hundred fifty families, scattered over twenty to thirty square miles. Geography, cultural diversity, and conditions of land purchase rendered these communities even more decentralized than the statistics indicate. Unlike the integrated nuclear villages of lower New England, backcountry towns consisted of several distinct neighborhoods often settled by persons of differing provenance. Traditional town government was transferred to the frontier, but the "consensual communalism" characteristic of mature New England towns did not develop in the new settlements. The hill town was a distinctly pluralistic social, cultural, and political entity from the beginnings of settlement and remained so through the early nineteenth century.[13]

The New England uplands permitted only a limited range of economic development. Subsistence farming was the norm for the vast majority of settlers. Low land prices enabled farmers to become independent freeholders with relative ease. But although many agreed with Samuel Williams that farming brought "the most flattering prospects and encouragement" for economic prosperity, simple subsistence with perhaps enough profit to secure additional land and to pay taxes was the hard reality of hill country farming. Residents and visitors alike noted "the uneven lands" and "unfavorable seasons" of the region.[14] Arable land was suitable for cropping in potatoes, fruit orchards, rye, and corn, but higher elevations were usable only as pasturage, at the cost of enormous labor. When frontier conditions finally gave way to subsistence farming, hill country settlers were still at the mercy of the weather. In 1788 and 1816 cold weather caused almost total failure of corn and hay crops. Nathan Perkins reported from Vermont in early 1789 that "it is supposed by ye more judicious and knowing that more than ¼ part of ye people will have neither bread nor meat for 8 weeks and that some will starve."[15] In 1816, known locally as "the cold year," "the famine year," or "eighteen hundred and froze to death," similar conditions prevailed. Despite the energy and determination of the New England farmer, the hill country remained in the best of times a marginal subsistence economy, in the worst of times an agricultural disaster.[16]

The backcountry also produced raw materials and some manufactured goods for commercial trade. Hill country maple sugaring rivaled the productivity of Louisana sugarcane by 1810, but by far the most important single industry was lumbering. Boom markets before and after the Revolution meant that in Maine and New Hampshire, "timber was king." Rapid market fluctuations and the need for credit, however, made lumbering an unstable enterprise. Jeremy Belknap observed in 1792 that lumbermen "generally work hard for little profit . . . They are always in debt and frequently at law."[17] Yet for many subsistence farmers, the woodlot was the only reliable way to sustain cash flow necessary for the operation of their homesteads.

It was a simple, almost mercantile economy, dependent on raw materials markets and imports of finished goods.[18] As such, the hill country was particularly vulnerable to larger economic trends. The disastrous inflation of the late 1770s and 1780s left farmers holding depreciating currency for payment of increasing debts, taxes, and prices. These problems were compounded by the crop failure of 1787–88, extending the region's economic depression into the 1790s. Eventually the favorable conditions of the Neutral Trade and increased farm production brought stability and prosperity to the region, but the dependent character of its economy persisted so that the Embargo of 1808 plunged the hill country into another depression, aggravated by the War of 1812 and the famine of 1816. The crisis of 1808–1816 resulted in wholesale abandonment of northern border towns, massive emigration west, and the passing of the Republic's first frontier.[19]

The basic facts of settlement fostered an egalitarian social structure in the hill country. Property was quite evenly distributed. The wealthiest 10 percent of the population controlled only one third of the region's property; the rest was owned by farmers and artisans in estates of under £500. Great wealth and landless poverty were significantly less than in the commerical farm and urban societies of southern New England. Backcountry people were "poor, but not in need," roughly equal in property and land. Classes were similarly undifferentiated. In frontier areas "class distinctions were minimized . . . Ordinarily no one of wealth was a resident. There might be a storekeeper, a minister, and perhaps a doctor; and there were a number of landless laborers. All the rest were farmers." With only slight difference, the same predominance of small farmers obtained in subsistence agricultural regions and even the commercial farming areas of rural New England's valleys.[20]

A second social dimension, the family, was also altered in the hill country. In southern New England nonfamilial institutions — town, church, and business — provided basic norms for societal life. The nuclear family, though still the indispensable context of everyday existence, had ceased to exercise its traditionally dominant influence. By Revolutionary times the effect of economic competition and partible inheritance had stripped the family's ability to provide security for its progeny. Increasing urbanization, a growing rural proletariat, and the maturation of commerce created a social environment in which extrafamilial status and deference hierarchies were determinative of life patterns.[21]

This trend temporarily reversed on the northern frontier. In the absence of reliable local institutions the family attained new importance as the basic economic, social, and cultural unit. Abundant land and scarce labor inverted the family economic equation, making child labor on farmsteads not only desirable but indispensable. Substantial opportunities for inheritance discouraged emigration from newly settled areas. These pressures resulted in a sharply increased birthrate and family size in the developing hill country.[22] Shorter generations and subsistence economics in turn led to the reappearance of the extended family. Jeremy Belknap reported from New Hampshire in 1784 that "an unmarried man of thirty years old is rarely to be found in our country towns. The women are grandmothers at forty, and it is not uncommon for a mother and daughter to have each a child at the breast at the same time, nor for a father, son, and grandson to be at work together in the same field."[23]

The family also provided primary identity, socialization, and cultural norms for rural life. "Most men, women, and children in this yeoman society continued to view the world through the prism of family values. This cultural outlook — this inbred pattern of behavior — set certain limits on personal autonomy, entrepreneurial activity, religious membership, and even political imagery." The lineal family constituted the central element in the mentality of the hill country, "an abiding core of symbolic and emotive meaning, and . . . a significant and reliable guide to behavior amid the uncertainties of the world."[24] Larger, more isolated, more economically necessary, and more culturally self-reliant than nuclear units to the south, the hill family became the social crucible in which a new regional style took shape.

The "new New England" of the late eighteenth century was a transformed traditional society. Its people, drawn from all parts of the region, were thrown together into new configurations of settlement in small communities. Its economy was underdeveloped and dependent on raw materials rather than shipping and commercial farming. Its social structure was egalitarian and familial. The effect of these conditions was a fragmentation of binding social and intellectual habits and the emergence of hybrid forms of culture congruent with the new realities of the hill country.

The cultural fragmentation of the hill country was most dramatically manifested in the realms of politics and religion, the two principal normative systems in late-eighteenth-century society. The basis of political order in New England was town government, and proprietors of the new settlements were charged to organize their communities as soon as possible. But throughout the Revolutionary period these towns lacked the coherence and effectiveness characteristic of other New England governments. The diversity and isolation of settlers made popular defiance of local elites common. Even the daily hum of town business was difficult to maintain in the "infant settlements," and when the crisis of revolution struck the hill country, only marginally effective institutions were available to deal with it.

The hill country was decisively Patriot in sympathy, but its conversion to the independence movement was late, and the presence of a large neutral population fostered suspicion and conflict. Toryism was not a serious threat, though many Tories did locate on the frontier seeking to avoid persecution without having to emigrate. Tension between Patriots, neutrals, and Tories was exacerbated by the location of most of the new settlements along principal invasion routes from Montreal and Quebec. In the absence of strong town governments, political authority was claimed by Committees of Safety and local militia units. These agencies were constantly occupied in defending the settlements from subversion and attack, real or imagined. Early in the Revolution the settlements also played a crucial military role, their troops and logistic support figuring large in the seizure of Ticonderoga, the invasion of Quebec, and the defeat of Burgoyne. From 1777 on, the military threat lessened, but the internal politics of the hill country became steadily more conflicted and chaotic.[25]

The development that caused the greatest disruption was the linkage of the ideology of national revolution to hill country demands for local political autonomy. Land titles in much of the northern frontier were in dispute before 1776. This circumstance, combined with the conviction that regimes in Boston, Portsmouth, and New York did not reflect rural interests, led settlers to claim the right of self-government while still remaining loyal to the Revolutionary cause.

The most explosive controversy involved jurisdiction over the New Hampshire Grants, the 124 townships in the Connecticut Valley and Green Mountains granted by New Hampshire Governor Benning Wentworth in the 1750s and early 1760s. New York's successful challenge to these patents in 1765 initiated a decade of simmering economic and political conflict between Yankees and Yorkers in the grants. On 17 January 1776, after the independence movement had brought the collapse of New York provincial government in the grants, a convention of towns west of the Connecticut River petitioned the Continental Congress for home rule. Ambiguous reaction by the Congress and the Declaration of Independence encouraged the grants towns to take matters into their own hands. In January 1777 the New Hampshire Grants Convention pronounced that the west bank "of right ought to be, and is hereby declared forever hereafter to be considered as a free and independent jurisdiction or state," to be known as Vermont.

The new state adopted a constitution — New England's most radically democratic — that reflected the sentiment of these egalitarian and localist "people out-of-doors" that "the more simple and the more immediately dependent the authority is upon the people, the better."[26]

Independent Vermont requested recognition by the Continental Congress, a move immediately and vociferously opposed by New York, New Hampshire, and Massachusetts, all of whom claimed title to the grants. After long debate, the Congress resolved on 24 September 1779 that all parties "suspend executing their laws over any of the inhabitants, except such of them, as shall profess allegiance to, and confess the jurisdiction of" the particular government in question. This plan amounted to plural government, and the consequence was virtual anarchy. "The state of society was very unhappy," Jeremy Belknap reported, "the majorities attempted to control the minorities; and these were disposed not to submit . . . Party rage, high words, and deep resentments were the effect of these clashing interests."[27]

Vermont, disappointed by the Congress, entered negotiations with the British command in Canada and in February 1781 annexed twelve New York districts and thirty-six New Hampshire towns that had petitioned to be "united with Vermont, in one independent government."[28] The Congress speedily condemned this action while New York and New Hampshire mustered militia units to the grants in December 1781. General George Washington personally appealed to Vermont to give up its new claims in order to "obtain an acknowledgement of independence and sovereignty." The Congress, however, again refused Vermont recognition, citing New York's title. Vermonters viewed this act as a betrayal, while Yorker settlers in southern Vermont saw it as a warrant to rebel against Green Mountain government. Yorker insurrection broke out in the summer of 1783, and Ethan Allen occupied Guilford, the center of unrest, in the fall of that year, but the rebellion was not broken until the decisive battle of 14 January 1784 in which several died.[29] On the east bank, armed resistance rose against the reassertion of New Hampshire sovereignty. Inferior Court at Keene was disrupted in September 1782 by pro-Vermont insurrectionists, and two hundred armed men mustered to "oppose the court" at the trial of the insurrection's leaders.[30]

Violence finally ended in the New Hampshire Grants in 1784, but for almost two decades the region had been a scene of fierce political conflict and struggle for self-determination. Nor was the matter settled in 1784. For eight more years Vermont remained independent, prevented by Congress and its own distrust of federalism from entering the Union until 1792. After admission, Vermont continued on its own political trajectory as an early bastion of Jeffersonianism in New England.

Resistance to the Revolutionary regime spread to other parts of the hill country after 1780. Agitation for statehood appeared in the District of Maine in 1785. There conflict raged between proprietors of new settlements and squatters. The three tiers of inland towns organized before 1800 were flooded by subsistence farmers who refused to pay for their land "either because they questioned the validity of the proprietors' title—they often deserved challenging—or because they had no money."[31] From the end of the Revolution, proprietors with the aid of Massachusetts officials established their claims, often taking possession without payment to settlers for improvements.

Squatters reacted to the expropriation of their farms with demands for land reform and Maine independence. On the coast, a down east elite of leading clergymen, physicians, and lawyers joined with the squatters in seeking to wrest political control away from Massachusetts. A convention of delegates from twenty towns issued a grievance circular in December 1785, citing inequitable districting, excise and impost, and improper fees and land transactions as intolerable abuses. Under the urging of Thomas B. Wait and his newspaper, the *Falmouth Gazette*, the convention on 6 September 1786 petitioned for separation from Massachusetts. Though crisis was averted by a series of reform bills enacted by the General Court between 1784 and 1788, the rural interior towns remained solidly anti-Boston and Antifederalist.[32]

Land problems persisted, however, into the nineteenth century. In 1808 squatter anger boiled over into widespread armed violence against proprietors, court officials, and civil officers that continued until the War of 1812. At the same time subsistence farmers found an effective political voice in the Jeffersonians, who made Maine independence their rallying cry in taking control of the district in 1805. The War of 1812 finally convinced a majority of Maine's citizens than neither state nor federal government would respond to their needs. It took six more years of political bargaining and constitutional debate, however, for Maine to gain statehood.

The most famed insurgency movement of the Revolutionary hill country was Shays' Rebellion of 1786 in western and central Massachusetts. Land title was not the primary issue, but regressive forms of taxation and the enforced collection of them during difficult economic times generated in Massachusetts the same sort of rural resistance movement as in the New Hampshire Grants and the District of Maine. The refusal by farmers and shopkeepers, many of them veterans of the Revolution, to pay excise and impost taxes while still in the grip of postwar inflation; their demand for emission of paper bills and suspension of county courts to ease the burden of debt; and their recourse to armed violence against court officers and the Commonwealth itself shocked the new nation and alerted it to the need for constitutional reform. In the hill country context, however, Shays' Rebellion was only the most violent and notable manifestation of post-Revolutionary unrest. The Shaysite constituency was similar in composition to that of the Vermont independence and Maine separation movements. Their objectives of tax relief, reduced spending, paper curency, judicial reform, and local control of government were those of hill country leaders everywhere. And underlying the rebellion was the cardinal backcountry assumption that citizens should resist or separate from governments that did not serve local interests.[33]

Shays' Rebellion drew its principal support from the four western counties of Massachusetts, but a similar movement also occurred in rural New Hampshire. Conventions in Grafton and Hillsborough counties petitioned the state assembly for an emission of bills on 13 September 1786. A week later, following the rejection of the petitions, two hundred armed insurrectionists entered the assembly meeting at Exeter to demand favorable action. The legislators refused to acquiesce, and after some tense hours of confrontation with the mustered citizens of Exeter, the insurrectionists withdrew. Forty leaders were arrested and subsequently confessed; eight were tried and released; militia officers among the rebels were cashiered; and the New Hampshire tax rebellion turned to more licit political processes. Though the violent stage of the Shaysite movement passed quickly, the opposition of rural folk in Massachusetts and New Hampshire to state governments and their ruling coastal elites continued in Jeffersonian form for the remainder of the eighteenth century and beyond.[34]

The political culture of the new settlements was formed in a context of internecine strife, unstable local institutions, and a regional search for self-determination. In the late 1770s and 1780s each major area of the northern frontier experienced a crisis that crystallized the ideology of revolution into resistance to the Revolutionary regime. The New Hampshire Grants question, Maine separation, and Shays' Rebellion fragmented loyalties and institutions in the new settlements until after 1790. Such conflicts, however, were the birth pangs of a new rural political stance deeply radical and democratic yet strongly localist and Antifederalist. To an extent unknown in southern New England, the new settlements employed Revolutionary ideas and techniques to break down the political traditions of the Puritan commonwealths and transform them into new principles of social order and self-government.

The cultural fragmentation of the hill country also affected matters of religion. It took surprising form in the failure of New Light Congregationalism to establish solid institutional domination in a region that could have been its exclusive province. The new settlements were overwhelmingly Evangelical in composition. The ubiquitous presence of settlers from Connecticut and Massachusetts guaranteed a strong Edwardsean theological environment and promised easy extension of New Light Congregationalism to the frontier. The earliest settlements in fact preserved the New England tradition of migration by congregational unit. In the Upper Connecticut Valley this pattern was strong enough to warrant organization of a ministerial association in Windham County, Vermont, on 17 October 1775. The valley also was the site of Dartmouth College, which was founded in 1769 by Eleazar Wheelock as an Indian school but which soon grew into a center for theological training of ministers.[35]

But these hopeful beginnings were overwhelmed by the effects of the Revolution. Wartime reductions in class size at New England colleges and disruption of private theological tutorials greatly diminished the supply of potential ministers and missionaries precisely at the time the hill country entered its most intense period of growth. Many ministers enlisted as officers or served as chaplains, often not returning to their pastorates. Even where rural churches retained their ministers, many were unable to finance them in the restricted economic circumstances of the 1770s and 1780s. In the new settlements, uncertain land titles and legal jurisdiction made provision of glebe lands for ministers a difficult matter. Legal controversy over glebe titles, though usually resolved in favor of the Congregationalists, hampered the recruitment and settlement of qualified ministers.[36]

The result of these multiple difficulties was the most serious degeneration of the parish system in the history of New England. In 1780, Ezra Stiles, president of Yale and overseer of the New Light ministry, counted 60 "destitute" parishes in Vermont, 60 in New Hampshire, and 80 in Massachusetts and Maine, most of them in the new settlements and rural areas. The magnitude of the crisis was underscored by his calculations that the vacancies represented over one third of all New England Congregationalist parishes and that at most eighty unsettled preachers were available even in principle to supply the 245 congregations "devoid of stated means of grace."[37]

The health of Congregationalism depended absolutely on the maintenance of the parish system, a network of congregations and settled ministers coextensive with and parallel to the organization of New England towns. In rural and frontier areas, revolution, migration, and isolation crippled parish development. After 1776 the organization of parishes began to fall behind the incorporation of towns. In Vermont, for example, between 1763 and 1820 church organization typically followed the legal recognition of towns by more than fifteen years.[38] Immigrants who had lived for generations under the aegis of local congregations regularly found themselves without an organized parish for more than a decade, with no recourse save an occasional itinerant minister to relieve their destitution.

The reversal of Congregationalist fortunes in the new settlements was dramatically illustrated in the *Minutes* of the General Association of Connecticut, New England's most powerful ecclesiastical organization. The association, solidly Edwardsean in theology and representing the churches of origin for most settlers of the New Hampshire Grants, confidently resolved in 1774 to fund two missionaries to "ye settlements now forming in the

Wilderness to the westward and northward of us." A year later, however, plans were suspended because "the perplexed and melancholy state of public affairs has been a discouragement to this design." By 1778 the condition of even well-established parishes in Connecticut itself had become so critical that the association feared for their very survival. It lamented "the discouragement lying upon candidates entering into the ministry, and the present distress and difficulties of them that are already in office," but it was unable to give them aid.[39]

By 1780 the need for "exertions to save the churches from ruin" produced a shrill alarm for "the awakening, instruction, and reformation of this stupid and backsliding generation." But despite jeremiads and apocalyptic threats, the decay continued. For more than a decade the general association was unable to provide significant relief for the many rural parishes that sought aid for "our destitute churches and congregations whose resettlement in the enjoyment of the gospel ordinances is improbable." At last in 1792 county associations began supplying missionaries to the beleaguered hill country; the next year the general association finally added its own itinerants, but organized relief did not appear until 1798 with the establishment of the Missionary Society of Connecticut.[40] The same inability of Congregationalists to organize frontier missions prevailed in Massachusetts and New Hampshire as well.

Deprived of the steady habits that undergirded it, the ministerial leadership that nurtured it, and the homogeneous constituency that supported it, the Congregationalist parish system languished in central and northern New England during the Revolutionary era. Evangelical divines continued to lament the "religious depression" until the turn of the century when the vigorous leadership of President Timothy Dwight of Yale animated a new generation of ministers to preach revival. In the meantime, Congregationalism lost its natural advantage as the traditional religion of hill country settlers. The failure of Congregationalists to provide intellectual leadership, missionary support, or material aid to fragile rural congregations in the 1770s and 1780s created a religious vacuum that was to be filled whether by family maintenance of traditional faith or by new religious options.

Congregationalism did not succumb entirely in the new settlements. A strong network of parishes developed in the Upper Connecticut Valley, and individual parishes flourished throughout northern New England. Yet this development was late in coming, as was the organization of ministerial associations. The Rutland and Royalton associations in Vermont did not form until 1788 and 1797 respectively. Maine's first association, Piscataqua, was established in 1781, but three others — Cumberland, Lincoln, and Hancock — appeared only shortly before the turn of the century. The General Association of Vermont was organized on 27 August 1795, but elsewhere Congregationalist cooperation remained locally based. The postwar recovery of Dartmouth College was similarly delayed, first by the death of founder Eleazar Wheelock in 1779 and later by the divisive policies of his son and successor, John Wheelock.[41] Intellectually, Congregationalism in the hill country, though overwhelmingly Edwardsean, became embroiled in theological debates not only with Arminians and Deists but also with Scottish Presbyterians who emigrated in sizable numbers to the Upper Connecticut. The Edwardseans remained on the theological defensive, seeking to combat growing liberalism and radicalism with their severe axioms of philosophical Calvinism.

Congregationalism was the majority religion of hill country settlers, but the New Light party to which most emigrants belonged proved unable to consolidate its advantage and create a reliable parish network. Alternatives to the New Lights in 1776 included the Radical Evangelicals, Quakers, Old Lights, and Deists. Before the Revolution Separates and Baptists had established only a few viable congregations. Baptists organized perhaps two dozen churches in the hill country, few of them allied with the Warren Association. Leaders of Baptist dissent were Samuel Shepard of Brentwood, New Hampshire, Valentine Rathbun of Pittsfield, Massachusetts, and Peletiah Tingley of Sanford, Maine. Separates were less well organized but still claimed thriving churches at locations like Bennington, Vermont. A modest network of Quaker meetings had long existed in the Connecticut and Piscataqua valleys, and many Friends were settling in the hill country by 1776. Arminian Old Light Congregationalists were located in the same areas and shared a similar development before the Revolution. Deism gained popularity among town elites, spurred on by Ethan Allen's well-known rationalism, which he committed to paper in his tract titled *Reason the Only Oracle of Man.*[42]

Each of these persuasions gained increased influence in the hill country owing to the absence of a comprehensive Congregationalist establishment. During the last quarter of the eighteenth century, dissenting religion developed rapidly in size and popularity, none more than Radical Evangelicalism. As early as 1778 signs of a major revival appeared among Baptists, Quakers, and New Lights. The awakening burst into full flower by 1780 and carried on unabated until the mid-1780s. This revival, known locally as "The New Light Stir," significantly altered the denominational balance of the hill country, elevating Baptists to almost equal numerical and institutional status with Congregationalists.

More important, the Stir loosed the innovative potential in Radical Evangelicalism, stimulating the appearance of new sects. Some of these remained strictly local in scope, but three of them — the Shakers, the Universalists, and the Freewill Baptists — quickly grew into regional religious movements. By the War of 1812 the radical sects constituted roughly one third of all churches in the new settlements. Between 1770 and 1815 the frontier became a stronghold not for traditional New England Congregationalism, but for Radical Evangelical dissent.

Northern New England in the late eighteenth century was a region in cultural crisis. Virtually none of the traditional patterns of life long established in colonial areas transferred to the hinterland without significant alteration. Compared with Nova Scotia or old New England, the hill country was more severely affected by the forces of change: Nova Scotia experienced frontier development but not revolution; old New England endured revolution but did not face the wilderness. The hill country was caught both in revolutionary political change and in the sweeping modifications necessitated by the frontier. This situation caused not only the breakdown of traditional ideals and institutions but also a search for new cultural forms expressive of the unprecedented realities of the new New England. The synthetic process was to be complex, molding tradition into new shapes dictated by emerging regional realities. The result might be termed Antifederalist culture, reflecting the localist, egalitarian, and tribal world view of the settlers and their institutions.

Around 1780 the hill country reached its maximum point of fluidity, a moment when environmental and cultural strain was at its highest, when the search for regional autonomy became most intense. For a decade all factors of change persisted undiminished. Stability was achieved around 1790, and for the next two decades the hill country enjoyed the zenith of prosperity and the flowering of its Antifederalist culture. The War of 1812, followed by the famine of 1816, plunged the region into a decline from which it never fully recovered. By 1820 the hill country was becoming an economic backwater, its agricultural boom spent, its population siphoned off to New York and the trans-Appalachian west, its cultural influence and vigor collapsing into dependence on urban centers to the south and east.

The development of religion in the new settlements was intimately related to this background of historic crisis. As a primary articulation of world view, religion was necessarily involved in the hill country's search for autonomy and identity. The traditional religion of most settlers was from the outset plagued by institutional weakness and intellectual anachronism. By 1780 Congregationalists had failed to provide channels to routinize and control new religious demands rising from revolution, economic hardship, and ecclesiastical destitution. The crisis point occurred almost exactly at the same time as the military threat of revolutionary war was alleviated by Burgoyne's defeat. For more than five years after 1777, revival inflamed the new settlements. Out of this paroxysm came new religions that indexed the cultural world of the Republic's first frontier and invested that world with radical ultimate meaning.

3

The New Light Stir

The most important religious event in rural New England during the Revolution was a revival that swept across the hill country and maritime Canada between 1776 and 1783. At the outbreak of hostilities all Evangelicals prescribed a new awakening, whether to purify Patriots and enlist God's aid in the struggle — as urged by New Light Congregationalists — or to proclaim as did Radicals "a spiritual assurance which rejected and transcended the tribulations of the secular world."[1] Rhetoric of the former kind buttressed the established order against ideological and institutional depredations of war and formed a powerful religious appeal to soldiers and citizens alike to persevere in revolutionary activity.[2]

The latter sort of evangelism sparked a renewal of charismatic religion and Radical Evangelical growth in the new settlements. The revival, called the New Light Stir in New England and the New Light Revival in Canada, established Baptists as a principal religious group on the frontier and also fostered the appearance of many local schismatic sects. Out of the Stir also came permanent indigenous religions of rural New England — Shakers, Universalists, and Freewill Baptists — each transmuting Radical Evangelicalism into new form under the combined force of revival, revolution, and frontier. The Stir was a declaration of identity for the new settlements, a religious analogue to the cultural and political turmoil assaulting the northern frontier. Its eventual consequence was the creation of new New England religions.

The revival began in the Yankee townships of Nova Scotia. The settlements of the Minas Basin were occupied primarily by Radical Evangelicals and New Lights during the 1760s and early 1770s. These settlers made up a constituency ripe for awakening when long-threatened war finally broke out. The latent power of charismatic religion was catalyzed by Henry Alline, an eccentric Radical who typified in many ways the rural leaders of the New Light Stir. Alline was born at Newport, Rhode Island, on 14 January 1748. His parents were descended from large and respected Plymouth Colony families, but like so many of their peers they had encountered economic and social limitations in southeastern New England by mid-century. Around 1760 the Alline family joined a party of 113 Connecticut and Rhode Island residents who removed to Falmouth, Nova Scotia. Alline's theological education was minimal, consisting of sermons by itinerant Baptists and Separates of the Minas Basin and reading in the Bible, spiritual autobiographies, and revival accounts, probably including Edwards's *Life of David Brainerd* and Whitefield's *Journals*.[3]

At the age of twenty he experienced sexual fantasies regarding a female acquaintance that plunged him into an extended period of conviction and depression. Seven years later, on 26 March 1775, while praying for divine mercy, he accidentally turned to the Thirty-eighth Psalm: "O Lord, rebuke me not in thy wrath: neither chasten me in thy hot displeasure." The text "took hold of me with such power, that it seemed to go through my whole soul, and read therein every thought of my heart, and raised my soul with groans and earnest cries to God, so that it seemed as if God was praying in, with, and for me!" In classic Evangelical fashion Alline yielded to this "impression," giving up "all to God" and willing "that God should reign in me and rule over me at his pleasure." Suddenly, "redeeming love broke into my soul with repeated scriptures with such power, that my whole soul seemed to be melted down with love."[4]

In short order Alline received by spiritual illumination a call to ministry and doctrinal insights including the absolute necessity of the New Birth, the near approach of the Second Coming, divine benevolence to sinners, and human free will and ability in the process of conversion. Armed with these beliefs and a powerful style of spiritual preaching, Alline set out as an unlicensed itinerant in the Minas Basin. He chose to begin his ministry on a symbolic day, 19 April 1776, the anniversary of Lexington and Concord, underscoring the pacifism of his charismatic message. Alline's evangelism bore all the hallmarks of the Whitefieldian style: "itinerant preaching in any available place; extemporaneous sermons designed for dramatic conversions; lay participation in religious services; emotional extravagance; and open confrontation with those who opposed evangelical principles."[5]

And there was ample opposition. Alline's own family rejected his ministry, as did many settlers who suspected an unlettered exhorter. The ministers of the Minas Basin publicly opposed Alline, particularly Jonathan Scott, a Presbyterian minister originally from Middleborough, Massachusetts. Scott took up the pen as well as the pulpit against Alline, publishing sermons, exposés, and polemics that denounced Alline's revivalism and doctrinal deviance. In addition, Alline encountered strong competition in the field from William Black, a Methodist itinerant who pressed the advantage of Arminian free will and perfectionism to draw off newly awakened converts into the Wesleyan persuasion.

Yet Alline was successful. He repeatedly toured the Minas Basin from 1776 to 1779, and during that period he personally gathered three churches that united in ordaining him an "itinerant Preacher" in April 1779. That fall Alline extended his successful labors to the St. John River valley and the Cumberland region of New Brunswick. In 1781 he visited the west and south coasts of Nova Scotia, and in 1782, Prince Edward Island. In 1783 he took his gospel to northern New England, where on 28 January 1784 he died of consumption in North Hampton, New Hampshire. Alline's evangelistic career was meteoric; everywhere he preached he gained converts and fomented intrachurch schism. He organized half a dozen congregations and coaxed divisions in a dozen more. After his death these churches spearheaded yet another revival in the 1790s that produced a vigorous and permanent Baptist presence in Nova Scotia after 1800. Almost single-handedly, Alline sparked a wave of mass revivalism unprecedented in maritime Canada, that region's own "Great Awakening."[6]

Alline's New Light movement was eclectic in doctrine and polity. His thought was shaped by the overwhelming personal experience of the New Birth rather than by the Edwardsean synthesis. He took as his intellectual task "to construct an alternative to Calvinistic theology as he understood it and . . . to transform mysticism from a personal tendency into an element of formal theology."[7] To do this, the evangelist developed an esoteric spiritual theology grounded in Calvinist tradition but heavily influenced by the Christian Platonism of William Law and the metaphysical speculations of John Fletcher. The social aspects of Alline's mission were no less unorthodox. He was an open-communion Radical Evangelical. In his hands, however, that doctrine became an invitation for Congregationalists, Separates, Baptists, and Presbyterians to withdraw from their communions and join his ecumenical conventicle. Yet Alline, like Whitefield, did not insist that his followers adopt the same position. Alline's ecclesiology demanded absolute congregational autonomy and voluntary payment to ministers. His moral teachings included pacifism and a prohibition of lawsuits among brethren. And as they had done in New England, these Radical Evangelical teachings brought schism as well as revival to Nova Scotia's churches.

The Nova Scotia revival set the pattern for the awakening of the northern frontier. It was centered on the ministry of a charismatic leader. His visionary experience, millennial expectations, and passionate gospel call stirred churched and unchurched alike to seek saving grace. Alline's demand for the New Birth was combined with anti-Calvinist beliefs and an explicitly schismatic strategy of evangelism. His revival exploited the institutional weakness of traditional religion and gained its converts at the price of wide-spread ecclesiastical disruption and doctrinal dispute. To fill the social void left by departure from familiar institutions, Alline acted as personal shepherd to intimate gathered communities of saints who governed one another in covenantal moral discipline.

In addition to these theological and social consequences, the New Light Revival also had clear political implications. Alline's gospel of pacifism spread through neutral Nova Scotia just after the most serious threat of American invasion had passed and British consolidation of the province was assured. Yet the revival was "an inadvertent counter-revolutionary force" at best, for Nova Scotian Yankees were opposed to war for independence before 1776 and stoutly maintained their neutrality thereafter. The revival rather served to confirm this stance by providing a new political and cultural identity for Canadian Yankees that was "at one time anti-British and anti-American, radical and counter-revolutionary."[8] Religion in effect replaced nationalism as a primary cultural identity, supplying the intellectual and social substance necessary for New Englanders to reorient themselves in an age of rapid and intense change.

Many of the same characteristics were exhibited in the New Light Stir in rural New England. The process of religious change there was far more complex, but essentially the same results of Radical Evangelical growth and sectarian innovation appeared in both sectors of the northern frontier. The first sign of large-scale revival in the New England hill country appeared in 1778 with a sudden growth of Quakerism in New Hampshire and Maine.

Leadership for Quaker expansion came from the Nine Partners Quarterly Meeting, located in New York's Oblong Patent in the eastern Hudson Valley. The influential leader at Nine Partners was David Ferriss, a Whitefieldian evangelist who helped to convert James Davenport at Yale in the 1730s and later converted to the Inner Light.[9] Ferriss and the Nine Partners Meeting periodically dispatched missionaries to southern New England through the early 1770s in hopes of kindling revivals among Friends. During the Revolution, Quakers' nonbelligerent status afforded opportunity for wider ministry to correligionists who needed ideological and spiritual support in time of war. In April 1777 Nine Partners Meeting named two of its young members Public Friends to tour "as far eastward as way might open." The leader of the mission was David Sands, a 1767 convert by vision from Presbyterianism who first "appeared in the ministry" during a tour of Connecticut and Rhode Island in 1772.

Sands and his colleague Aaron Lancaster spent the summer and fall of 1777 touring the area served by the Salem, Massachusetts, and Kittery, Maine, Monthly Meetings. During these months they performed the normal functions of Public Friends, exhorting and disciplining existing meetings, visiting isolated Quaker families, and preaching publicly on occasion. But in 1778 and 1779 Sands traveled alone into western Maine and the Kennebec Valley preaching openly to Friend and non-Friend alike. The warm reception he received in "this wild new country" convinced him that "Friends here, if they keep their place, will increase."[10]

Sands's preaching emphasized the revivalistic and perfectionistic implications of Quaker Inner Light. He insisted that carnality could be overcome and pure spirituality attained in this life through the experience of immediate revelation. As he put it, "the old heaven" of doctrinal error and worldly sin could be "dissolved" and "a new earth" of spirit and discipline created "through the melting power of truth."[11] His message of spiritual renewal and pacifism, delivered in vigorous Whitefieldian rhetoric, created an exciting religious option for many Radical Evangelicals as well as "destitute" Quakers. At Leicester, Maine, for example, "divers people not of our Society" attended Sands's preaching, "and the Lord's power was over all, and the witness in many hearts seemed to be reached."[12]

Through such itinerant evangelism Sands "convinced" many Radical Evangelical settlers to embrace Quakerism while pressing his particularly revivalistic style on traditionally quietistic Yankee Friends. His tour revitalized Friends' meetings from Boston to Kittery and generated new meetings in the backcountry. Sands personally gathered more than a dozen congregations that soon organized into the Windham, New Hampshire, and Vassalborough, Maine, Monthly Meetings. But even more important, Sands's success indicated the readiness of settlers on the frontier to modify their beliefs and follow a faith that promised spiritual transformation and sanctified community.[13]

The Quaker revival of 1778 was but the prelude to a far larger "time of refreshing" among Baptists, Separates, and New Light Congregationalists. Despite the severe disruptions of wartime, a number of Congregationalist ministers were able to itinerate briefly in the hill country. Many of these were pastors visiting former parishioners who had removed to the frontier. Following the urging of ministerial associations and denominational leaders, these itinerants promoted revival on the frontier as at home. Their mission was indisputably successful in New Hampshire, western Massachusetts, and the Connecticut Valley. In 1778 evidence of growing Congregationalist strength appeared in the form of eight new hill country parishes. Expansion continued with nine more churches the next year, a peak of twelve in 1780, and an additional ten in 1781.

By 1782, however, the brief Congregationalist phase of the New Light Stir was over. Baptist and sectarian evangelism soon encroached on the newly organized parishes and the chronic shortage of ministers left them destitute for long periods. Under such circumstances the promising network of New Light churches failed to mature, and little further Congregationalist growth occurred in the hill country during the 1780s. Nonetheless, the creation of forty churches between 1778 and 1781 was the largest increment of growth for Congregationalism between the Great Awakening and the Second Great Awakening.[14]

Separates were also active in the New Light Stir, though without the benefit of fixed institutions. The leaders of the Separate revival were rural exhorters Joseph Marshall, David Avery, and Ithimar Hibbard, who itinerated widely in the Green Mountains and Connecticut Valley. But Separate revivalism was often a lay enterprise conducted in isolated conditions among friendship circles. In this context, Separates' charismatic and visionary religion easily broke up into a profusion of local sects during the Stir. Thus the Separates played their characteristically radical and dissenting part in the hill country revival that would mark their last major appearance in New England religion.[15]

It was the Baptists who were most successful in the New Light Stir. In 1778 Caleb Blood, an elder from Marlow, New Hampshire, wrote to the Warren Association describing a rich missionary field in the Connecticut Valley. The association responded by appointing four missionaries to the north, of whom "very agreeable accounts were received of their free reception in many places" during 1778 "and in some instances of very remarkable and glorious effects of the Gospel."[16] Four more missionaries were dispatched in 1779, and late in the year Samuel Stillman's Circular Letter singled out "the Westward and Northern frontier settlements of our country, where God's people have been quickened and built up in their most holy faith, and many careless sinners awakened and turned to God in the year past."[17] By 1780 Baptists had gathered six new churches in the valley and had formed informal congregations in at least a dozen more towns.[18]

The revival impulse soon spread to the east. Hezekiah Smith of Haverhill, Massachusetts, found time between tours as chaplain in the Continental army to coax a revival in his home church and to gather two new congregations in New Hampshire during 1779. To the north, Smith's protégé Samuel Shepard of Brentwood, New Hampshire, itinerated widely in 1780 and a year later reported to Isaac Backus "some hundreds of souls are hopefully converted in the counties of Rockingham, Strafford, and Grafton in New Hampshire, within a year past."[19] Shepard's mission produced a dozen new churches, ample evidence for his claim that "there appears to be a general increase of the Baptist principles, through all the Eastern parts of New England."

The New Light Stir brought a dramatic increase in membership to the Warren Association. In 1779 Warren numbered 1,876 members. But the next year the association reported 542 baptisms and 796 new members. These figures represented the greatest annual growth for New England Baptists until the Second Great Awakening. In 1781 there were 470 more baptisms and 441 new members. In little more than two years the Warren Association almost doubled its membership, consolidated its organization, and forged revivalism into an effective tool for mission on the frontier.[20]

Although the Warren Association ministered successfully to all New England east of the Connecticut Valley, the Green Mountain area of Vermont remained too isolated for even its zealots to reach regularly. Nonetheless, revival struck southwestern Vermont soon after the Battle of Bennington in 1777. With apparently no coordinated missionary effort, five churches were gathered around Shaftesbury between 1779 and 1781. Three of these along with the area's two pre-Revolutionary churches formed the Shaftesbury Baptist Association on 12 June 1780.[21] Shaftesbury soon adopted the principles and plan of the Philadelphia Baptist Association of 1707 and entered into close ties with the Warren Association. As the revival continued Shaftesbury undertook the normal functions of doctrinal advice, ordination, and general oversight, and by the mid-1780s it had brought coherence and order to the fast-growing Baptist denomination throughout western New England.[22]

By Isaac Backus's count, a century and a half of Baptist history in New England had produced only fifty-three churches before 1778. Thirty-six more were founded during the revival years 1778 through 1782. By the latter year the entire frontier had been opened up to Baptist evangelism, and the foundations had been laid for effective organization. In the west the Shaftesbury Association of 1780 was followed by the Woodstock and Vermont associations in 1783 and 1785; in the White Mountains the New Hampshire and Meredith associations were organized in 1785; and in Maine the Bowdoinham Association formed in 1788.[23]

The New Light Stir thus was predominantly a Radical Evangelical event, and as such it reflected the Whitefieldian themes of the New Birth, charismatic gifts, separation from the world, and the gathered church. But above all the rural revivalists seized on millennialism and perfectionism as vehicles of persuasion. Belief in the imminent Second Coming of Christ and the concomitant search for complete sanctification among the "saved remnant" in the Last Days were irresistible and effective themes for evangelists responding to revolutionary "wars and rumors of war."

Congregationalist divines also proclaimed "the promised day of the Lord," but there was a significant and revealing difference between the two visions of the future. The Congregationalist view, typified by Ezra Stiles's 1783 sermon *The United States Elevated to Glory and Honor,* focused on America as the chosen nation of God, blessed by the Lord with millennial holiness, virtue, prosperity, and empire. Proceeding from this endorsement and support of the Revolution, Congregationalists articulated a sanguine expectation for an earthly millennial kingdom in America.[24] Radical Evangelicals, on the other hand, held to the notion that war confirmed human sinfulness and depravity and that the revival itself signaled the speedy end of history and the imminent establishment of the otherworldly kingdom of the New Jerusalem.

It was a conflict between premillennialism and postmillennialism—

whether the thousand-year reign of the saints would precede or follow the cataclysmic Second Coming of Christ. The rural saints of the New Light Stir were certain that their reign would commence only after the imminent return of Christ, and instead of finding hope and solace in America's military triumph they sought "the signs of the times" in political events and natural omens to discern the moment of millennial dawn.

One such event—the Dark Day of 1780—occurred about midway through the Stir and served to drive it to new heights of chiliastic fervor. On 19 May 1780, from early morning in the Hudson Valley to mid-afternoon as far east as Casco Bay, Maine, all of New England was plunged into an eerie and profound darkness. At Worcester, "the Obscurity was so great that those who had good eyesight could scarcely see to read common print; the birds and fowls in many places retired to roost as tho' it had been actually night, and people were obliged to light candles to dine by." Accounts from Amenia, New York; Rupert, Vermont; Ipswich, Massachusetts; Portsmouth, Maine; and elsewhere all confirmed the story, amplifying it with reports of distant thunderings and other omens. At Newport, for example, "a Ball of fire was seen to pass swiftly and southerly over the water" in the afternoon darkness.[25]

The impact of the Dark Day was electric: To the already indubitable millennial signs of war and revival, God had added yet another through dramatic natural omens. Even in sophisticated New Haven, Ezra Stiles reported that "the inhabitants were thrown into a Consternation, as if the appearance was preternatural." Observers in other urban centers registered similar popular dismay; on the frontier the message of the darkness was even more fearful and compelling. Even Stiles himself, though convinced that the condition was caused by smoke from slash-and-burn land clearing on the northern frontier, could not resist speculation about the meaning of the event. "It is not recollected from History," he mused, "that a darkness of equal Intenseness & Duration has ever happened in any parts of the world, except in Egypt, and at the miraculous Eclipse at the Crucifixion of our Blessed Savior."[26] Stiles did not follow the implication that New England might soon see the climax of the divine drama begun with Exodus and the Crucifixion, but he did mirror the reaction of many that "the unusual appearances in the Natural World ought to lead our Tho'ts up to the Author of Nature, & the Energies of his irresistable power, that we may be filled with reverential awe of the divine majesty."[27]

For rural revivalists, the Dark Day, the wartime atmosphere, and the revival itself all were indications of prophetic fulfillment portending the Last Days. Understanding themselves as experiencing the narrative of the Book of Revelation, revivalists urged their hearers to join the last witnesses to the gospel and claim the powers of spiritual and physical perfection granted to the apostolic remnant. The theme of millennial expectation suffused the New Light Stir. The larger and more intense the awakening became, the

more self-validating evidence it provided that Divine Providence was preparing to introduce "the period so often spoken of in God's word, when the
earth shall be full of the knowledge of the Lord, as the waters cover the sea."
Radical Evangelicals vigorously pursued their mission of proclaiming the
Last Days of grace to rural New Englanders, urging them to join the hosts
of saints "crying in union, come Lord Jesus, come quickly."[28]

The New Light Stir gradually weakened after 1782, but significant local
revivals continued sporadically throughout the 1780s and 1790s. The Stir
thus introduced revivalism as a permanent element in the religious culture
of the northern frontier. It also provided a participatory mode of expression
for Radical Evangelical dissent from dominant Revolutionary politics and
ideology. New England Baptists, Separates, and New Lights, like their
Nova Scotian counterparts, utilized revival to articulate political neutrality
and solidarity with sacred rather than secular reality. It was not a matter of
replacing politics with religion; it was one of reasserting religion's primacy
in a time of political conflict and cultural change. In the process, however,
the very norms of the Radical Evangelical heritage were themselves transformed into new shapes that reflected the particular intellectual, emotional,
and social demands of time and place. These transformations first became
visible in the form of local sectarian movements that flourished widely in
rural New England from 1780 until the Second Great Awakening.

The largest and best-known local sect was the Universal Friends, led by
the prophetess Jemima Wilkinson, which flourished in Rhode Island and
Connecticut from 1776 to 1789. Wilkinson was born in 1752 at Cumberland, Rhode Island, the eighth child of a prosperous Quaker family. She
came under Radical Evangelical influence during the late 1760s quite possi-
bly through the itinerancy of George Whitefield. By 1776 she had rejected
the plain style of Quakerism and embraced the charismatic faith of a Separate congregation at nearby Abbott Run. The year of revolution was a time
of religious and moral turmoil in the Wilkinson family. Jemima's elder sister, Patience, was dismissed from Smithfield Lower Friends Meeting in
1776 for bearing an illegitimate child, and three elder brothers were expelled the same year because they frequented "Trainings for Military Service and endeavor[ed] to Justify the Same."[29]

Amidst this disintegration of familial and religious bonds Jemima experienced renewed conviction and ascetic physical mortification. In October
1776 she contracted an "illness" during which "she appeared to meet the
Shock of Death." In her delirium she saw two archangels who announced
that the Last Days were come and that "the Spirit of Life from God, had descended to earth, to warn a lost and guilty, perishing and dying world, to
flee from the wrath to come." The Spirit "was waiting to assume the body
which God had prepared," the body of Jemima Wilkinson. She experienced
the departure of her own soul to heaven and its replacement by "the Spirit

of Life from God," which henceforth "took full possession" of her.[30] Immediately Wilkinson began to exhort and itinerate, wearing a clerical costume of robes and cravat-bands, surmounted by a high-crowned white Quaker hat. She called herself "the Public Universal Friend," a minister whose mission was to witness to the Spirit within her and preach salvation to all who would listen in "the eleventh hour."

Wilkinson preached an Arminian theology that each soul enjoyed a "day of grace" in which it was free to choose salvation or damnation. Millennialism and perfectionism were also salient dimensions of Wilkinson's message. To war-ravaged Narragansett society she offered a life of holiness and moral discipline in preparation for the Last Judgment. "As in war an Error is death," she proclaimed, "so in death an Error is damnation. Therefore live as you intend to die and die as you intend to live."[31] The decisive element in Wilkinson's ministry, however, was her personal charisma. "She exhorts in a pathetic manner," reported an early convert, "with great Confidence and Boldness . . . says that she has an immediate Revelation for all she delivers." Wilkinson's sermons, usually delivered at taverns or private homes, were often accompanied by prophecies, ecstatic prayer, and the gift of spiritual discernment. Her gender, costume, meticulous appearance, and social skills also contributed to her messianic impact on hearers. Although stopping short of asserting the power to judge and forgive sin, Wilkinson presented herself as an infallible, inspired guide in all matters of human life, possessing "the Voice that spake as never Man spake."[32]

Wilkinson's first converts were members of her immediate family. Her father, four sisters ranging in age from twelve to twenty-nine, and a younger brother who had served in the military all professed faith in her by the end of 1777. But the most important early convert was Judge William Potter of South Kingston, Rhode Island, a wealthy and distinguished member of the Narragansett elite. Potter, whose household included thirteen children and twelve slaves in 1774, built a fourteen-room addition to the family mansion to house the Public Universal Friend. From this social base Wilkinson was able to gather other families into the sect: the Hathaways, a prominent Tory family of New Bedford; the Smith family of Stonington and Groton, Connecticut; the five sons of Benjamin Brown of New London and their families; and several clans at East Greenwich and New Milford, Connecticut.

These first converts gathered into typical Radical Evangelical congregations. In 1783 the Universal Friends built a meetinghouse at East Greenwich and issued a public declaration of faith stating "that it was by obeying the Divine Counsil Spoken to us by & through the Dear Universal Friend of friends that we are redeemed from wrath to come and are brought into Union with God & his holy one."[33] Similar congregations appeared at South Kingston, Stonington, and New Milford in the mid-1780s. The center of community life was worship and moral discipline. Universal

Friends worshiped daily in a variety of formats: silent meetings, sermonic meetings, and prayer meetings. These sessions embodied a synthesis of Quaker and Separate spirituality and emphasized the exercise of charismatic gifts. During one meeting Wilkinson was inspired to perform a healing; during another, Alice Potter Hazard cast devils out of her mentally ill brother.[34]

At an early date, however, Universal Friends' congregations developed into more intimate biological communities. "Four of Jemima Wilkinson's sisters, her earliest converts, married members of the society. Thus the Wilkinsons of Cumberland were allied with the Potters of South Kingston and the Botsfords married Hathaways from New Bedford. Eventually all the leading families in the society of Universal Friends were linked together by ties of marriage."[35]

The prophetess was resistant to familism, however, enjoining celibacy on her followers as the spiritually purest way of life. Yet she did not forbid marriage and took a more positive tack on the question by rewarding continent members, especially females, with special responsibilities for mission, worship, and moral oversight. Intermarriage paradoxically enforced another aspect of Wilkinson's communal leadership. With members living in such close physical and biological proximity, every aspect of their behavior was prescribed. The prophetess issued detailed rules for personal hygiene, dress, food preparation, indoor and outdoor labor, social contact, and all other matters of life-style. The sect thus became an unusual social composition, a kinship network of nuclear families governed by a charismatic celibate matriarchy. This tribal organization lent stability and discipline to the commitment of members and reflected the manner in which sectarian religion constructed new forms of primary community.

Jemima Wilkinson's vision extended beyond New England. Seeking additional converts among Quakers, she began itinerating in and around Philadelphia in 1782; within a few years she had gathered another network of converts there. Obeying a revelation to unite her followers, Wilkinson planned an independent communal settlement in the wilderness where Universal Friends could initiate the millennial kingdom. In 1788 the sect purchased land in the Seneca Lake region of New York; the next year they founded their settlement, aptly named New Jerusalem. The most dedicated Universal Friends followed Wilkinson there and created a prosperous utopian community that, however, did not long survive the death of the prophetess in 1819.

Another Radical sect appeared around 1775 at Harvard, Massachusetts, "a typical subsistence community" thirty miles west of Boston. Harvard experienced a classic pattern of religious pluralization after the Great Awakening. Separates organized in 1753, calling Charlestown pipefitter Shadrach Ireland as their minister. By 1776, however, a sizable proportion of the Separates had become Baptists, and in that year they organized a congregation under their local leader Isaiah Parker. Ireland, meanwhile, became increasingly eccentric and extreme in his religious teaching. Around 1770 he abandoned his wife and family and professed the doctrine of "spiritual wifery." Ireland persuaded his followers to construct "the Square House," a large brick dwelling in which Ireland resided with his new spiritual wife and a retinue of other female disciples.[36] About 1775 he proclaimed himself immortal and urged followers to obey his instructions so that they too would achieve physical and spiritual perfection. Included in his rules were a ban on marriage for single converts and a demand for married partners "not to lodge with each other." The Irelandites abandoned the biological family and occupied the Square House, where the prophet molded them into a celibate perfectionist sect.[37]

Ireland's movement flourished for two more years, until his failing health made it impossible to sustain his claim to immortality. In preparing the community for his death, Ireland shifted to an apocalyptic focus, predicting the imminent arrival of Christ. According to Isaac Backus, Ireland pronounced on his deathbed, "I am going but don't bury me; for the time is short; God is coming to take the church." After his death in September 1778, Ireland's disciples obeyed, leaving his corpse reposing in a lime-filled box for more than six weeks before finally burying it. Utilizing their esoteric interpretations to the fullest, the disciples regarded Ireland's departure as a prophetic sign of the Second Coming, and the sect survived its founder. Irelandites remained at the Square House until 1781, when many of them were converted by the Shakers.[38]

Other kinds of local sectarian activity took place elsewhere in the hill country during the New Light Stir. In Maine, New Light immigration produced tension in rural parishes originally of Old Light persuasion. At Gorham in 1773, New Lights protested paying the salary of Old Light Josiah Thacher and two years later began independent meetings where "all who had the gift should preach." Into this unsettled situation came returning young veterans "carrying rather unsettled notions of religion." As the New Light Stir spread into Gorham, these veterans "almost to a man" joined the "Come-Outers" and fueled their enthusiasm to new heights.

By 1779 the Come-Outers were practicing ecstatic worship quite reminiscent of James Davenport's followers in the Great Awakening. The charismatic leaders were "generally females" who "wrought themselves up to complete frenzy, even to frothing at the mouth, dancing, stamping, and whirling around." This exercise eventuated in a trance state that they regarded as "holding communion with God." When conscious again these charismatics confronted individual sinners, "assailing them with a torrent of invectives . . . not forgetting to remind the poor culprit of each and every known fault, or deviation from the path of right, which he had been known to take from his infancy."[39]

At its peak the Come-Outer movement embraced "strange notions" of physical and spiritual perfection as well as pacifism. The sectarians also embraced a radical life-style marked by shunning, separation from the world, and strict sumptuary codes. "Ribbons, ruffles, jewelry, and ornaments of all kinds were in their estimation especially articles of temptation used by the devil to work evil and ruin the soul of the wearer."

In 1780 the Come-Outers continued their campaign against the Old Lights, locking the parish church, rioting, and disrupting services. They in turn were beaten and stoned for their pacifism and radical deviance. The violence ended only with the assertion of civil and military order, along with "an epidemic of some sort" that forced cooperation between the competing religious groups. Active hostility subsided after 1781, but Gorham remained permanently divided on religious grounds.[40]

Other short-lived sectarian manifestations occurred in western New England during the Stir. The revival struck with particular power throughout the Berkshire Hills and the Taconic Range. Its course at New Lebanon, New York, six miles west of the Massachusetts line, was typical. "Operations" broke out among unchurched New Light settlers. The focal point of the New Lebanon revival was the imminent return of Christ and the search for millennial perfection. The millenarians coalesced into a local sect, holding protracted meetings in which glossolalia, visions, and prophecy were prominent gifts. The leader of the New Light sect was Joseph Meacham, son of a Baptist elder from Enfield, Connecticut. Meacham had been active in the Enfield church as a young man in the 1760s and early 1770s. By 1775 he had begun preaching as a lay exhorter. But in that year dissension appeared in the congregation that caused Meacham to doubt the validity of their profession of faith. "Seeing . . . those who professed to be Brethren, and followers of the Prince of peace, destroying, ravaging, and rending each other miserable as was in their power," Meacham left Enfield in 1776 and spent several years in spiritual and physical pilgrimage. He had arrived in New Lebanon not long before the outbreak of the New Light Stir.[41]

Under Meacham's leadership, the millennial fervor of the revival reached its peak with daily meetings in 1779 during which the New Lights awaited the Second Coming amidst ecstatic worship, perfectionist preaching, and other charismatic gifts. Mary Andrus, a participant in the revival, recalled that Meacham and other exhorters "testified that the latter day of glory was near at hand, and that Christ would shortly set up his kingdom on earth and make an end of sin."[42] When Christ did not appear in 1779, the congregation, and especially Meacham, suffered a severe spiritual depression that left them troubled about their erroneous interpretation of signs, yet still certain that God had indisputably signaled the end of the world. "The revival which was so powerful during the summer of 1779 seemed to die away in the fall, and the extraordinary operations ceased. Still the people retained a firm belief that Christ would shortly appear, but in what manner they knew not. They continued to come together as well as they could, to keep their faith and not be discouraged, tho their meetings seemed powerless and heavy."[43] The New Lebanon New Lights illustrated both the volatile millennial potential of the Stir and the social and theological consequences of the revival in rural communities. Unchecked enthusiasm and charisma easily led to apocalyptic expectations, but after a short period of feverish intensity, such local sects lapsed into religious anxiety and doubt. Left with heightened existential concern, the New Lebanon New Lights along with many similar communities in western Massachusetts continued to seek dramatic demonstration of spiritual power, especially the millennial sign of "actual freedom from all committed sin."

Similar movements occurred in Maine at New Gloucester, Alfred, and Sanford. In Sanford the Radicals were called "the Merry Dancers" for their unbridled ecstasy. Made up mainly of young war veterans, the Merry Dancers repeatedly disrupted the Congregationalist parish before gathering their own meeting in 1780. The perfectionism of this youthful group soon grew out of hand, bringing about "drinking to excess . . . and indecent and immoral practices." The Dancers also engaged in strange antics such as "hooting the Devil." Members dressed in strange garb while screaming, "Woe! Woe! Woe!" which was "audible in the stillness of the evening nearly the distance of one mile." The Merry Dancers explained such excesses as purification rites for perfection, "a sort of carnal slough through which they were doomed to pass, preparatory to spiritual regeneration."[44]

The Come-Outers, Merry Dancers, and New Lebanon New Lights illustrated the process of sect development on the northern frontier. Renewed religious concern, a rapid influx of settlers, and returning veterans created unstable socioreligious conditions, characterized by mounting division between New Lights and Old Lights. When revival struck in such circumstances, institutional fluidity permitted swift growth of heterodox doctrine and charismatic experience. Young men and women emerged as sectarian leaders on the basis of their extraordinary gifts while millennial expectation, new communal identity, and Old Light opposition kept revival at fever pitch. Typically these sectarian movements rose to a paroxysm of ecstatic deviance — chiliasm, orgiastic purification, violence. These episodes often passed quickly, leaving the sects in an ambiguous position that they resolved by either returning to the larger community or remaining apart in a kind of spiritual limbo, awaiting "further light."

Sectarian localism continued to flourish along with sporadic revivals until 1800 and beyond. The Dorrellites, for example, were a community of perfectionists that arose in the Yorker communities of Guilford, Vermont, and Leyden and Bernardston, Massachusetts, in the late eighteenth century. The leader of the sect was William Dorrell, a Tory who fought with Burgoyne at Saratoga. Upon returning to Vermont after the war, he received a visionary commission to prophesy and exhort sinners to perfection. But it was not until about 1794 that Dorrell proclaimed his own immortality and physical invulnerability. His preaching soon thereafter drew a number of converts who "discarded all revelations except what their leader received."[45]

The group adopted a semicommunal social organization, living in close proximity on contiguous farms. Dorrell demanded firm discipline from his followers, including "no eating or use of anything at the expense of life." Such strict discipline contrasted with the excess of Dorrellite public worship, which attracted "some very respectable families from all neighboring towns" to meetings for "eating, drinking, singing and dancing, and hearing lectures" from the prophet. Dorrell's teaching seems to have been a sort of pentecostal Deism: The prophet attributed his revelations not to God or Christ, but "the light of nature." Followers apparently took his visionary experiences to be a heightened form of natural perception, a belief that implied a human capacity to transcend physical laws when empowered by God.[46]

The Dorrellites flourished for several years before the prophet was publicly disgraced in 1798. When Dorrell announced at a meeting that "no man can harm me," an outraged visitor assaulted him, bloodying his nose. Bereft in the most dramatic way of his principal claim, Dorrell nonetheless was able to hold together a small group of believers into the nineteenth century. In 1802 members of the sect still lived together on Frizzel Hill in Guilford, continuing to "speak as though they meant to go to hell, sooner than obey the teaching of any man which comes outside of the revelation of God they pretend to have themselves."[47]

A different pattern of local sectarianism appeared in the rise of the New Israelites of Middletown, Vermont. This community was inspired by Nathaniel Wood, a Separate from Norwich, Connecticut, who was one of Middletown's original settlers and sire of its leading family. During the 1780s Wood's sons, Jacob, Ephraim, and Nathaniel, served the new settlement in most elective capacities including state representative, justice of the peace, and selectman. The Woods also had been prominent in the founding of the Middletown Congregationalist Church in 1780, but nine years later Nathaniel Wood was expelled for censoriousness and heterodoxy. "He had gotten up a new system of religious doctrine, and seemed determined it should prevail at all events." His three sons and their families allied with the patriarch and withdrew from the church.[48]

The new family sect soon assumed a menacing tone, pronouncing "supernatural agencies and special judgments of God" on local citizens. This defensive posture was elaborated into theological terms with "Priest" Wood's assertion that his followers were "modern Israelites or Jews, who were under the special guardianship of the Almighty while the Gentiles—all who were opposed to them—would suffer from their hostility." For about ten years Priest Wood and his New Israelites adopted rigorous dietary and sumptuary codes based on their reading of the Mosaic Law and manifested prophetic and other spiritual gifts. During this period the sect grew to a modest size, including in its numbers Joseph Smith, Sr., father of the Mormon prophet, and Oliver Cowdery, Sr., father of one of the three Mormon Witnesses.[49]

Around 1799 the New Israelites came under the influnce of a diviner named Wingate who convinced the Woods that secret prophecies and miraculous root medicines could be discovered by use of divining rods. Priest Wood pronounced the rods to be instruments of God's judgment and used their powers to make increasingly bizarre demands on his followers. For example, the rods revealed to Wood that Satan was inhabiting the clothes of two adolescent females in the sect, who were then directed to strip and hike naked over a nearby mountain to purify themselves. A temple was built and then abandoned by command of the rods, and for several years New Israelites spent their summers digging for treasure under their guidance.

This sectarian jumble of divination, prophecy, and alienation crystallized in Wood's prediction that "the destroyer would pass through the land and slay a portion of unbelievers" on the night of 14 January 1801 and that a great earthquake would obliterate the remaining unfaithful. The New Israelites recognized the prophecy as a second Passover preparatory to the end of the world. They abandoned their homes, painting over the doorposts the slogan "Jesus our passover was sacrificed for us" as a sign for their possessions to be spared. They then gathered in a schoolhouse to observe the Passover by fasting, prayer, and exhortation. The local militia was mustered to meet any insurrectionary action by the New Israelites, but the night passed quietly. Wood announced a slight miscalculation, then eight weeks later instructed believers to contribute their specie to pave the streets of the New Jerusalem.[50] At this point the diviner Wingate was exposed as a convicted counterfeiter, and the movement collapsed. The Wood, Smith, and Cowdery families left Middletown in disgrace for upstate New York, where their religious enthusiasm passed to a new generation.

Still other, less documented sects flourished in the hill country. During the 1790s Thomas Fessenden of Walpole, New Hampshire, gathered several congregations around his unorthodox "science of sanctity." Around 1805 William Bullard, a Vermont prophet, organized an ascetic community of "pilgrims" in the central Green Mountains. Perhaps the most elusive sect was the Annihilationists, also called Nothingarians, who believed that the souls of the unjust were not damned, but rather exterminated at death. This particular tenet, which assumed that the elect were the only immortal and truly alive beings on earth, was popular especially in the upper Connecticut Valley.[51]

The evidence, though fragmentary, suggests that literally dozens of local sects were spawned in rural New England by the New Light Stir and its aftermath. Revivalism is an uncontrollable form of religious transformation, an when it struck an already fragmented culture in the hill country the result was an explosion of enthusiasm and heterodoxy. A region mired in the throes of war, political struggle for self-determination, precarious economic conditions, and frontier isolation did not possess the means to routinize religious renewal into stable institutional form. The Congregationalists who first called for revival in the new settlements were paradoxically weakened by the rise of Radical Evangelicalism in the New Light Stir. Baptists and Separates who most vigorously promoted the Stir were in turn victimized by local sectarian movements that attracted many converts away from their organizational efforts.

Yet despite warnings from Congregationalists and Baptists that the sects were "as dangerous to the heedless passengers as Scylla and Charybodes are to the unskilful mariner," many rural New Englanders embraced them.[52] This was understandable, for the sects articulated basic social and intellectual discontent with colonial religion in all its forms and pointed toward new religious identities appropriate to unprecedented circumstances. Three interlocking dimensions of this emerging identity seem particularly important. First, the sects expressed an overwhelming need for deep and transforming personal religious experience. Virtually all the local sects were charismatic. They displayed a range and variety of gifts limited only by the imagination and creativity of the sectarians themselves. Their spirituality was so intense that it extended into the realm of sensory and physical reality, transforming even sexuality into an instrument for divine use, whether through celibacy, continence, or spiritual wifery. For the sectarians, religion was above all an experiential mode that gave access to new spiritual understanding and physical powers of sinlessness.

The sects also undertook to redefine social and economic order through the model of the extended family. They practiced separation from the world and built new social practices upon the kinship networks that comprised most of their membership. Marginal economic conditions helped extend this social reorientation through collective farming and communal property arrangements. Local sects tended to be economically egalitarian and socially authoritarian, with the charismatic leadership functioning often as symbolic "spiritual parents" to believing children. Extensive rituals and detailed prescription of daily activity followed from such an arrangement, providing concrete social and economic behaviors through which spiritual authority could be mediated. These characteristics suggest that rural sectarians absorbed the most distinctive social and economic traits of their environment — clans and friendship circles, egalitarian class structure, and cooperative subsistence economics — into their visions of religious community, thereby sacralizing and legitimating the life patterns of the new New England.

Finally, the local sects unmistakably modified the Calvinist theological tradition. Each group based its beliefs on a rejection of some salient feature of post-Awakening Calvinist thought, and no matter how bizarre the protests seemed, they contained serious intellectual content. Jemima Wilkinson, Shadrach Ireland, and William Dorrell challenged the uneasy Calvinist anthropology of innate depravity and spiritual sensation, claiming an essentially Arminian perfectionism. Annihilationists and Nothingarians, Merry Dancers and Come-Outers applied the logic of determinism in alternative ways, the former arguing that the damned had no existence after death, the latter that the elect were doomed to sin as a precondition for grace. Nathaniel Wood stood Evangelical Calvinist exegesis on its head, claiming that the Old rather than the New Testament was the norm for Christian faith and practice. Joseph Meacham surveyed the signs of the times and asserted that the gradual earthly appearance of Christ's kingdom argued by Edwards was erroneous. Rather, a violent and sudden Second Advent was about to commence.

These doctrines originating from the unexpected quarter of Radical Evangelicalism represented the intellectual breakdown of Calvinism. Proceeding from Whitefieldian assumptions heightened by revivalism, frontier isolation, war, and millennial expectations, the sectarians challenged the Calvinist tradition as logically restrictive and spiritually dead. The local sects typically retained much of the Calvinist theological edifice, but at key points such as the definition of human nature, revelation, or the soul's destiny they substituted new notions of divine truth. In most cases the theological implications of such revisions were not consciously elaborated. But the overall tendency was clearly toward greater human capacity and responsibility in the economy of salvation, a more benevolent conception of God, and a simplified gospel stripped of logical paradox and tortuous exegesis. The sects thus reflected the same intellectual orientation toward optimism, common sense, and certainty that characterized late-eighteenth-century Arminianism. But their gospels were not directly influenced by theological liberalism; rather they were an indigenous rural synthesis of extreme experientialism and intellectual rebellion against received Calvinism, a new theological identity for evanescent new religions.

Local sectarianism indicated the potential of the New Light Stir as a source for new religious forms. For at least some rural New Englanders, the visionary faiths of local prophets became the vehicle for vivid experience, intimate community, and eternal security. At the same time the sects preserved much of the Radical Evangelical tradition that informed northern settlers and blossomed in the New Light Stir. In addition, the local sects inaugurated an era of religious creativity and innovation in the new settlements that paralleled the fragmentation and synthesis of other cultural elements on the frontier. Out of the chaos of the Stir came these many indicators that the new New England would have a religious character as distinctive as its political, economic, and social life.

In the aftermath of the New Light Stir, Samuel Elsworth of Arlington,

Vermont, wrote a poem about the Dark Day that vividly articulated the impact of revivalism and sectarianism on the new settlements. The composition, titled "True Account of Appearances in the Heavens Seen by the Inhabitants of New England," was written from the perspective of a dismayed Congregationalist seeking to understand the meaning of his society's headlong rush to enthusiasm and heterodoxy. Elsworth identified the factors that were unhinging Calvinism: dissenting revivalism, biblical speculation, war, millennial expectation, natural omens, and proliferating sects. But it was the poet's conclusion that such disarray could only herald "the Second Coming of the Lord" that made his stanzas not only a complete summary but also a representative statement of the uncontrolled religious upheaval that was the New Light Stir.

Attend O Christians far and near,
And you the strangest truths shall hear,
That has for ages past befel,
This earthly globe on which we dwell.

Oft has the sacred truth been told,
By priests and prophets new and old,
That e'er the dreadful judgment day,
E'er nature moulders to decay,

Strange signs shall to the world arise,
And dreadful omens fill the skies.
The moon shall shroud her glim'ring light,
The sun shall be as dark as night.

Imposters shall in clouds appear,
And preach Lo Christ is there or here,
And thousands shall be led astray,
And perish from the heavenly way.

Now let us for a while attend,
The voice of Christ our heavenly friend.
Do not our present troubles shew,
His words are holy, just, and true.

Have not false preachers lately given,
A new and easy way to heaven,
And taught by practice and by word,
Blasphemous doctrines 'gainst the Lord.

How many sects entirely new,
Are daily springing into view,
Claiming exclusively a sight,
To Christ and heavenly glory bright.
Thus far the sacred truth's fulfilled,
As all are forced assent to yield

But now the solemn text is found,
To force conviction from the ground.

Earthquakes the solid world hath shook,
To ratify the sacred book,
Strange sights have fill'd the lofty sky,
And struck with dread th' admiring eye.

Strange noises likewise have been heard,
As is by men of truth declared,
And sounds of battle in the air,
And horrid deeds of arms declare.

The wonders of our threatened land,
Bespeak the Lord Jehovah's hand,
And shew if we believe his word,
The Second Coming of the Lord.[53]

PART

Two

Freewill
Baptists,
Universalists,
and
Shakers

4

Gifts of the Spirit

The many factors of religious change abroad in rural New England coalesced most dramatically and permanently in the rise of three major sects: the Freewill Baptists, the Universalists, and the Shakers. Each of these groups attained substantial size before 1800 and went far beyond the tentative innovations of the local sects to completely detailed polities, theologies, and liturgies. By 1815 they were "established sects," independent denominations that had introduced a new level of diversity and pluralism into the formerly homogeneous religious culture of Calvinist New England. In that year each sect numbered more than 100 congregations or the equivalent and commanded four to six thousand members, plus an indeterminate number of adherents and temporary followers. Such figures compared well with the other alternatives in the hill country. Congregationalists and Baptists each numbered 300 congregations by 1815. The new sects placed both of these Calvinist communions in a new world of pluralized beliefs and religious competition. At the same time the sects were the primary religious creation of the Revolutionary generation: Their heterodoxy and social structure translated into religious terms many of the pressing cultural concerns of a pioneer community.

The origins of the three sects illustrated the complexity and range of Radical Evangelicalism as an Anglo-American movement. In many ways the principal sects resembled their smaller local counterparts at least at first. The ultimate source for each was the charismatic, visionary experience of prophetic leaders. But these leaders, unlike the other rural prophets, possessed a more diverse theological background, were more directly influenced by the Evangelicalism of the wider British world—especially Whitefields later ministry — and in the new revelations and moral duties they proclaimed, they struck more fundamentally at the problematic aspects of Calvinist tradition.

The Freewill Baptist movement began with the end of George Whitefield's long itinerant career: Benjamin Randel, the sect's founder, was one of the Grand Itinerant's last converts. Randel, a tailor and sailmaker from Newcastle, New Hampshire, was born in 1749 and reared in an Old Light Congregationalist family. Though much opposed to the "delusion and enthusiasm" of revivalism, he was persuaded by friends to hear the venerable Whitefield at Portsmouth on 25 and 26 September 1770. After hearing three sermons at the packed meetinghouse of Harvard's President Samuel Langdon, Randel confirmed his opinion of the Grand Itinerant as "a worthless, noisy fellow."

A week later, however, news of the evangelist's death at Newburyport deeply disturbed Randel. "An arrow from the quiver of the Almighty struck through my heart," he recalled, "and a mental voice sounded through my ears." Randel became obsessed with the thought that "Whitefield is now in heaven, while I am in the road to hell." He quickly fell under conviction for his sins and "continued in this unutterable horror more than three weeks." Randel eventually "despaired of obtaining salvation from any, or all of my former religious duties." In this state of humiliation, however, the text of Hebrews 9:26 impressed itself on his mind: "But once in the end of the world hath he appeared to put away sin by the sacrifice of himself." "As I was meditating on this passage," he reported, "my load and burden of sin went off." Realizing that "the world and all its vanities" had suddenly become "loathsome" and that he "loved God and longed after righteousness," Randel concluded that "this is what I read of in the scriptures, being born again."[1]

The young convert joined Samuel Chase's Old Light congregation in Newcastle, but he soon discovered that it "was all in disorder — that some of its members were men of intemperance, and of corrupt or ungodly lives, and without reproof were suffered and allowed to come to the communion table every month." Randel objected to these irregularities, and in 1773 he organized a biweekly meeting "for the purpose of singing, praying, and reading a sermon or other good book." Samuel Chase and the Newcastle Old Lights promptly complained about "the old Whitefield sound" of the meeting. Conflict ensued that resulted in Randel's withdrawal from the church in 1775.[2]

In this period of controversy Randel married Jane Oram, a New Light convert like himself. She did not follow him, however, in separating from Congregationalism. The birth of their first child in May 1776 presented the couple with a difficult theological and liturgical dilemma: She desired infant baptism, but he, coming under the influence of Baptist William Hooper of

Madbury, New Hampshire, had become convinced that "believers were the only proper subjects of baptism." A serious domestic quarrel ensued. Jane Oram Randel became "very urgent to have the child christened, and wished Mr. Randel to carry it to the meeting and have it done. He told her it would do no good. Upon hearing this answer, she appeared to be affrightened and said, 'I don't know what you will become!' " Randel permitted the infant baptism of the child, but the dispute helped determine his own decision to be rebaptized. Randel was immersed and admitted to the Madbury Baptist Church in June 1776.[3]

Revolutionary war presented Randel with another serious religious question. As a strong Patriot he supported the cause of liberty, but he scrupled against bearing arms as a violation of Christian morality. He served briefly in a noncombatant role during late 1776 and early 1777, then returned to Newcastle where he dedicated his life to the "gospel ministry" vowing "to wear out my life in God's cause." As an itinerant licentiate of the Madbury Baptist Church, Randel sparked a small revival in early 1777 that met the intense ecclesiastical and political opposition of Old Lights. Wearing their antirevival orthodoxy as a badge of civic unity and patriotism, Newcastle's Old Lights accused Randel of disloyalty for fomenting religious dissent in time of war. After a series of assaults, stonings, and mobbings, Randel only narrowly escaped being tarred and feathered by the selectmen of Newcastle and nearby Rye. Allegations of Toryism continued as Randel fearlessly preached the priority of spiritual over temporal concerns. Trouble ceased only after the preacher faced down a hostile crowd at Newcastle and categorically refused to give up his calling. His evangelism was henceforth permitted, but as a social pariah Randel lost effectiveness and began looking elsewhere for a responsive audience.[4]

In the early stages of the New Light Stir Randel itinerated for the Madbury Baptist Church in the Portsmouth hinterland, and in 1779 he received a call from the hill country town of New Durham near the Maine border. Many of the New Durham Baptists, like Randel himself, possessed Old Light origins; to them his Arminianism seemed unobjectionable because it was accompanied by a vigorous demand for experiential piety and strict moral discipline. The Separate Baptist elders of the region, however, were strict Calvinists on matters of atonement and regeneration. When they questioned him on the doctrine of predestination and election, Randel readily admitted that he did not believe it or understand it. Shortly after accepting the New Durham call he was denounced and dismissed from the Baptist communion at Madbury. Randel was shocked to discover that his own religious development apparently had been flawed by incorrect doctrine. The New Durham congregation grew uneasy with his sermons, and soon he withdrew from the pulpit in confusion and acute distress.[5]

The period from 1773 to 1779 was deeply disturbing for the young preacher. He faced familial challenges, political opposition, and ecclesiastical sanction for his faith. Now the communion that had seemed to welcome him with the pure gospel had rejected him. Not only was his vow of ministerial service apparently invalid, but the very substance of his belief as well. He retired to his farm for an extended season of prayer "in which he cried constantly to the Lord to be taught." One day while praying in his cornfield, Randel demanded to know of God why he was kept in doctrinal darkness. "And the answer was, 'because thou hast too many right hands, and too many right eyes.' I said, Lord, what are my right hands and right eyes? And it appeared to me that they were my traditions, which I still held, and my old brethren who I had come out from."[6] In the opaque language of personal revelation Randel had discovered that the demand of true spirituality was greater than he had realized. "I was too much encumbered with natural connexions. I saw that I needed much purifying and refining." The ties of family, marriage, community, and religious tradition all had to be sacrificed to attain the true understanding he sought.

At this crucial moment Randel yielded to the power of the Spirit. The following sequence of psychological events was to become the most determinative in Randel's life. "O! the flaming power, which instantly passed through my soul . . . I had no feeling of any thing, but the great and awful, terrible and dreadful majesty of God, which sunk me, as it were, to nothing."[7] He was left in a state of "perfect calm, awful reverence, and solemn fear" in which he was literally unable to remember or feel any attachment to earthly reality. "I never could tell whether I was in the body or not," he recalled. In this condition Randel began to receive visual and aural impressions. "I saw a white robe brought down and put over me, which covered me, and I appeared as white as snow."[8] A Bible also appeared that contained the key to knowledge that he had so strenuously pursued. "I saw that [the Scripture] ran in perfect connection with the universal love of God to men — the universal atonement in the work of redemption by Jesus Christ who tasted death for every man — the universal appearance of grace to all men, and with the universal call of the gospel." These anti-Calvinist beliefs were confirmed by the ultimate test of Evangelical piety — the personal experience of the Spirit.

Randel returned to waking consciousness, "all flowing with sweat, and was so weak I could hardly stand up." He estimated that the "exercise" had lasted one and a half hours, and it seems likely that physical manifestations accompanied the ecstasy. In any case Randel left his cornfield a charismatic prophet. His experience had revealed a new theological framework for understanding the gospel and had provided indubitable evidence for his call to the ministry.[9]

Randel resumed preaching at New Durham and itinerated among New Hampshire Baptist congregations recently gathered by Samuel Shepard of Brentwood. His message was infused with millennial expectation, the claim of free will, and the demand for Christian perfection. In many congregations Randel met hostility and rejection. At Gilmanton his preaching of "general provision"—universal atonement and a universal day of grace— led a disputant to break fellowship with him publicly in the midst of worship. Randel's reaction was as unambiguous as it was radical: "I makes no odds with me who disowns me," he said, "so long as I know the Lord owns me." Such conflicts eventually had positive consequences for Randel's movement. In the heat of the New Light Stir, influential Baptist lay members and several licensed preachers were converted by his evangel. In August 1779 a recently formed branch of the Madbury church at Strafford, New Hampshire, rejected Calvinism and installed Tosier Lord, a Randelite convert, to their pulpit. In December the Gilmanton church lost Edward Lock, one of its two licensed itinerants, and John Shepard, its ruling elder and nephew of Samuel Shepard, to the new movement. They brought with them the small Loudon-Canterbury branch of the Gilmanton church that they recently had organized. Lord, Lock, and Shepard ordained Randel over the New Durham congregation on 5 April 1780. A few months later Pelatiah Tingley, a minister at the Sanford, Maine, Baptist Church, abrogated his relationship with the Warren Association and joined his congregation to the Randelites. Samuel Weeks, another Baptist licentiate at Gilmanton, converted to "freewill principles" and was ordained over the Randelite congregation there in June 1780.[10]

Late in 1780 Randel convened a series of intense week-long conferences with the leading converts to his new movement. At these meetings doctrinal and ecclesiological differences were resolved by prayer, meditation, scripture study, and argument. By the end of the year a dozen ministers and several whole congregations had joined the sect. A provisional doctrinal consensus had been established, and the outlines of a charismatic leadership hierarchy were visible. After several years of vigorous evangelism, however, Randel again experienced theological difficulties. His movement had grown large enough to demand a more thorough and systematic rendering of the gospel of free will. At this crucial juncture, in 1783, Randel encountered Henry Alline, the Nova Scotian revivalist, who had traveled to New England to redeem it from error. In one of the curious interfaces of international Radical Evangelicalism, Randel embraced Alline's mystical theology. Alline's thought helped fill the intellectual void left by Randel's lack of theological training, and when the Nova Scotian died early in 1784, it was Randel, the Freewill Baptist, who assumed his spiritual and intellectual mantle.[11]

By 1784 Benjamin Randel's fourteen-year spiritual odyssey was at last over. He had synthesized Old Light tradition, Whitefield's New Birth, Baptist practice, and Henry Alline's theology into a unique New England form of Radical Evangelical sectarianism. The message he developed would blossom before the end of the century into the hill country's largest indigenous religion.

New England Universalism was far more complex in origin than the Freewill Baptist movement. Its diverse Anglo-American prophets included John Murray, a British Whitefieldian; Elhanan Winchester and Adams Streeter, New England Baptist elders; Isaac Davis, a Separate lay exhorter; and Caleb Rich, a rural Radical Evangelical prophet. Universalist tradition honors Murray and Winchester as the founders of the movement, and they indeed were significant figures in post-Revolutionary urban Universalism. Their biographies reveal sectarianism's rich Radical Evangelical background. But the numerical and cultural center of New England Universalism was in the hill country. There Streeter, Davis, and especially Rich developed an independent form of Universalism that was embraced by thousands of rural folk.

John Murray was born in 1741 at Alton, Hampshire, England, into a "very rigid Calvinist" family of modest means. The Murrays moved to Dublin in 1753 where they came under the influence of Wesleyan missionaries. About 1760 young Murray was converted, and he temporarily itinerated as an "approved preacher" for the Irish Wesleyans. But he soon reaffirmed his Calvinist origins and moved to London to join Whitefield's congregation at Moorfields Tabernacle. From 1763 he preached widely in London to Baptists and Independents, demonstrating a Whitefieldian ecumenism in his evangelistic efforts.[12]

In 1768 Murray undertook to oppose the "blasphemies" of James Relly, an influential former Whitefieldian whose Universalist preaching was gathering a steady stream of converts from Moorfields. Though determined to discredit Relly's arguments, Murray instead found himself "astonished and delighted" with the spiritual speculations and exegesis of the Universalist's major work, *Union, Or a Treatise on the Consanguinity and Affinity between Christ and His Church*. Relly taught that Christ's atonement on the cross had the purpose and effect of uniting the entire human race to Him both physically and spiritually. Hence the promises of mercy and salvation contained in the gospel must apply to the whole of humanity. Bonded to the Saviour by common blood and common spirit, all human beings participate in his life, death, and resurrection, finally sharing the Christ nature eternally in the heavenly kingdom.[13] These theological ideas appealed to Murray, and Relly's powerful preaching was even more persuasive. In short order Relly's "rational and scriptural discourse" convinced Murray to reject Whitefield's Calvinism and embrace the new gospel. Relly immediately befriended Murray and urged him to evangelize for the cause.[14]

While considering Relly's call, Murray endured a series of personal shocks that altered the course of his life. Eliza, his wife of five years and spiritual companion through his religious transformation, died of consumption early in 1770. Murray was unable to pay her medical bills and served a brief prison term for debt. Release only brought more despair, and Murray decided to immigrate to America "to close my life in solitude, in the most complete retirement." This vow was not to be fulfilled. Murray's ship ran aground in Barnegat Bay, New Jersey, on 21 July 1770. His rescuer was, most improbably, one Thomas Potter, a well-to-do eccentric Radical Evangelical who had built a meetinghouse in the belief that "God will send one who shall deliver unto me his own truth—who shall speak of Jesus Christ and his salvation." Potter was certain that Murray was the promised messenger, and at length he convinced Murray himself that "God, in his providence, is committing to me a dispensation of the Gospel" in America.[15]

Murray was an instant success in coastal New Jersey and soon was itinerating the middle colonies preaching his own amalgam of Calvinist doctrine, Whitefieldian New Birth, and Rellyan exegesis without explicitly proclaiming the tenet of universal salvation. In 1773 and 1774 he evangelized the coast of New England from Milford, Connecticut, to Portsmouth, New Hampshire, following the route of Whitefield's 1770 tour. Among New Lights, Separates, and Baptists alike Murray was acclaimed "for manner and matter, a second Whitefield." This first flush of popularity, however, disintegrated when he publicly avowed Universalism early in 1775.[16]

In that year Murray settled in Gloucester, Massachusetts, the site of his largest following. He established good political credentials as chaplain to Nathaniel Greene's Rhode Island Brigade and as Gloucester's distributor of relief funds. But public opposition rose against his Universalist preaching. He was arrested for vagrancy, cursed and stoned by angry crowds, and threatened with deportation. Congregationalist opponents produced letters accusing Murray of Toryism, espionage, and immorality. One from Ezra Stiles indicted him as "a Romanist in disguise, endeavoring to excite confusion in our churches." The harassment ceased when Murray obtained a statement from Greene declaring him to be "an honest man and good citizen."

Murray formally organized a congregation at Gloucester in 1779 and extended his outreach to churches at Boston, Salem, and Portsmouth in the early 1780s. His theological position found a loyal urban constituency, and his forceful leadership and strict moral code provided a strong institutional framework for converts. Murray also published many polemic works defending the Rellyan scheme. But despite an active pen and constant itinerancy, he was unable to extend his influence beyond New England's commercial centers. His imperious personality would brook no compromises, and after the rise of other Universalist movements in the hill country and elsewhere, his intransigence divided the movement and isolated him from the rural majority. Yet Murray, like Benjamin Randel, illustrated the complex international dynamics of Radical Evangelicalism, endured political and cultural opposition for religious beliefs, and introduced into New England a hybrid of non-Calvinist belief and Whitefieldian style.

Perhaps the most able native New England founder of Universalism was

Elhanan Winchester of Brookline, Massachusetts. Born in 1751, Winchester was a child prodigy whose father was an inveterate religious seeker. The elder Winchester passed from Old Light to New Light Congregationalism, thence to the Baptists and Universalists, and died a Shaker. His son, the eldest of fifteen children, followed a similar though less spectacular pattern. At the age of nineteen he experienced the New Birth and joined an open-communion Baptist church; within a year he accepted the ministerial call of the Rehoboth, Massachusetts, Baptists Church. But during the early 1770s Winchester became progressively more Calvinistic, first embracing close communion, then the "hyper-Calvinist" theology of John Gill. These developments caused his dismissal from Rehoboth, and the young preacher turned itinerant, settling at last in 1774 at Welsh Neck, South Carolina, where he quickly established himself as an effective revivalist.[17]

Winchester's conversion to Universalism began with a book. In 1778 a friend at Welsh Neck asked Winchester to read and comment upon *The Everlasting Covenant,* written in 1710 by the German exegete Paul Siegvolck and published in English in 1753 by the Philadephia mystic George de Benneville. Siegvolck argued "that there would be a final end of sin and misery, and that all fallen creatures would be restored by Jesus Christ to a state of holiness and happiness, after such as were rebellious had suffered in proportion to their crimes." His position was based on the logical impossibility of good and evil perpetually coexisting in the universe and on the assertion that scripture spoke only of finite "periodical eternities" of punishment for sin. The logical clarity of "universal restoration" and Siegvolck's impressive linguistic scholarship appealed to Winchester. He explored the doctrine further while on a lengthy visit to New England in 1779–80 during which he gained renewed notoriety as a Baptist evangelist in the New Light Stir.[18]

In the fall of 1780 Winchester received an unexpected call to the pastorate of the prestigious First Baptist Church of Philadelphia, the largest Baptist church in America. Though he accepted the post, Winchester was by now "half a convert to the doctrine of the Restoration." In cosmopolitan Philadelphia he was exposed to the liberalizing influence of de Benneville, Jacob Duché, and Benjamin Rush. Word of Winchester's sentiments swiftly spread through the Philadelphia congregation. After bitter conflicts and public debates, Winchester and one hundred followers were dismissed from the church, whereupon they organized the Society of Christian Baptists to promulgate their faith.[19] On 22 April 1781 Winchester "openly asserted the doctrine of the final and Universal Restoration of all fallen intelligences" for the first time. He argued that God created humans for a good end, which Christ would attain for them "by destroying the evil principle, or sin, out of the universe."[20] In succeeding years Winchester became a successful itinerant, employing his revivalistic homiletics to convince many converts. In 1787 he sailed for London to take the pulpit of James Relly's congregation after Relly's death. In London Winchester wrote *The Universal Restoration,* a highly popular defense of Universalism in dialogue form, and *A Course of Lectures on the Prophecies that Remain to be Fulfilled,* an elaborate eschatological scheme reconciling future punishment with universal salvation. Winchester returned to America in 1794 and for several years he enjoyed extraordinary success itinerating in New England and the middle colonies. But his always-fragile health declined rapidly in 1796, and the next year he died while on tour at Hartford, Connecticut.[21]

The careers of Winchester and Murray illustrate the complexity of Universalist origins. Each man took a similar trajectory through Radical Evangelicalism, yet they had irreconcilable theological differences. Murray was Calvinistic, Rellyan, doctrinaire, and imperious; Winchester was Arminian, restorationist, rationalistic, and irenic. Murray's theology was fundamentally Christological while Winchester's was rooted in eschatological speculation. But their roles in the rise of New England Universalism were similar. Both were conduits for innovative theological views from the Old World that they publicized through preaching and publication. Both were erratic in their organization and leadership of their followers. Their constituencies were largely limited to sophisticated liberal-minded citizens in urban centers. And though their ideas contributed to the theological ferment of post-Revolutionary New England, their gospels did not penetrate deeply into the region's geographical and ecclesiastical hinterland.

That task was performed by three rural prophets, Isaac Davis, Adams Streeter, and Caleb Rich. Little is known about Isaac Davis, a physician who was born at Windsor, Connecticut, around 1700. In the early 1770s he began to "teach Universal Salvation and deny the existence of hell or devils." Itinerating from his home at Somers, Connecticut, Davis had his greatest impact on the Connecticut Valley and the Worcester County towns of Oxford, Douglas, and Milford, Massachusetts. As early as 1775, a number of "Davisonians" withdrew from the Oxford Congregationalist Church, forming the base for permanent Universalist strength in that region after Davis's death in 1777.

Davis's theology seems to have developed from a Separate or New Light background. In his one published work, *What Love Jesus Christ Has for Sinners,* he asserted that Adam's fall produced "a natural, spiritual, and eternal death" for all humans. God's covenant of salvation with Abraham did not obviate the universal curse, according to Davis. Only the substitutionary atonement of Christ could do so. The full imputation of sin onto Christ established the infinite justice of God and gave pardon to all sinners. Such a universal atonement, Davis concluded, was the final salvation of all intelligent beings.[22] Davis's thought had certain affinities with John Murray's, and a historical connection between the two men cannot be ruled out. But unlike Murray, Davis was centrally concerned with the logic of original sin and the radical need for redemption that it created. This Whitefieldian scenario was complemented by Davis's outspoken criticism of unconverted ministers who spent their time in salary disputes rather than preaching the gospel. "I would to God," he wrote, "that our preachers had a genuine sense of woe that Paul pronounced against [false] preachers. They would throw by their preaching and go to hoeing corn, for Christ never called anyone but to an honest calling." Isaac Davis thus may have been the earliest New England Universalist, deriving his doctrine from Radical Evangelical roots and gathering around him a local sect.[23]

Adams Streeter continued Davis's work in central New England. Born in 1735 and raised in Worcester County, he became a Separate, then a Baptist elder, and then converted to Universalism, perhaps under Davis's influence, around 1777. Streeter gave new organization and direction to the Oxford Universalists, who reported in 1785 that they "have for a number of years past assembled on the Sabbath-day for public worship, and have attended to the instructions of Rev. Adams Streeter." From about 1780 until his death in 1786, Streeter served on a circuit that included Milford and Oxford, Massachusetts, and Providence, Rhode Island. Murray welcomed Streeter into the Rellyan circle at Boston, and this personal tie helped bring together the far-flung Universalist constituency in times of crisis. Little is known of Streeter's theology, but it may be safely assumed to have been, like that of all the Universalist founders, of Radical Evangelical cast. Streeter's ministry successfully preserved the Worcester County mission and provided a much-needed social cohesion for the early Universalist movement.[24]

The most important native New England Universalist leader was Caleb Rich. Born at Sutton, Massachusetts, in 1750 into a large and influential clan of Separates and Baptists, young Rich was early exposed to strict Calvinist beliefs. But it was not until his father joined the strife-torn Second Baptist Church of Sutton in 1768 that Rich became seriously involved in religion. As the congregation debated the standards of baptism and communion, and the content of "sound faith," Rich came under conviction, assiduously studied the Bible, and prayed "that God would give me understanding in the scriptures . . . to make me wise unto salvation." But he received no relief from his growing spiritual disease.[25]

In 1771 Rich moved with his brothers Nathaniel and Thomas to Warwick, Massachusetts, a rural hill town on the New Hampshire border. Here he at last experienced conversion through the impression of a saving scriptural text. At this time Rich's beliefs were fluid, tending toward annihilationism — the tenet that the souls of the reprobate were destroyed after death — and toward a limited "day of atonement" for every soul. His predestinarianism brought a number of challenges, none more serious than from his brother Nathaniel. In 1772, while discussing the "day of grace," Nathaniel denied that there was a finite period of time during which the gospel was offered to the soul. Moreover, Nathaniel asserted, if God in fact did ever present grace to the soul, it should be irresistible and require no preparatory time of blindness or the ultimate destruction of souls. Rich was deeply disturbed by this rupture in his most intimate spiritual and familial relationship. After the conversation he resolved "not to give sleep to my eyes until I had found mercy," and within an hour began the series of visionary and charismatic experiences that were to lead him to Universalism.[26]

First Rich heard "a still small voice" that explained, "your motive is from selfish principles, for fear of future and endless misery; you always have been and now are excited to pray from the same false motives." He was reduced to a state of utter humiliation before God; "a great calm overspread my mind and my passions all subsided. Instantly I saw a vision." A "celestial guide" appeared who showed Rich an incomplete stone wall and told him that he was as a stone "placed by unerring wisdom into God's building before the foundation of the world." The vision confirmed Rich's own salvation, bolstered his determinism, and taught him that "slavish fear, tormenting doubts, self love, and self-righteousness, or dependence on their own agency, produced spurious conversion and begat hypocrites."[27]

Shortly after this experience Rich has a second "vision of the night," in which he ascended Mount Zion, again accompanied by a "celestial friend." The angel admonished him to avoid the tracks of the Baptists. "Follow no man any further," the angel instructed, "though they follow Christ." Guided by "a staff called faith," Rich arrived at the mountain's summit, "the house of God and the gate of heaven."[28] He awoke "with joyful surprise" and immediately received a number of scriptural texts verifying that his vision was an "outpouring of the spirit of God." The experience confirmed that Rich was called to explore further his own innovative beliefs and lead the Baptists out of the wilderness. His scripture study increased, out of which he developed an annihilationist scheme of double predestination. In this scheme the elect were "created in Adam . . . and fell or died with him in the Fall," and the reprobate were nonimmortal creatures who would cease to exist after the death of the body. On the basis of these speculations he denied "endless misery" for unregenerate sinners. Christ's redemption was universal for those who had been first created in Adam; sinners were a second class of human beings to whom the notion of future rewards and punishments simply did not apply.[29]

When Rich shared his ideas with local Baptist elders, they denounced him as a heretic. Rich, his two brothers, and his friend Joseph Goodell were banished from the newly organized Warwick Baptist Church. The dissidents organized a "new religious society" in 1773, and soon a number of converts were attracted through Rich's preaching and Bible teaching. By 1776 Rich had gathered additional followers at Sutton, Oxford, and Douglas, Massachusetts, and in 1777 he formed a "general society" of his adherents in and around Richmond, New Hampshire. These congregations flourished during the Revolution despite the itinerant's eight-month tour of duty in 1778. During this time Rich's personal life became further linked to the new gospel when the woman he began courting in 1777 and her Baptist family opposed his "wild and false religious principles." Rich converted the entire family and in January 1778 the couple was married.[30]

For Caleb Rich the 1770s were a time of spiritual search, political involvement, and sociopsychological maturation. These elements set the context for the decisive charismatic episodes of 1778. After retiring one April evening, Rich saw "a person, or the likeness of one," enter his house carrying a Bible. The visitor, who had luminous but indistinguishable features, spoke on the text of Galatians 4:22–31, the difference between "the children of the bond woman" Hagar, who were bound by a covenant of works and a spirit of fear, self-righteousness, and formalism, and "the children of the free woman" Sarah, who were heirs to the covenant of grace made by God to Abraham. These differences, the angel taught, were only superficial. Rich's error was that he had consigned the children of bondage to extinction. The atonement of Jesus Christ the Second Adam guaranteed that "the first Adam and every individual of his posterity from the beginning of this world to the end" would "truly and positively" pass "from death unto life." Christians, however, had become the children of the bond woman. "There was not one formal church among them," the angel announced, "that stood in the Apostolic rectitude or that contended for the Faith once delivered to the saints—Abraham, Isaac, and Jacob." Furthermore, the Second Coming was fast approaching, to "sweep and cleanse . . . sin, death, hell, pain, sorrow, or evil" from the universe. On this apocalyptic note, the visitor assured Rich that he had a call "to proclaim the same gospel" and then disappeared.[31]

Rich was certain that the messenger was sent from God, but the next day further charismatic gifts confirmed his conclusion. While meditating he suddenly "felt as it were a shock of electricity, my lips quivered, my flesh trembled, and felt a tremour throughout my whole frame for several days, which was noticed by my wife." Any remaining doubt was removed soon afterward by yet another "vision of the night while in deep sleep" in which Rich was visited by "Jesus the Christ of God" himself.

The Lord was "a beautiful personage" possessed of "an unspeakable grace, mercy, meekness, mildness, loving kindness, gentleness, and compassion" that "beamed in his countenance." Christ conversed "with the sociability of an equal, and all that tenderness and pity of a tender mother to a young child." He gave Rich "two small portions of food resembling corn" and said, "Eat sufficiently of it thyself; and of it feed my sheep and lambs, and it will never exhaust, it will be sufficient for thee at all times." This explicit call and Christ's humble example set Rich on a life of evangelism to oppose "anything that savours in the least degree of pomposity or worldly grandeur in a professed gospel minister." Rich's message of divine benevolence and universal salvation was henceforth couched in the most extreme claim of Radical Evangelicalism: "I could say in truth that the gospel that was preached by me, was not after man; for I neither received it of man, neither was I taught it by man, but by the revelation of Jesus Christ, through the medium of the Holy Spirit in opening my understanding to understand the scriptures.[32]

By 1780 Universalism had appeared as a viable sectarian movement in rural New England. Separated both geographically and theologically from the influence of John Murray and Elhanan Winchester, the hill country prophets, Isaac Davis, Adams Streeter, and Caleb Rich, followed their personal quests for a critique of Radical Evangelicalism that was intellectually satisfying and spiritually convincing. In Rich the movement found its principal early leader, a charismatically gifted preacher who laid solid theological and institutional foundations for the spectacular growth of the gospel of universal salvation in the New England hinterland.

The first Shakers were a splinter group of enthusiasts from an English working-class Friends Meeting in Manchester, Lancashire. In the 1740s the meeting's leaders, tailors Jane and James Wardley, broke with the Society of Friends in search of a more vivid experience of the Inner Light than was available in the quietistic sect. Almost immediately the Wardley group was swept into the Evangelical Revival in England. The burgeoning working class of Lancashire had become a rich pool of converts for Methodism. John and Charles Wesley visited the district regularly, and from 1749 Manchester was a regular station on George Whitefield's northern circuit.

While the Wardleys were competing with the Methodist itinerants for converts, they came under the influence of the French Prophets, a group of exiled Huguenot *inspirés* who combined doctrinaire Calvinism with ecstatic spirituality that included "fasts, trances, agitations of head and limbs, prophecies concerning the Second Coming of Christ, calls for repentance, miracles of heavenly voices, lights in the sky, and other signs."[33] By 1747 the Wardleys had adopted the stance of the French Prophets, and a great wave of Lancashire revivalism in the early 1750s provided a steady stream of Methodist converts to the sect. A decade after their independency, the "Shaking Quakers" maintained a modest but committed membership under the leadership of Jane Wardley, now styled "Mother Jane," their spiritual virtuoso.

One of their converts was Ann Lee, the Manchester fur cutter and laborer who became the leader of New England Shakerism. Lee was born in Manchester in 1736 to a poor working-class family. As a child she exhibited great moral sensitivity, particularly in regard to sexuality. Around 1750 she came under the influence of Whitefield, regarding him as an authentic prophet endowed with "great powers and gifts of God."[34] It is not clear whether Lee ever attended Methodist meetings in Manchester with any regularity, but her Radical Evangelical piety provided the motivation to seek fellowship in conventicles like the Wardley society. By 1758 the charismatic gifts, public confessions, and female leadership of the Shaking Quakers persuaded Lee to join their company.

Domestic problems, however, developed for the young convert. Her father, John Lee, seeking to provide economic security for his daughter, arranged a marriage for her with his apprentice, the blacksmith Abraham Standerin. Their union proved biologically disastrous, producing four offspring who died in either infancy or early childhood. Following the death of the fourth child, Elizabeth, in 1766, Ann Lee underwent a six-month period of severe physical decline and psychological depression. She was revolted by the sexual union that had brought such misery and regarded herself as hopelessly mired in carnal corruption. "She sought deliverance from the bondage of sin, and gave herself no rest, day or night, but often spent whole nights in laboring and crying to God for deliverance from sin." Her anxiety was finally relieved by Mother Jane Wardley who prescribed celibacy; "James and I lodge together but we do not touch each other any more than two babes," she told her, "You may return and do likewise."[35]

This episode cemented Lee's loyalty to the Shaking Quakers, and soon she became a leading member, converting her husband, her father, her brother William and sister Elizabeth, and her niece Nancy. Ann Lee herself undertook a life of extreme asceticism and public proclamation of her faith. She was arrested several times for profaning the Sabbath and disturbing the peace. While in prison in 1770 she experienced "astonishing visions and divine manifestations" of "the whole spiritual world." The crucial revelation was that sexual intercourse was the original sin of Adam and Eve, the cause of all human evil and suffering. The vision taught that only through sexual purity and public confession of all carnality could the sinner hope to receive divine grace and salvation.

Lee aggressively proclaimed this celibate gospel and drew both converts and opposition. Her family; James and Daniel Whittaker, youths whom she had raised from childhood; John Townley and John Hocknell, well-to-do Methodists from the textile trade; and James Shepard and Mary Partington followed Lee into the new ascetic life and became her inner circle of followers.[36] The prophetess grew increasingly extreme in her denunciation of all other religions, and she resorted to disrupting Anglican services in Manchester. For this offense she was mobbed, stoned, repeatedly arrested, and finally committed to an insane asylum. There she experienced yet another vision, this time of "the Lord Jesus Christ in his glory." Christ announced that she was to proclaim the celibate gospel as his successor and would receive the indwelling of his spirit to empower her ministry. "I feel the blood of Christ running through my soul and body! I feel him present with me, as sensibly as I feel my hands together . . . It is not I that speak. It is Christ who dwells in me." The other Shakers accepted her visionary commission and Ann Lee became Mother Ann, the second manifestation of Christ's spirit on earth.[37]

Through the early 1770s Mother Ann continued to proclaim her eccentric message and endure political and ecclesiastical persecution. Influenced by a number of factors, including Whitefield's *Journals* and the news of the independence movement, Ann Lee began to contemplate a move to America. Sometime in 1772 she received a vision of "a place that had been prepared" for the Shakers to "open the gospel" and gather a church in New England. James Whittaker also had a waking dream of a tree "whose leaves shone with such a brightness as made it appear like a burning torch," guiding the way to Christ's kingdom in the New World. Others also received charismatic confirmation of the plan, and preparations for the migration went forward.[38]

On 6 August 1774 Mother Ann arrived at New York with eight of her closest followers: Abraham Standerin, William Lee, Nancy Lee, John and Richard Hocknell, James Whittaker, Mary Partington, and James Shepard. The Shakers found employment as domestic servants and laborers in New York, and in 1775 they purchased a wilderness homestead at Niskeyuna eight miles northwest of Albany. During this period the marriage of Ann Lee and Abraham Standerin finally collapsed, and early in 1776 Mother Ann led the tiny sect from war-torn New York to the millennial kingdom of Niskeyuna.

At Niskeyuna the Shakers rapidly developed their beliefs and charismatic practices into more elaborate form. Leadership functions were divided among three principal figures: Mother Ann remained the inspired guide, primary charistmatic, and embodiment of sinless perfection; her brother William Lee took the lead in worship, employing gifts of song and movement to develop Shaker ecstasies into dramatic new forms; and James Whittaker emerged as the sect's primary exhorter, biblical interpreter, and liaison with the outside world. From the beginning of the Shaker mission in New England, these three—"Mother Ann and the Elders"—were regarded as a separate class of spiritual hierarchs.[39]

The intellectual development of Shakerism was extensive during the early Revolutionary years. The basic tenets of celibacy and mutual confession remained, but Mother Ann became increasingly apocalyptic awaiting a sign to begin her mission of redemption in the Last Days. The Shakers became convinced that the Second Coming had already begun, not through a physical reappearance of Jesus but through the manifestation of the "Christ spirit" in their souls. Mother Ann and the Elders were regarded as having attained "the resurrection state." Their role as confessors came to include the actual forgiveness of sins as the first representatives of the millennial kingdom. These new functions combined with ongoing visionary gifts and scriptural reflection to produce a series of doctrines "which struck against all former ideas of religion."

Amos Taylor, an early convert and close observer of the Shakers, published an extensive list of their beliefs in 1782. These tenets occupied the same Radical Evangelical spectrum as the revelations of Benjamin Randel and Caleb Rich. According to Taylor, the Shakers held that God was merciful to human beings and that through Christ He "enlightens every man that cometh into the world without distinction." On the question of free will they, like Rich and Randel, believed that "every man is a free agent to walk in the true light, and so to choose or reject the truth of God within him." They were equally liberal regarding eternal punishment, following an almost Winchesterite view that "the word 'everlasting' when applied to the punishment of the wicked refers only to a limited space of time" and that "every man suffers personally . . . inexpressible woe and misery for sins not repented of until final redemption."[40]

The center of early Shaker doctrine, however, concerned the nature and necessity of the New Birth. The Shakers postulated the Radical Evangelical tenet of behavioral as well as spiritual transformation in response to the Spirit. Access to full regeneration was available only through the pardoning of confessed sins by Christ, who was embodied in the Shaker leaders: "All sin which is committed against God, is done against them, and must be pardoned for Christ's sake through them, for which confession must be made to them." After confession and forgiveness, movement toward complete perfection required that converts "come out of the order of natural generation to be as Christ was." Through celibacy and sexual abstinence they "loose their sensual or earthly relation to Adam the first, and come to be transparent in their ideas in the bright and heavenly visions of God . . . Heaven begins upon earth."[41]

For pragmatic as well as theological reasons Mother Ann did not authorize any public evangelism during the worst years of military crisis. Niskeyuna was located along Burgoyne's invasion route, and even after his defeat the Hudson Valley remained a major zone of armed Tory activity. Regular terrorist attacks and subversive counterinsurgency plagued Continental forces based at Albany. Amid this sort of military tension, the arrival of the British émigrés did not go unnoticed. But Mother Ann's long-awaited sign of mission finally arrived on the Dark Day of 19 May 1780. Observing the "Egyptian darkness," she declared the opening of the gospel of Christ's second appearing and began local evangelism. Immediately the combined impact of the Dark Day enthusiasm, the New Light Stir, and the Shaker gospel produced converts. The largest group was taken from Joseph Meacham's disappointed New Lights from New Lebanon, New York. Meacham himself visited Niskeyuna and was convinced by the Shakers' physical exercises and spiritual gifts that they were "the people of God." Mother Ann in turn hailed him as her "first born in America."

The stumbling block to Meacham's conversion was Paul's prohibition of women leaders in the church. In response to Meacham's direct question on the matter, Mother Ann offered a spiritual interpretation of "the natural creation" as "a figure of the order of God." "As the order of nature requires a man and a woman to produce offspring," she said, "so where they both stand in their proper order, the man is the first and the woman the second in the government of the family. But when the man is gone, the right of Government belongs to the woman; so is the family of Christ." In this concise statement Mother Ann articulated her concept of the Shakers as a spiritual family and her own messianic role as ruler of that family both according to natural law and according to her divine calling as the second embodiment of Christ's spirit. Meacham immediately declared his faith and confessed to Mother Ann.[42]

Early converts also shared charismatic endowments under the guidance of Shaker leaders. Valentine Rathbun, a Baptist elder at Pittsfield, Massachusetts, and a temporary convert, described the same sort of physical manifestation that affected Caleb Rich: "I found a power come over me different from what I had ever felt before and made me feel very weak and maugre, and in a little time it so affected my nerves that they gave a twitch, as sudden as a flash of lightening . . . I can compare it to nothing nearer its feelings, than the operations of an electerising machine."[43] "The power of God" affected Mary Andrus of New Lebanon in a similar way: "It struck me first upon my tung, and extended thru my head and over my whole body, and seemed to wash me from head to foot, like a shower of warm water." Another believer "shook and trembled mightily, was signed [sic] about and carried here and there and shook till her hair was thrown every way."[44] Still others joined the Shaker virtuosos in experiencing waking visions, premonitory dreams, and omens.

Mother Ann and the Elders invited converts to move to Niskeyuna or to organize locally into communal cooperatives. As soon as the movement of families, goods, and stock began, however, the Albany Committee of Safety received reports of suspicious activity among the Shakers. When it became clear that Mother Ann was preaching pacifism as well as claiming to usher in a new millennial kingdom, she, William Lee, James Whittaker, John Hocknell, and three converts were arrested by the militia. In July 1780 they were convicted of "being enemies to the country" and imprisoned at Albany's Old Fort. Other converts suffered injury and confiscation of property at the hands of Continental forces.

The Shakers proselytized among the Tories and British regulars at Albany. Political as well as religious debates raged in the prison, and the Shakers soon gathered a few converts. Typical of Mother Ann's prison converts was Zadok Wright, a Tory regular from Hartland, Vermont, and one of the first settlers and leading members of that community. Wright accepted the Shaker testimony but was unable to join the Niskeyuna community upon his release because he was to be deported. When Wright took leave of Mother Ann to immigrate to Canada, she correctly prophesied that he would "be released from that bondage"; Wright's ship had already departed when he arrived to embark. He returned to Mother Ann and was instructed by her to return home "trusting in God and Mother's word."[45]

Such charismatic displays and the local converts' constant attendance on Mother Ann made the Shakers a public prodigy at Albany. After a short time it became apparent to military authorities that the Shakers were a nuisance to order but harmless to the Revolutionary cause. All were released except Mother Ann, who remained in jail for four months before a personal appeal by James Whittaker to Governor George Clinton obtained her release in December 1780. By the beginning of 1781 the Shaker community at Niskeyuna was restored. Mother Ann had gathered an inner circle of American converts headed by Joseph Meacham; the sect had developed a rudimentary communal economy, a clear charismatic hierarchy, and an elaborate theology. Ann Lee's dream of a millennial kingdom in New England had passed through its crucial stage. The "opening of the gospel of Christ's second appearing" had begun.

The founders of Freewill Baptist, Universalist, and Shaker faith exhibited in their experiences a diversity and range far beyond the prophets and seers of local New England sects. They were in most cases products of the wider Anglo-American realm of Radical Evangelicalism. Benjamin Randel, John Murray, and Ann Lee were each directly and profoundly influenced by the later ministry of George Whitefield. All the leaders traversed a lengthy course of religious development, moving through many byways of Radical Evangelicalism before finding the goal of their quest in personal revelation and enlightenment.

In addition to this amplitude of protean religiousness, the sectarian founders also had life histories replete with emotional crisis. Each of them translated deep psychological, familial, or vocational problems into intensified religious concern. Mother Ann Lee's traumatic experiences with sexuality were the clearest example of such life problems, but John Murray's loss of his wife almost immediately after his conversion; Benjamin Randel's conflicts with his wife and his ministerial calling; and Caleb Rich's ruptures with his brother, his fiancée, and her family all had the same effect of challenging, then eventually confirming their personal spiritual pilgrimages.

The wider-ranging religious and personal experiences of Randel, Rich, Murray, Winchester, and Lee seem to have contributed to their prophetic virtuosity. The most distinguishing mark of their leadership was a superior grasp of the doctrinal implications of their charismatic endowments. Each of them received direct personal confirmation of their unique and world-saving mission through visionary and providential experiences. Unlike the local prophets, the major founders were personally called in vision by Christ himself. But beyond this, they also received explicit cognitive insights into the nature of true religion: Ann Lee's vision of original sin; Benjamin Randel's vision of the open Bible; Caleb Rich's angelic visitors. The doctrinal innovations they comprehended through such charismatic means were aimed at crucial aspects of the Calvinist tradition—the Fall, the Atonement, and the process of conversion. In their hands these new beliefs would become the keys to unlock new evangels for rural New Englanders.

5

Evangelism and Community

The development of the sects into organized religious collectivities did not happen automatically. Rather, the foundations of sectarian community were laid by a disorganized, ill-documented process of proselytism, intra-church disputes, debates, and small-group interaction that can be best grouped under the rubric "evangelism." During the early 1780s the Freewill Baptists, Universalists, and Shakers experimentally developed forms of evangelism specially adapted to their message and social environment. From that time until the early nineteenth century these remained in use as the main agencies of sectarian growth.

In evangelism as in spirituality the sectarians borrowed from Radical Evangelical practice, modifying it to meet the requirements of religious communication in a revolutionary frontier society. More important, in the evangelistic process the sects gradually elaborated their doctrines and biblical interpretations, identified a permanent constituency, and became aware of the need for social institutions to nurture the faith of their converts. Evangelism, by its creation of standardized communications and social formats, thus performed an essential role in the development of New England's experimental religions.

The sectarians were aware of the animosity they would face in rural New England even before they began to evangelize. Mother Ann had predicted persecution for the Shakers because of their celibacy and pacifism. Benjamin Randel knew in 1780 that he "would be a stranger in a strange land, and it was unusual for a minister to go about and preach, such being regarded with suspicion on the part of many."[1] Caleb Rich had an even clearer sense of the problem of sectarian evangelism: "In reflecting upon entering the gospel ministry," he wrote, "I foresaw that against me would be arrayed all formal church establishments, all the prejudices of education, all the superstition of the age."[2]

But while cognizant of these liabilities, the sectarians responded to them with the conviction born of personal religious experience. The primary method they used in the "dispensation of the gospel" was itinerant preaching. The sectarian itinerants saw their homiletic role to be "expounding the Scriptures," drawing types and figures from text upon text in a "spiritualized" interpretation to defend their doctrinal innovations. Such preaching reduced the new gospels to the simplest, least offensive, most accessible terms as "scripture doctrine," illustrated with masses of proof-texts from unassailable biblical authority.[3]

Despite the intensity and artistry of sectarian preaching, however, this sort of appeal was not automatically successful. Its reception depended upon the credence given it by the audience. In the absence of institutions that selected out receptive hearers, the early itinerants had to choose their audiences carefully. For example, Benjamin Randel's first missionary venture was undertaken in August 1781, "in response to an invitation" from "friends" at Little Falls on Maine's Saco River. Randel and other sectarian itinerants would not normally enter an unfamiliar town unless some reliable information or personal acquaintance suggested a favorable reception. "When Randel's convictions of duty were not clear," wrote his biographer, "or his access to the people was doubtful, no man was more cautious."[4] Caleb Rich's ministry was even more careful. Until 1783 he restricted his outreach to the communities of Worcester county and the Connecticut Valley where he was already known. Mother Ann also selected locations for Shaker evangelism carefully and employed local converts "to prepare the people for her reception." This prudent exercise of itinerancy indicated the sectarians' reluctance to face hostile communities without ample preparation and known support.

The sectarians thus began their evangelism guided by the Radical Evangelical tradition of itinerant exhortation. They were soon forced, however, to adapt these traditions to hill country circumstance. In the flush of the New Light Stir the nascent sects gravitated toward one or another aspect of the Radical Evangelical manner of evangelism and elaborated it into their own characteristic style of mission. Their differing message and clientele coalesced converts into distinctively different social groupings. The Universalists concentrated their efforts on itinerancy and the creation of informal preaching stations. The Freewill Baptists fomented schism in Separate, Baptist, and Congregationalist churches, while the Shakers combined itinerant preaching with a unique kind of residential evangelism aimed at pockets of New Light radicalism. These proselytizing techniques and the converts gathered thereby constituted the foundation for distinctive sectarian institutions.

Universalist itinerants usually taught at homes of sympathetic local residents. Occasionally a town meetinghouse could be secured despite the opposition of settled clergy. Early Universalist gatherings in the hill country typically were made up of unchurched Separates or Baptists eager to hear preaching different from the locally available Congregationalist variety. But after such meetings there was no institutional format to channel favorable response. Further conversation and persuasion devolved upon families and friendship circles. These informal networks constituted the all-but-invisible center of Universalist mission.

Caleb Rich's preaching around Richmond, New Hampshire, set the type for Universalist itinerancy. The town had been settled in 1757 by Baptists and Quakers from Rhode Island and southeastern Massachusetts. Rich's principal audience was the Richmond Baptist Church, the town's largest congregation, which had ordained Maturin Ballou its pastor in 1770. Through the 1770s this flourishing church served as the northwestern outpost for the Warren Baptist Association. But Rich's evangelism drew off many Baptists and compelled Ballou to resign in 1780. One convert recalled that when Rich first preached, "the doctrine of Universal salvation excited horror, mingled with disgust, and was denounced as the most dangerous heresy ever propagated."[5] The new gospel was widely discussed in social circles throughout the community and a sizable group of Baptists followed Rich into Universalism. Their revivallike meetings rehearsed the Radical Evangelical manner: "Each read, or prayed, or sung, or spoke as the Spirit directed, and all were edified." Rich took the role of scripture teacher. He taught extempore and by inspiration, delivering discourses "largely made up of scripture quotations, explanations and comparisons, and arguments aimed at the contradictions, unreasonableness, unscriptural doctrines, and irreligion of the dominant theology."[6]

To the curious and the religiously concerned, such social and homiletic styles were appealing. The conversions of Thomas and Mary Fletcher Barnes of Jaffrey, New Hampshire, in 1782 illustrated the role of informal family interaction as a primary factor in the evangelistic process. Thomas Barnes, a Baptist convert in 1770, was drawn first by curiosity, then by conviction to Rich's meetings. His wife, Mary, however, regarded Rich's gospel as "a fatal error." When she urged her husband to stop attending the meetings he asked "Can you set bounds to the love of God?" Thomas departed for Richmond, and Mary was left contemplating his crucial question. "At length she found it impossible to set bounds on the love of God. The more she tried, the more she found this love overleaping every barrier until it overcame sin and death."[7] Meanwhile Thomas became fully convinced by Caleb Rich's arguments at Richmond. "On her husband's return, Mrs. Barnes communicated to him her unsuccessful efforts to set bounds to the love of God, and of her hopes in a world's redemption; and after a prayerful examination of the Holy Scriptures, they both openly avowed themselves Universalists."[8]

The initial economy of Universalist evangelism was the commerce of teachers like Rich with people like Thomas and Mary Barnes. In the absence of a resident church community, persons who were attracted to sectarian claims reviewed those arguments at length with their primary social groups, especially with family and friendship circles. When the itinerant returned, perhaps months later, the filtration of his message through such familial, occupational, and political groupings in a given town often had produced several individual or family conversions.[9]

Given the intense quality of religious commitment during the New Light Stir, such converts were ripe for a call to the ministry. This was the case with Thomas Barnes himself, who began preaching soon after his conversion. The appearance of a local advocate for sectarian views in towns like Jaffrey—population 404 in 1786—set off yet another round of popular discussion and disputation that gained further adherents. Thus after Barnes began preaching at Jaffrey, "many people received [Universalism] as the truth, felt its sweet and mellowing influence upon their hearts, and many more hastened to hear what could be said in its defence."[10] This sort of restricted itinerancy by a known local figure became typical of Universalist evangelism.

The technique also provided a self-perpetuating ministry. Through the 1780s and 1790s articulate converts moving into newly settled areas rehearsed the process of persuasion. Thomas Barnes, for example, moved to New Fane, Vermont, in 1786, where he "continued preaching wherever he was invited, with or without remuneration."[11] In 1798 Barnes moved again to New Gloucester, Maine, where he served as Universalist apostle to eastern Maine until his death in 1816. One result of Barnes's and Rich's combined ministry was the conversion of William Farwell of Charlestown, New Hampshire, in 1788. Farwell became the leading Universalist itinerant in Vermont between 1790 and 1820.

Another Rich convert was Hosea Ballou of Richmond, New Hampshire. By the late 1790s Ballou was minister to a circuit of five Universalist meetings in central Vermont, and after 1800 he was the paramount leader of New England Universalism. Rich himself removed to New Haven, Vermont, in 1803, where he continued to influence the second generation of rural Universalists until his death in 1821. Rich, Barnes, Farwell, and Ballou provided the leadership for New England Universalism through their practice of consistent and well-focused itinerancy in the hill country.

Such was the kind of community that Universalist evangelism characteristically produced. Travelling evangelists first gained adherents by expounding the scriptures to small informal gatherings throughout the hill country. The sectarian message was then reviewed, criticized, and elaborated at length in family and friendship circles. Individuals and clan groups who converted under these circumstances simply gathered themselves into informal house-churches for worship and mutual support.

Such house-churches mobilized local leaders and resources for small-scale local proselytizing. Until 1815 this pattern of house-churches, lay leadership, and itinerant visitation was the primary manner in which Universalist evangelism drew together converts into social cohesion.

A second form of early sectarian evangelism was systematic expansion by intrachurch schism. This approach to proselytizing focused on established Baptist and Congregationalist churches in which sectarian beliefs were embraced by a subgroup that eventually created a new congregation of its own. Evangelists in this situation, most common among the Freewill Baptists, did not have to rely on ad hoc and informal social processes to produce strong responses to their message. Discontented members of Radical Evangelical congregations easily made the transition to Freewill beliefs while still preserving their traditional style of religious life. Thus the Freewill Baptists could utilize the strength of their Radical Evangelical background to strategic advantage in channeling converts into new church organizations.

The Freewill movement began in schism and subversion. Benjamin Randel's 1780 call to New Durham was facilitated by the inability of the town to support the Congregationalist minister, Joel Porter, whom it had ordained in 1773. Porter was dismissed in 1777, and when the New Light Stir struck New Durham, Randel was able to bring most of the Congregationalists over to his gospel. Randel and his Freewill colleagues also benefited from their popularity as former itinerants for Samuel Shepard's Brentwood Baptist Church. By virtue of their familiarity with Shepard's followers, the Freewill elders were able to make heavy inroads into the Brentwood-influenced congregations. In addition, because all the early Freewill Baptists shared the Brentwood style of revivalism, church organization, and discipline, the nascent sect had unusually clear models for its evangelistic practice. The Randelites were thus fully prepared to carry out an effective and tested sort of evangelism immediately upon their separation from the Calvinistic Baptists in 1780.

At New Gloucester, Maine, for example, the revival had created a group of charismatics that provided fertile soil for Freewill evangelism. Randel preached there during his tour of Maine in 1782. He consciously aimed his message at emergent schismatic groups like the one at New Gloucester, which had tentatively withdrawn from the town's New Light Congregationalist parish. Lay exhortation, protracted charismatic meetings, and rampant emotionalism had prepared the ground for Randel's message of free salvation, freedom from sin, and the near approach of the Second Coming.[12] Randel sent for Tozier Lord and Peletiah Tingley to assist him in evangelizing the New Gloucester group, and within a few weeks they converted as a body. Randel made them a congregation of "the Church of Christ at New Durham" on 1 July 1782 by mass baptism. And Randel did not leave the New Gloucester converts leaderless. His evangelism had persuaded Daniel Hibbard, a local Baptist elder, to join the Freewill movement. Randel charged Hibbard with oversight of the New Gloucester congregation; and Nathan Merrill, leader of the schismatics, became Hibbard's assistant.[13]

This was the basic pattern of Freewill institution-oriented evangelism. Employing its exploitative technique the Freewill Baptists established more than a dozen churches in less than two years.[14] A second instance of Freewill evangelism at Woolwich, Maine, illustrated even more clearly why Baptists and Congregationalists regarded the Freewillers as "wolves in sheep's clothing" and found it difficult to combat their tactics. "A number of devoted Christians of free sentiments" lived at Woolwich, members of the Old Light Congregationalist parish pastored since 1765 by Josiah Winship. By 1780 these Radicals "had become tired of the old lifeless religious forms among them, and had been earnestly praying for some evangelist to visit them and preach a free salvation and a heartfelt religion."[15]

This combination was precisely what Randel had to offer. On his first visit to Woolwich, the first of any itinerant in the New Light Stir, he was able to gather a sizable congregation at the town meetinghouse for a sermon on the Song of Solomon 1:7-8, "Tell me . . . where thou feedest, where thou makest thy flock to rest at noon; for why should I be as one that turned aside to the flocks of thy companions?" The text and sermon were designed to propose an alternative "place of rest" for dissident locals, one different from "the flocks of their companions." This was a strategic message for the Woolwich situation and it was right on the mark. The first meeting produced charismatic manifestations, and by the next day a town-wide process of conviction and revival was under way. "This marvelous display of Immanuel's power excited almost universal attention," Randel recalled, "and the people of all ranks turned out to hear the new preachers."[16]

An anecdote from the Woolwich revival indicates the sort of tactics used by Freewill sectarians to exploit parish divisions. A large crowd had gathered at the town meetinghouse to hear Randel for a second time when "the parson," Josiah Winship, demanded an explanation for his actions. Randel replied that he was called on his mission by God. Winship retorted that such revelatory calls must be accompanied by miracles as they had been with Moses and the prophets, and that Randel would oblige him by turning his riding whip into a snake. Before Randel could respond, a voice from the crowd commented loudly, "I think if he were to do so, you would be the first one to run from it." The joke set off an uproar that Randel controlled by moving off to the town burial ground. Echoing his mentor Whitefield, Randel defiantly declared, "The most high dwelleth not in temples made with hands. I will have this grave for my pulpit, and the heavens for my sounding board."[17]

Woolwich was by now in the throes of a classic revival, which Randel culminated by employing the Freewill Baptists' most novel and sensatial evangelistic device, baptism by immersion. "Although there were about three hundred persons present," Randel noted, "there were no more than three that ever before saw baptism administered by immersion."[18] In towns like Woolwich, where Congregationalism was completely dominant, Freewill Baptists emphasized the necessity of baptism by immersion as an emblem of true New Testament faith. Baptism, moreover, provided an ideal initiation rite by which the core of a new congregation could be identified and organized. At Woolwich, the original five converts were soon joined by several more on Randel's return visit. These people were immediately "embodied" into a church by Randel, who gave them "suitable instructions, with respect to church discipline."[19] The infant church then undertook to maintain evangelism in the area, aided by similar small communities Randel had set up at nearby Edgecomb and Georgetown.

Capitalizing on the New Light Stir, Freewill Baptists forged a potent method of evangelism addressed to nascent dissenting communities of Radical Evangelicals in the new settlements. They recruited whole congregations and local leaders on the spot while employing their arsenal of persuasive devices. In Calvinistic Baptist churches they emphasized free will and universal atonement, liberal doctrinal positions that when grafted onto vigorous revivalism often split young Baptist communities. In Congregationalist contexts, whether Old Light or New Light, the same qualities of Arminian revivalism proved effective when combined with defiance of the established order and the rite of believers' baptism. The Freewill technique worked. By 1785 Randel's movement was the largest hill country sect, and it retained that position until after 1815. Baptists and Congregationalists regularly denounced Freewillers. The Bowdoinham Baptist Association, for example, depicted itself as "a fold in the midst of wolves, or a defenceless flock surrounded with . . . prowling multitudes" in the face of Freewill expansion.[20] But they were helpless to resist. With a strong corps of leaders and an effective method of institutional evangelism, the Freewill Baptist movement took shape as a close-knit communion of congregations drawn primarily from intrachurch schisms.

When the Shakers dramatically opened their public evangelism on the Dark Day of 1780, they discovered that it was their community—the sharing of goods, spiritual gifts, and discipline—that had the most impact on New Englanders. When it became clear that the social ambience at Niskeyuna was convincing many that the Shakers were "the people of God," it was but a short step to conclude that the best means of spreading the gospel was to bring the community to prospective converts. This, in essence, was what Mother Ann and the rest of the Niskeyuna community did in their major evangelistic effort, an extended tour of New England between 1781 and 1784. The intention of their proselytizing, like that of all sectarians, was to replicate their spiritual and social experiences among prospective converts. But rather than rely on haphazard itinerancy or on institutional combat, the Shakers developed the unusual technique of moving the Niskeyuna community from town to town, living with converts for considerable periods and initiating them firsthand into the detailed practice of their new faith.

During 1780 and 1781 visitors flocked to the Niskeyuna community, spurring the development of that commune into a staging area for proselytizing. Hospitality was an important feature of Shaker residential evangelism. Mother Ann insisted that all visitors, regardless of their religious convictions, be offered food and lodging. Valentine Rathbun reported that Mother Ann would not even consent to an interview with him until he had been fed and warmed. These gestures impressed Rathbun, and doubtless other visitors, as prima facie evidence of extraordinary piety and Christian charity,[21] which in turn promoted a favorable disposition toward the Shakers and their gospel. To present their faith, the Shakers created an elaborate environment of personal interviews, reproofs, exhortations, and charismatic episodes designed to initiate the curious into their gospel. Visitors questioned the Shakers individually and collectively about the nature of their experience, the necessity of repentance and celibacy, the interpretation of scripture, and "the travel to perfection." In the informal household atmosphere at Niskeyuna several Shaker spokespersons responded to such inquiries, sometimes cutting off conversation with a prophetic non sequitur, a vision, a trance, or an exhortation.[22] Although Mother Ann was the central figure in the community, the other charismatics, particularly William Lee and James Whittaker, also contributed to the group process.

The picture that emerges from the Niskeyuna community is that of a fluid and continuous social process of religious communication that the Shaker leaders controlled by a kind of ensemble improvisation. The contours of the group changed constantly. Mother Ann often engaged in intense private interviews with visitors while Elder James carried on a group doctrinal discussion and Elder William interviewed a prospective convert outdoors or elsewhere on the homestead. When these various transactions were completed, new configurations would appear as the principal Shakers circulated through the whole group.[23] In this manner, the proselytizing was constant, varied, and intense.

At crucial times when the possibility of conversion appeared, the Shakers moved into charismatic worship, a disorganized exercise of visions, trances, prophecies, bodily effects, singing, and dancing, which brought group attention to rest on a single focus. Participation in Shaker worship was not mandatory for visitors, though it was required for confirmed Believers. The varied gifts displayed by the worshipers, however, did give prospective converts easy access to the group. In these moments of high group emotion a person who had become intellectually convinced of the

Shaker gospel could abandon himself or herself to a relatively fluid form of ritual self-expression.

The most important procedure developed at Niskeyuna, however, was the confession of sins. After the elaborate and continuous evangelism of the sect had made its impression for several days, prospective converts were exhorted to confess all their sins to the Shaker leaders. This was done through intimate spiritual interviews with Mother Ann, Elder James Whittaker, or Elder William Lee, in which the penitent confessed all sins ever consciously committed and was forgiven for them. This intimate procedure brought the convert to a new level of trust and commitment to the sect and at the same time verified the Shaker claims to prophetic and visionary powers. Thus confession was the culmination of Shaker residential evangelism. It could not have succeeded, however, without the elaborate series of individual, subgroup, and collective transactions—interviews, discussions, meals, and worship—that created a richly textured spiritual environment in which confession became natural, meaningful, and effective.[24]

In the spring of 1781 Mother Ann and the Niskeyuna community set out to discover "the place in this country" shown to her in vision as the site of the Shaker millennial kingdom. Though the Shakers often preached in the Whitefieldian manner on the tour, their chief effort was to reproduce in detail, at each location they visited, the residential style that had already developed at Niskeyuna. Converts were dispatched to prepare each locality for the Shakers' arrival. At Tucconock, Massachusetts, the first stop on the tour, the curious and the faithful flocked to worship, receive "the power of God" in charisma, and hear the message of Mother Ann and the Elders. The Shakers remained at Tucconock "about ten days, in continual labors with the people," residing at the homes of converts Jonathan Slosson and Benjamin Osborn where those under conviction were also housed and initiated.[25]

The Shakers routinized this pattern of evangelism as they moved eastward. They spent a week at Enfield, Connecticut, and several days at Grafton and Upton, Massachusetts. At each place a local Believer who had been converted at Niskeyuna served as liaison to the town community and provided a residential center for mission activity. Similar evangelism was undertaken for periods up to several months at Petersham, Ashfield, Rehoboth, and Norton in Massachusetts and at Stonington, Preston, Windham, and Cheshire in Connecticut. In June 1781, nearing Harvard, Massachusetts, Mother Ann received a vision of angels leading the Shakers through a mob into a large brick house. She promptly proclaimed that Harvard was "the place and the people which had been shown her in vision while in England."[26] The mission had found its destination.

Founded in 1737, Harvard experienced a history of political radicalism and religious conflict common in rural New England during the Revolutionary period. Its Congregationalist minister, Daniel Johnson, died in 1777 while serving as a chaplain in the Revolutionary army. It was not until 1782 that the town could summon the means to issue a new call, this time to Ebenezer Grosvenor. During this hiatus the New Light Stir precipitated the organization of a Baptist church "in the easterly part of town" that petitioned unsuccessfully to be set off as an independent community. In 1781 and 1782 the Baptists were denied abatement of ministerial taxes, and they issued new calls for home rule. Harvard was also the home of Shadrach Ireland's perfectionist sect, leaderless since 1778. The vacancy in the parish pulpit, the hostility of the Baptists, and the threatening presence of the Irelandites polarized the Harvard community and presented Mother Ann with fertile ground for her mission.

Mother Ann's initial strategy was to preempt the leaderless Ireland movement. She pronounced that "God has a people in this place; he had heard their cries; they have had great light. Their leader got overcome; God has taken him away and sent me here."[27] She also claimed to see and "make labours" with Ireland's departed spirit. Mother Ann informed his followers that "he will never be released [from the wages of sin] until some of his people find their redemption." Mother Ann's convincing clairvoyance coupled with the vigor of Shaker evangelism and charisma soon persuaded most of the Irelandites to convert. Within weeks Mother Ann and the Elders occupied Ireland's headquarters at the Square House.

As large numbers of Baptists and New Light Congregationalists visited the Square House, the residential pattern of evangelism again appeared. Work went forward on several fronts. Elder James Whittaker, the leading Shaker preacher, and Mother Ann preached publicly at Shirley, Woburn, Littleton, and Petersham, "where numbers had already embraced the testimony" and "the sound of the gospel awakened serious inquiry" by others. In large outdoor meetings Whittaker's message took on an enthusiastic Whitefieldian air. At Shirley, for example, Elder James proclaimed, "This is the gospel, and see ye to it, what kind of use you make of it . . . Treasure up the word, for the time will come when there will be a famine, not of bread, nor of water, but of the Word of the Lord. You will see the time when you will be willing to crawl on your hands and knees to hear the word of the Lord."[28] Whittaker's incendiary preaching was accompanied by Mother Ann's presence as adviser, confessor, seer, charismatic virtuoso, and leader. "Tho her words were few," her converts reported, "yet they always seemed adapted to the occasion, and it did not appear that she ever spoke in vain."[29]

At the Square House, the more intimate and intense processes of residential evangelism were taken up. "They spared no pains by day or night, and frequently spent whole nights in continued labors teaching and instructing the people, and ministering the power of the resurrection to lost souls."[30] The improvised style of teaching, conversation, and confession continued unmodified at the Square House, there as elsewhere capitalizing on the immediate, the unexpected, and the sensational.

The conversion of Jemima Blanchard at Harvard illustrated the intimacy and directness of Shaker evangelism. Blanchard had fled to friends in Holliston, Massachusetts, to avoid being "taking in" by the Shakers and was pursued there by convert Daniel Wood and persuaded to return. At the house of Zaccheus Stevens she viewed old acquaintances "with wonder, and saw the power of God visible on their faces, and even on the clothes of the Believers. It looked perfectly white and run in veins."[31] At Isaac Willard's home and elsewhere Blanchard found similar transformations and preternatural appearances that so impressed her that she went to the Square House "to see for myself what had caused such a change in all my acquaintances."

At the Square House she met two friends who "talked very lovingly to me" and invited her into the kitchen where Mother Ann was washing. "She turned and looked at me with such a pleasant heavenly countenance, that it absorbed my whole soul . . . She took me by the arm and said 'Wilt thou be a daughter of Zion, and be searched as Jerusalem with candles?' I answered not, for I knew not what to say; her word seemed to me like the voice of God."[32] Mother Ann conducted Jemima "into meeting" and watched the young woman with such intensity that it seemed "that she could see through me." When Blanchard attempted to leave the Square House that afternoon, she was unable to disengage from "the beautiful, and god-like woman." Suddenly Mother Ann suggested that Blanchard confess her sins. When Jemima evidenced reluctance, Mother Ann asked, "Don't you want the people of God to pray for you?" Jemima replied that she did, and "in an instant her arms were around my waist and we were both on our knees. I shook so that the windows clattered, but I did not know what it was for some minutes . . . After this I thought no more of going home, being exercised almost constantly by the power of God for many days."

Hospitality was maintained at Harvard, and it became a powerful evangelistic device in itself. "Vast numbers of people came from various parts to visit them and great crowds were almost daily fed there." But the sheer size of the mission soon demanded the organization of food procurement and preparation. A communal farming operation began in 1782 with Jonathan Slosson in charge, and Mother Ann personally managed the household. In the same year David Meacham led the establishment of craft shops that enhanced Shaker self-sufficiency.

As the Shaker mission succeeded, it encountered increasing opposition from Harvard's citizens, who were especially aroused by the possibility that the Shakers were fomenting counterrevolution. The Believers disclaimed any interest or partisanship in the war, but the stocking of provisions at the Square House led to rumors and then charges of sedition. On at least half a dozen occasions mobs were raised against the Shakers. The most violent episode occurred in August 1782 during the first general convocation of Believers. A large mob led by Captain Phinehas Farnsworth and Lieutenant Jonathan Houghton seized the Shakers and drove them under whips seven miles out of town. The visitors were dispersed, the Harvard Shakers publicly whipped for collaboration with traitors.[33]

Mother Ann shifted the residential center to Ashfield for the winter of 1782-83. She returned to Harvard in the spring, but the belief that she was "a British emissary, dressed in a woman's habit, for seditious purposes" would not abate. The mission was finally abandoned late in 1783 after yet another mob led by the same Farnsworth captured William Lee and James Whittaker, tied them to trees, and whipped them "with sticks cut from the bushes." The Shakers returned to Niskeyuna, visiting on the way the small communities of converts in western New England.

The residential method of evangelism thus was markedly successful in gaining new converts, but it also roused much more serious opposition than simple preaching or even church subversion did for other sectarians. Doubtless the English Shaker leaders caused much of the hysteria, but had Mother Ann or James Whittaker appeared alone in Harvard or any other town, they would not have met with such violence. It was the successful team ministry and overt residential evangelism of the sect that brought it into such serious conflict with local military, political, and religious leaders.

By Mother Ann's return to Niskeyuna in 1784, the Shakers had demonstrated the effectiveness of residential evangelism. Mother Ann and the Elders had made hundreds of converts and gathered them into household communities modeled after Niskeyuna. Evangelistic teams sent to New Hampshire, Vermont, and Maine had similar success among many local sects formed during the New Light Stir. The Shakers reversed the whole rationale of itinerancy by creating a religious prodigy that attracted visitors to it. By supplying hospitality and continuous informal evangelism, the Shakers added another dimension to the evangelistic effort. Like Freewill Baptists and Universalists, the Shakers attempted to foster new spiritual communities. But instead of relying on traditional notions of church discipline to organize converts, they simply incorporated families of new Believers into the traveling Niskeyuna community on the spot.

During Shaker evangelistic visitations, the converted began living as a new community immediately. They were given every conceivable kind of instruction, reprimand, exhortation, and inspiration. The Shaker style of evangelism thus imparted not only a revival spark of new doctrine to its proselytes; new Believers received a complete set of social cues and roles by which they were to embark on their celibate and sinless lives. It was around this residential evangelism that a distinctive type of Shaker community developed. At once hierarchic and egalitarian, communal and familial, charismatic and ascetic, millennial and this-worldly, the Believers constructed a network of convert centers across rural New England. Following the pattern for daily and religious life set at Niskeyuna, the Shaker converts set out as spiritual families to reproduce Mother Ann's model of sinless perfection and social cooperation down to the minutest detail.

The models of sectarian mission that developed in the early 1780s continued to be effective methods of growth until the War of 1812. Each sect thus established a solid constituency in a subregion of the hill country before 1790. Universalists were strongest in the upper Connecticut Valley and the Worcester Highlands; Freewill Baptists gained the bulk of their membership in Maine and central New Hampshire. The Shakers were the widest-ranging sect, owing to Mother Ann's tour and the efforts of the evangelistic teams she sent to distant New Light groups. Shakerism was concentrated in the Berkshire Hills, but it also found numerous converts in the Connecticut Valley, in Worcester County, in central New Hampshire, and in Maine.

The revivalistic character of the sects' evangelism resulted in growth patterns that were remarkably similar. After the spectacular increases during the New Light Stir, conversions continued to mount until around 1790. For the next decade or so accessions continued on a much reduced scale. Then in the late 1790s the sects capitalized on the first stirrings of the Second Great Awakening, reaping a rich harvest of new members through the first two decades of the nineteenth century. The relative and absolute size of the sects, however, is difficult to estimate. On the basis of available evidence the Freewill Baptists seem to have been the largest sect, having organized more than one hundred fifty congregations in New England by 1815. The Universalists were only slightly behind, claiming more than seventy churches by 1794 and more than one hundred twenty-five by 1815. The Shakers organized far fewer societies — only twelve in New England — but each of these was a large centralized entity. Each Shaker society contained as many as six semi-independent communities numbering from fifty to one hundred persons per "family." In addition, Shaker records did not indicate the sizable number of informal adherents and "outfamilies" — at Cheshire and Savoy, Massachusetts; Guilford and Pittsford, Vermont; Tuftonboro, New Hampshire; Saybrook, Connecticut; Gorham, Maine, and elsewhere — that should be included in their aggregate. A minimum estimate of the three sects' membership and regular adherents by 1815 is six thousand Freewill Baptists, five thousand Universalists, and four thousand Shakers.

This estimate of 15,000 sectarians in the New England hinterland by 1815 compares well with the strength of Congregationalist and Baptist communions. In 1813 David Benedict counted 315 Baptist churches in the same region with a total of 20,497 members. Congregationalist strength is less precisely gauged. Modern scholars have estimated 50 Congregationalist parishes in Maine; 146 in Vermont; 153 in New Hampshire; and perhaps 100 in western Massachusetts by 1815. The ministerial shortage of the Revolutionary period was never overcome, however, by rural Congregationalists. For example, 50 of 153 New Hampshire pulpits were vacant in 1815. Moreover, these estimates include parishes from older coastal regions in their totals. Rural Congregationalism probably included 350 to 400 active parishes byt 1815; reckoning 50 or so members per parish—the New Hampshire average between 1783 and 1828—the total membership in rural Congregationalist churches in all likelihood did not exceed 20,000. Thus the sectarians, minimally estimated at 15,000 adherents and geographically distributed across the whole hill country, constituted a fully competitive religious presence in the region.[34]

Who were these converts? Their religious background has already been established. They were Radical Evangelicals, primarily Baptists, Separates, New Light Congregationalists, or local sectarians. Further evidence is provided by the predominance of former Baptist elders among the sects' leaders. Freewill leaders Randel, Tingley, Lord, Lock, Ephraim Stinchfield, and John Buzzell were all Baptist elders before their conversions. Among Universalists, Caleb Rich, Adams Streeter, Zephaniah Lathe, Elhanan Winchester, and Hosea Ballou emerged from positions of Baptist leadership to become converts and missionaries. Joseph Meacham was the most notable ex-Baptist leader of the Shakers, but the sect also included at one time Valentine and Daniel Rathbun, leaders of the Pittsfield Baptist Church, the largest in the Berkshires.

But what can be said about the social and economic characteristics of the sectarian constituency? A correlation between enthusiastic religion and economic dispossession has been widely posited by historians and social scientists.[35] In the present case, treatment of the question is severely hampered by the fragmentary nature of sectarian records and the high geographical mobility of converts. Where collection of reasonably complete lists of membership is possible, the correlative economic and social information is often lacking. But in three cases—Harvard, Massachusetts; Langdon, New Hampshire; and New Durham, New Hampshire—the requisite evidence is present, and some preliminary conclusions may be drawn. It seems clear than the sectarians constituted a typical and representative socioeconomic group in rural New England. They were not dispossessed, nor were they socially ostracized. They occupied a normal range of incomes and participated in town offices commensurate with their class. They were Patriots and Loyalists, Revolutionary veterans and neutrals. To understand the significance of these generalizations they must be placed in the specific contexts of the three towns under examination.

Harvard, Massachusetts, incorporated in 1737, was a typical subsistence farm community of rural New England.[36] Three sources exist that reconstruct the early Shaker constituency there: a list of thirty contributors who helped Mother Ann buy Shadrach Ireland's Square House on 29 April 1782; a list of subscribers to the construction of the Shaker meetinghouse in 1791; and a running list of members kept by the Harvard Shaker elders.

The names on these records were compared with those on the Harvard tax assessment of 1781, which was levied to fund the town's military and logistics quota for the Continental army.[37] The comparison reveals that the Shaker constituency was economically quite similar to that of the town in general. The 20 Shakers who appeared among the 385 polls on the 1781 assessment were taxed an average of £45. The town average was slightly less, at £39. The Shakers thus represented a slightly wealthier aggregate group than did the average Harvard citizen. The income range of Shakers was also typical of Harvard's taxpayers. The largest taxes were £253 on Captain Isaac Gates and £237 on Oliver Atherton. These men were the leaders of Harvard's wealthiest and most prominent families; they were the only persons to be charged more than £200. Forty men, roughly one tenth of the polls, were assessed between £100 and £200. Two Shaker adherents—Zaccheus Stevens (£120) and Jonathan Wetherbee (£116)—were among this group. In addition, a number of other Shakers of substantial worth appeared on the 1781 list, including Jonathan Clark (£71), Jonathan Clark, Jr. (£55), Jonathan Cooper (£60), Simon Cooper (£65), Isaac Willard (£83), and Jeremiah Willard (£85). All these men represented "the better sort" of people, the small group of farmers who lived above subsistence in rural New England towns. The remaining Shakers occupied the lower ranges of the 1781 assessment. Most of them—Samuel Cooper, Samuel Cooper, Jr., William Safford, David Crouch, and John Warner—joined the majority of Harvard polls assessed between £20 and £30. Two others, David Melvin and Eleazar Rand, were included among the more than one hundred males listed but not taxed. Economically the Harvard Shakers were virtually indistinguishable from the rest of the community. Although none of the wealthiest dozen men were Shakers, several of the town's more substantial citizens were. Most of the Harvard Shakers were persons of solid middle income, and the dependents and poor among them were fewer in proportion to the larger community.

The social standing and political status of the Shakers was commensurate with their economic role. Zaccheus Stevens and Jonathan Wetherbee were town selectmen in the 1770s and 1780s; Reuben Dodge and Simon Cooper were Revolutionary officers. Eleven of the twenty Shakers served in the militia or the Continental army before their conversion. Thus the Harvard Shakers drew their converts from some of the town's oldest and largest families, from officers and enlisted soldiers, from town officials and average taxpayers. Though they embraced a radical gospel of millenarian perfectionism, the Shakers were not a dispossessed or socially deviant constituency. Their experience at Harvard and elsewhere indicates that sectarian beliefs could appeal to a representative cross section of rural New England society.

What was true of sectarians at Harvard was also true in newer areas of settlement to the north and west. A good example was New Durham, New Hampshire, the site of Benjamin Randel's original Freewill Baptist congregation. New Durham lies on the New Hampshire-Maine border in the hill country thirty-five miles inland from Portsmouth. It was settled after the French and Indian War by Louisbourg veterans. The earliest settlers quickly established themselves as a permanent social and economic elite that maintained its control through the Revolutionary period.[38]

A town inventory of 1784, taken to finance New Durham's military quota, contained the names of nine men who were original signers of Randel's first New Durham covenant.[39] These 9 persons constitute a small but revealing sample of the 112 rated polls. The comparison of the average wealth of these Freewill Baptists with the New Durham per capita inventory reveals both the typicality of the sectarians and the classic subsistence economy of the town:

	Oxen	Cows	Horses	Tillage	Mowing	Pasture	Wild
Freewill Baptists	2	1.67	2.75	1.22	4.6	1.88	90.3
New Durham per capita	1.15	1.57	1.33	1.1	3.15	2.25	83.35

The Freewill Baptists were slightly above average in total wealth, and within even their small numbers there existed a representatively wide range of property. The Freewillers numbered among their converts some of the town's wealthiest citizens, like Shadrach Allard, owner of four oxen, three cows, nine horses, and 287 acres, seventeen of them cleared. On the other hand there were also poor members of Randel's congregation, like Widow Susannah York, who owned one cow and no land in 1784.

A few men in New Durham were richer than Shadrach Allard, but none of them could match him and the other Freewill converts in community standing. Allard was selected selectman in 1766 and served annually until 1773; he also was a lieutenant in the militia. Ebenezer Bickford, an early settler who served as selectman from 1768 to 1772, was another charter Freewiller. A third notable convert was Colonel Thomas Tash, selectman at the town's first meeting in 1765, its first state representative in 1778, and again selectman from 1780 to 1784. Most influential of all, however, was Robert Boody, assessor, former constable, town clerk, selectman from 1771 to 1784, and militia captain. Boody went on to become one of the leading ministers and missionaries of the Freewill movement in the 1780s and 1790s. In a hill town like New Durham, early settlers like Tash, Bickford, Allard, and Boody constituted the social and economic infrastructure. Through their carefully calibrated evangelism, Benjamin Randel and other Freewill itinerants were able to attract such leaders as well as average subsistence farmers, creating a sectarian community of respectable rural citizens.

A final example taken from the upper Connecticut Valley illustrates how the phenomenon of sectarian typicality continued through time and space. Langdon, New Hampshire, is located five miles east of the Connecticut River and twenty miles north of the Massachusetts border. Not settled until 1773, the town was incorporated in 1787. Langdon's first church was Universalist, gathered in 1791 by Zebulon Streeter, cousin of Adams Streeter. A small Congregationalist parish coexisted with the Universalists until 1805, when both merged under the ministry of Universalist Abner Kneeland.[40] Langdon conducted a tax inventory for revaluation in 1809 that listed 130 polls, 23 of whom had signed the 1791 or 1805 Universalist church covenants.[41] A comparison of the average wealth of these Universalists and Langdon per capita income again illustrates sectarian typicality amidst a marginal economy.

	Oxen	Cows	Horses	Cattle	Tillage	Mowing	Pasture	Wild
Universalists	1.05	2.3	1.0	3.3	1.8	1.5	9.5	34.6
Langdon per capita	.75	1.7	.9	2.15	1.4	2.5	7.3	29.6

At Langdon as elsewhere, sectarians owned slightly above-average amounts of property and claimed members of economic prominence. Benjamin Palmer owned 85 acres, 13 of them improved, four oxen, six cows, and eleven cattle; Daniel Prouty held 62 acres, 12 of them improved, two oxen, five cows, and thirteen cattle; and John Sartwell possessed 52 acres, 13 of them improved, two oxen, five cows, and nine cattle. Universalists Jeremiah Howard and James Egerton were among the wealthiest citizens of Langdon. The former held 120 acres, 15 of them improved including a two-acre orchard, and the latter owned 87 acres, four oxen, five cows, and seven cattle. Such men made up a substantial economic constituency and a considerable sociopolitical group as well. James Egerton, for example, was a revered early settler, perennial town moderator and selectman. Daniel Prouty, John and Obadiah Sartwell, Jeremiah Howard, and Isaac Walker also served regularly in elected office around the turn of the nineteenth century.

Langdon Universalists also included poorer persons as well, like Darwin Royce, whose inventory included only two oxen and one cow; Isaachar Johnson, who owned only fifty acres of unimproved land; William Benton, owner of two oxen and three cows; or Thomas Kenny, who held one cow, three cattle, and did not even own a horse. But these men were simply characteristic of the lower end of the economic scale in a marginal local economy. At Langdon in 1809, as at New Durham in 1784 and Harvard in 1781, the evidence overwhelmingly indicates the normality and representative nature of the sectarian constituency.

The typicality of sectarian converts is also indicated by the important role played by extended families in the nascent sects. The hill towns where sectarian itinerants gathered converts were fragile societies in which kinship groups were the central social organization. Over one third of the taxable polls of Harvard, Massachusetts, in 1781, for example, were members of the Willard family. When sectarian prophets made an inroad into such a massive clan network, the process of conversion often spread to include a large proportion of the kinship group.

A classic illustration is provided by the Ballou family of Richmond, New Hampshire. A hill town on the Massachusetts border ten miles east of the Connecticut River, Richmond was first settled in 1757 by Baptists and Quakers from Rhode Island and eastern Massachusetts. In 1767 Maturin Ballou, a Baptist farmer from Cumberland, Rhode Island, moved to Richmond with his wife and children. Ballou, who had become a Separate-Baptist in 1752, soon emerged as the leader of Richmond's Baptists and was ordained elder there in 1770. But by 1780 Caleb Rich's vigorous evangelism had hopelessly divided the church and forced Ballou's resignation. Through the 1780s Rich continued to carry off most of Ballou's former congregation, and in 1790 the Baptist elder's youngest son, Hosea, renounced the family faith for Rich's Universalism.[42]

Through Hosea's efforts most of Maturin's ten children were converted, along with many members of two other branches of the Ballou clan that had recently arrived in Richmond. Three of Maturin's sons, Hosea, Benjamin, and David, became Universalist elders. Two others, Nathan and Stephen, converted but remained lay. In addition, Maturin's nephew Silas, a Richmond resident, was a notable early Universalist leader who published the sect's first hymnal in 1785. The Ballou family, like many sectarian clans, continued to produce leaders in succeeding generations. Among the children of Hosea's siblings were three more elders; five sons of the next generation were also ordained to the Universalist ministry. This one extended family from rural New Hampshire thus provided almost a dozen ministers and more than one hundred converts in three short generations. In the words of the family's genealogist, "these seem to be uncommonly rich findings for the Universalists to derive from one Calvinistic Baptist name."[43]

But though exceptional in scale, the experience of the Ballous was common enough in kind among New England sectarians. Within Universalism, for example, the Streeter family also contributed three first-generation elders, Adams, Zebulon, and Sebastian, as well as prominent ministers in the next generation and a host of lay members. The Freewill Baptists were even more influenced by such clan conversions. No less than eight families in New Hampshire and Maine—Buzzell, Blaisdell, Dudley, Elliott, Hutchinson, Knowlton, Lord, and Whitney—supplied three or more Freewill elders before 1815. Behind these numbers stood the same kind of wholesale familial conversions experienced by the Ballous in Richmond.[44]

The most striking examples of clan influence were found among the Shakers. With their policy of residential evangelism, the early Shakers encouraged entire family groups to mold their households into model celibate communities. The records of the Shaker society at New Gloucester, Maine, indicate just how important such familial conversions could be.[45] For example, two brothers, Ephraim and Barnanas Briggs, and their wives, Naomi and Lettice, became Shaker Believers in 1784. The Briggs couples were in their forties when they converted, and they brought with them families of ten children each into the faith. Thus from the conversion of four adults in 1784 came no less than twenty-four new Shakers. Nor was this case unusual. The Holmes family, a migrant clan from Plymouth County, Massachusetts, joined the New Gloucester Shakers with seven adults — three married couples and one unmarried female — and a total of twenty-two children. The largest family was the Merrill clan, one of the earliest families to settle in New Gloucester. In 1784 James Merrill, his wife, Sarah, and their eight children became the town's second family to convert to Shakerism. Of the children, two males, Nathan and Edmund, had married previously. Nathan and his wife, Rachel, had six children; Edmund and his wife, Charity Proctor, had seven. All these offspring followed their parents and grandparents into celibate Shaker life. Five other Merrill females were also recorded as Shaker members, for a total of thirty-two Merrills among the New Gloucester Shakers before 1796. And as with the other sects, these large families exercised important leadership functions, controlling both the eldership and the diaconate at New Gloucester for two decades.[46]

The constituency attracted by sectarianism was typical of hill country citizens in its social, political, economic, and religious characteristics. Sectarians occupied all economic levels in roughly the same distribution as the general population. Many of them served in the militia or the Continental army, some as officers. Numerous converts served in public office and were long-standing respected citizens of their towns. And the new adherents often joined en masse as extended families, bringing this major characteristic of the society at large into the nascent sects as a powerful shaping influence on community development. The sectarian converts were not socially, economically, or politically deviant. Rather, the new gospels of the Shakers, Universalists, and Freewill Baptists were acceptable to converts precisely because they addressed those religious problems that were widely felt during the New Light Stir by people of all ranks: free grace, freedom from sin, and the coming end of the world. The new gospels brought together a microcosm of all the new settlements around novel religious ideas and traditionally valued charismatic leadership. The decisive factor in the gathering of the sects was not social or economic or political; it was the intrinsic religious message of the founders broadcast in compelling evangelistic strategies to the settlers of the hill country. The success of that evangelism created new indigenous communities in the early 1780s that soon found themselves launched on the perilous search for permanent religious cultures.

6

Improvisation and Crisis

By 1784 the Universalist, Shaker, and Freewill Baptist movements had become small sects with the beginnings of a regional constituency. Their incisive religious claims and effective methods of evangelization had brought strong positive response from many Radical Evangelicals in rural New England. But with success came a series of new problems, the most pressing of which was the need for institutional structure. With hundreds of converts widely scattered in the hill country, the sects were in danger of swift disintegration unless they provided discipline, organization, and unity.

The sectarian founders, however, did not possess clear visions of institutional order. They relied on the assumptions of Radical Evangelicalism, which called for a covenanted, gathered church of the elect effortlessly guided by the unifying influence of the Holy Spirit. Mother Ann Lee also enjoined strict rules of ascetic life-style while Benjamin Randel experimented with mutual discipline. But the late 1780s were a time when social needs presented the sects with new problems for which they were largely unprepared. Each sect confronted the task of social maturation in a different way, and for a complex set of reasons each failed at first to deal with the problem. By 1790 the groups were suffering from uncertain leadership, unchecked diffusion of membership, and unresolved institutional disorder. They sought to relieve the troubles by essentially improvising new social arrangements from the Radical Evangelical tradition and from their brief evangelistic experience. But the course of religious development in post-Revolutionary New England required creative and thoroughly rationalized institutions. This need became fully apparent only after an extended period of organizational confusion and finally crisis.

Of the three sects, the Freewill Baptists at first possessed the clearest ecclesiastical standard. Virtually all its early members were Baptists, and
under the leadership of Randel, Lord, and Tingley they readily could have
established an associational polity of gathered churches modeled on the
Warren Baptist Association. But Randel was a neophyte to religious leadership, and his visionary faith inclined strongly toward a radically noncreedal
polity in the Quaker mold. At New Durham Randel took the position that
the Scriptures required no further human elaboration; but after his ordination a majority of the congregation was "still of the opinion that there must
be some written articles of faith and a written covenant."

Randel complied by providing thirteen articles and a brief constitution in
1780. The articles, of which no copy is extant, set out Randel's theology of
free will and universal atonement. The covenant endorsed the articles and
pledged members "to give ourselves to one another in love and fellowship,
and agree to take the Scriptures of truth as our rule of faith and practice,
respecting our duty to God, our neighbors, and ourselves."[1] But his commitment to a biblicist life-style was modified by an insistence on the primacy of the Holy Spirit in all Christian activity. "All the commands and ordinances of the New Testament"—including the articles—were to be
obeyed only "so far as they are, or shall be made known to us, by the light of
the Holy Spirit without which we cannot attain to the true knowledge
thereof."

Members also covenanted to "bear one another's burdens" both spiritual
and material through charity and Christian community. Organizationally
New Durham followed Radical Evangelical precedent in dividing church
offices among ruling elders, teaching elders, and deacons. The congregation made liberal provisions for "the improvement of the gifts of the brethren" and stipulated that no one could enter this gathered community "except he give a satisfactory account of a change of life and heart; and shall
also promise to submit to the order and discipline as above."[2]

The first New Durham covenant did not claim to be authoritative for
other Freewill congregations, nor was it accepted as such. But it did articulate with precision the earliest ecclesiastical notions of the sect. The docu-
ment followed Radical Evangelical precedent in most details and was inspired by the ideal of the unity of the Spirit through which the community
could carry out its discipline and good works. There was a strong sense in
Randel's formula that the Holy Spirit would lead the sect to further insights
and rules for Christian life, and the door to more unorthodox forms of polity was left quite open. But the most revealing thing about the 1780 articles
and covenant was precisely its Radical Evangelical typicality. At the outset,
the Freewill Baptists had no idea that their gospel and constituency would
require modification of received Separate and Baptist norms. The institutional structure was therefore kept to an absolute minimum, no congregational subordination to larger denominational organizations was contem-

plated, and ultimate confidence was placed on the Holy Spirit's guidance of the entire enterprise.

New Durham's congregational stability was the exception rather than the rule. Most early congregations were schismatic groups generated by the New Light Stir. They lacked ministerial expertise and often were divided by converts of differing ecclesiastical origin. In these frontier churches the need for organization was acute and resources for order were minimal. The congregations were forced to improvise whatever structures they could devise from their rich but confused background. At Loudon, New Hampshire, for example, a large Freewill congregation was organized by John Shepard of Gilmanton in 1780. The church adopted an oral covenant, elected ruling elders, and ordained a deacon. The latter officer was empowered to make an inventory of members' economic worth and establish an "equality" or percentage contribution for each member. The Loudon church dealt with all fiscal and disciplinary matters on an ad hoc basis. The results were first inconsistent, then disastrous. The congregation voted not to bear arms as a Christian duty, then decided not to expel those members who "went to training and answered to their names." They spent large sums building houses for needy members, but soon found it difficult to collect the equalities. By 1781 doctrinal controversies had split the congregation, and during the next year many members were drawn off to Shakerism. In the face of these problems the Loudon church could muster only cumbersome and ineffective discipline. Inexperienced leaders failed; membership swiftly declined. So recently a leader in the nascent sect, the church was compelled to disband in June 1782.[3]

The Freewill Baptists thus discovered in the mid-1780s that converts were as easy to lose as to gain and that without some oversight their fragile local church structures would suffer the same fate as Loudon. To meet such pressing needs a group of itinerants and lay representatives, led by Benjamin Randel, convened at Hollis, Maine, in October 1783. They agreed to meet quarterly on a rotating basis at Hollis; New Gloucester, Maine; New Durham; and Woolwich, Maine. On 6 December the Freewill Baptist Quarterly Meeting was formally organized "to ascertain the state of the churches—consult upon the general interests of religion—adjust difficulties—inquire into the fellowship of those present—examine candidates for ministry, and ordain them if advisable—and engage in public worship and the celebration of the ordinances."[4]

Aside from its more frequent meetings, the Quarterly Meeting closely resembled Baptist associations in powers and procedures. It issued no disciplinary judgments at all in its early years but did vigorously pursue other avenues of unification among "the Connection" of Freewill congregations. It urged a day of fasting and prayer on 13 October 1784 to combat the effects of Shakerism; it authorized publication of anti-Calvinist tracts. The most effective action of the Quarterly Meeting, however, was the drafting and circulation of epistles to the churches admonishing them in Pauline rhetoric to "live up to their profession." One of the earliest such circulars concluded with a typically millennialist exhortation to "Live like children of the King of Kings. Let your light shine. Live always ready, like servants, waiting for the coming of the Lord."[5] These letters were read to all Freewill congregations in hopes that such communications would bolster their resolve to pursue the apostolic life. It was a poor substitute for competent ministerial assistance, but circular letters and itinerants were virtually the only resources available to the struggling sect.

Local institutions were so weak that the Quarterly Meeting soon emerged as the most important early ecclesiastical organization. Originally conceived as a representative body comprising ministers and "messengers chosen and sent by the churches," the Quarterly Meeting soon abandoned this associational composition and became a mass "convention of all present" at the meeting site. In keeping with this popular makeup, the sessions became more devotional than administrative. Meetings normally lasted five days and consisted primarily of revival sermons by the sect's best preachers, preparatory to the culminating performance of the ordinances—the Lord's Supper, baptism, and foot-washing. As the excitement of the New Light Stir began to cool, the Freewill Baptists thus sought to preserve its intensity and their own enthusiastic origins through mass religious meetings, a New England precedent for the frontier camp meetings of the Second Great Awakening.[6]

As the largest Freewill institution the Quarterly Meeting served a unifying function for the whole sect. As early as December 1785 it established a liberal policy of open communion, welcoming "all such persons as give a satisfactory evidence that they are united to Christ by a living union to him."[7] Meetings began with a laborious process of establishing "fellowship and union" among all attending either by vote "affirming the entire fellowship of the members with each other" or by individual testimonies to that effect. If any disagreement on doctrine, moral duty, or behavior appeared, all business was suspended until "Christian union" was established. The process of prayer, exhortation, and public confession often took an entire day. More important, it became the cornerstone of a developing consensualism that soon became a major characteristic of Freewill practice.

The Quarterly Meeting was the most significant early Freewill institutional experiment, but neither it nor congregational organization achieved structural adequacy before 1790. The Quarterly Meeting was an improvised hybrid of Baptist and Quaker principles, grounded in a spiritual union with the Holy Spirit and animated by the drive to preserve revivalistic zeal after the New Light Stir. Local congregations had varying structures based on written and oral covenants derived from Evangelical roots, but they lacked a strong disciplinary and doctrinal foundation. This two-tiered polity was unsystematic and at times contradictory. It did not survive the internal pressures and external attacks on the sect that began around 1785.

In that year, for example, the Little River, Maine, church split over the validity of "the predestinarian plan" because the congregation could achieve consensus only on the statement "he that believeth and is baptized shall be saved, but he that believeth not shall be damned." Its dispirited remnant sadly wished "that all beliefs, but a belief in Jesus, as the scripture hath said, were rooted out of the world."[8] By 1787 other doctrinal disputes had appeared in local congregations, particularly over the validity of foot-washing as an ordinance, which cost the Connection several congregations. From outside, the Shakers and the better-organized and more numerous Brentwood Baptists took a heavy toll of Freewill believers. Only nine new churches were gathered by the sect between 1783 and 1791. And as the revival zeal of Freewill believers declined, the limited effectiveness of their institutions likewise collapsed.

By 1790 "schisms and discords" were rife throughout the Connection and in November of that year the consensus of the Quarterly Meeting at Gorham was shattered "by a number of heady, highminded, selfconceited professors, who came into their meetings and disturbed them, both in the time of our worship and business."[9] The worst blow of all, however, was the collapse of the New Durham church. In pursuing his minimalist ideal of church order, Benjamin Randel had allowed discipline to falter and doctrinal dispute to continue without taking definitive measures to remedy these chronic problems. In May 1791 the New Durham congregation announced to a stunned Connection that "our covenant obligations are broken, we are no longer a church in visible standing, and we believe it most for the glory of God that a public declaration be made to that effect."[10]

By 1791 the Freewill experiment was on the verge of failure. The lack of doctrinal standards or structures of authority had become critical. Randel and his ministerial colleagues were largely responsible for the breakdown. The founder's reluctance to build uniform institutions came both from his primitivist convictions and from his lack of inspirational gifts regarding church order. No other leader emerged among early ministers, therefore clerical control of the Quarterly Meeting and local congregations did not materialize. As competition increased from Shakers and Baptists, Randel's followers and even the prophet himself began to doubt whether the Holy Spirit continued to lead them. By 1791, with their chief congregation disbanded, their connectional body a scene of argument and schism, their founder bereft of his charismatic leadership, and as many as half of their converts drawn off to other faiths, the Freewill Baptists indeed endured "the most dark and trying time that ever these people experienced."[11]

From the outset, Universalist congregations in New England experienced difficulties in agreeing to uniform church structures. In the 1780s rival plans for local order were debated as theological diversity grew. An attempt in 1785 to organize the congregations into a common body proved temporary; thereafter personal and theological differences rapidly increased, and by 1790 virtually no effective cooperation existed at all. John Murray's first formal church organization in New England was the Independent Christian Society of Gloucester, gathered in 1779. The society's Articles of Faith combined Radical Evangelical covenantalism with an aggressive "declaration of intention," claiming that God was "revealing to them his secret" truth. The Independents pledged themselves to a life of separation from the world, "determining by God's grace no more to be entangled by any yoke of bondage." The articles also asserted radical political and doctrinal freedom. Although acknowledging "obedience to every ordinance of man, for God's sake," the Independents flatly refused to compromise their liberty of conscience. The Gloucester Articles also named John Murray their prophet and affirmed that he preached "the same gospel" proclaimed by "the first preachers of Jesus Christ." Yet even Murray was to be judged by "the word and the spirit" manifested to the congregation through "the promise of the divine presence," and if he deviated from the truth they promised "to consider him a stranger."[12]

The Independents were guided by the Radical Evangelical principles of primitivism and minimalism. They covenanted to pray, praise, hear the Word, and "freely to communicate whatever God shall please to manifest to us for our mutual edification." In these activities they endorsed the "improvement of gifts" among all members. Matters of discipline and financial responsibility were regarded as private affairs, with no special officers to perform or coordinate these functions. Each member simply agreed to hold "a serious regard" for the "exhortations, admonitions, and instructions" of the apostolic epistles. The distinctive element of the Gloucester Articles was a distrust of organizational hierarchy. The covenant emphasized individualism over unity, perhaps because of the egalitarianism inherent in the message of universal salvation. Whatever the reason, from the very beginning of Universalist institutionalization, individualism and minimalism were dominant characteristics.[13]

A similar impulse is visible from the fragmentary early records of Universalist churches in the hill country. In 1777 Caleb Rich's congregations at Richmond, Warwick, and Jaffrey united into a single society. "For the purpose of strengthening and confirming the believers," they adopted "numerous articles . . . expressing and explaining their faith, their views of church government, and their personal and social duties." Rich composed the formula, which was "very prolix and unwieldy." No extant copy of the Richmond Articles exists, though their characteristics can be ascertained from nineteenth-century accounts. "They contained not only a full statement of the doctrine they embraced, but the arguments and scripture proofs, also the duties of Christians, distinctly and forceably presented. There was no laxity in this respect. They claimed the purest system of morals of any sect in Christendom as a necessary result of the doctrine."[14]

The Richmond Articles seem to have followed Radical Evangelical lines in most particulars, and certainly in form. But in several aspects Rich introduced distinctive Universalist notions. Despite their common covenantal bond, Rich refused to permit the three congregations to consolidate. He insisted on separate meetings with locally elected ruling elders that he served in circuit as scripture teacher. Even after his ordination in 1781, Rich refused to accept traditional ministerial authority, preferring informal spiritual Bible teaching to reasoned discourse "in the normal manner." The most revealing aspect of this first rural Universalist community was its liberalism regarding liturgical participation. "Each person was made a member of the church in full fellowship, free to accept the outward ordinances or not." This provision indicates not only deeply rooted individualism but also a radical attitude toward ritual performance itself. Rural Universalism was primarily a cognitive faith based on innovative biblical interpretation. This emphasis was so strong that even baptism and the Lord's Supper, essential exercises in piety and apostolic imitation, were jettisoned as unnecessary for saving faith. But the fact that even in its earliest stages the Universalist movement exhibited such liturgical optionality was the strongest sort of testimony confirming a highly individualistic style of collective life.

In the 1780s a theologically diverse Universalism spawned a varied set of local institutions improvised from differing contexts in rural and coastal areas. Before 1785 the Richite and Murrayite branches were completely autonomous. But in that year they were called together as a result of legal action against Murray and the Gloucester Independents. Gloucester's Congregationalists claimed that the Murrayites were "a mere jumble of detached members" and in 1779 sued them for nonpayment of ministerial taxes. When the property of three Independents was auctioned for tax payment, Murray, represented by Rufus King, countersued for return of the confiscated goods. The legal process dragged on into 1785, draining the congregation of its financial resources and political support. The needs of the Independents moved Adams Streeter to propose an associational meeting at Oxford, Massachusetts, on 14 September 1785. "Our strength," he wrote in his call, "depends on our being cemented together in one united body, in order to anticipate any embarrassment of our Constitutional Rights."[15]

The Oxford Association was thus brought into being from considerations of political expediency rather than ecclesiology. It was attended by lay delegates from five Richite churches along with Murray, Rich, Streeter, and Elhanan Winchester. Their agenda contemplated permanent organization: "We deliberated, first, on a name; secondly, on the propriety of being united in our common defence; thirdly, upon the utility of an annual meeting of representatives from the different societies; and fourthly, upon keeping up a constant correspondence by letter."[16] The results were less promising. The association did adopt the name Independent Christian Society, "commonly called 'Universalists,' " as the standard for all the represented churches, but this and all other actions were referred back to the constituent congregations for ratification.

The one substantive action of the association was unanimous approval of a "charter of compact" adopted only the week before by the Gloucester church. The new charter replaced the exclusivism and militancy of the earlier Gloucester Articles with Whig rhetoric in an effort to establish political legitimacy. Citing the importance to society that citizens "form themselves in a way which is most happyfying and secure in the great matters of Religion and Morality," the Independents established a "select committee" chaired by a clerk "for the purpose of supporting a teacher or teachers of piety, religion, and morality, and for the purpose of assisting poor and distressed brethren." This language was borrowed from Article III of the Massachusetts Constitution in an effort to claim its protection in court. The charter also bound the congregation "to afford all legal measures" necessary to free any member suffering from "persecution from an unlawful exercise of power."[17]

The adoption of the Gloucester Charter by the Oxford Association was an expedient move to provide Murray's people with financial, moral, and legal support. The effectiveness of this action ended with the Independents' court victory in 1786. In that year the congregations under Murray's direct influence embraced the charter, but Rich's congregations did not. The Oxford Association thus failed to unify New England Universalism behind Murray's leadership. In fact, the association collapsed as soon as the crisis had passed.

After this temporary political alliance Universalists reverted to their pattern of noncooperation and coexistence. During the late 1780s the theological differences between Rich, Winchester, and Murray became more intense and obvious. The rapid and completely uncoordinated growth of the sect, especially in the hill country, invited institutional confusion and protracted disputes. As these problems grew the sect became increasingly fragmented, particularly in rural areas, and retired into localism. Though not in any real danger of collapse, New England Universalism by 1790 was mired in endemic conflict and had lost any real sense of institutional cohesion.

Shaker efforts to organize permanent communities were severely hampered by a crisis of leadership in the 1780s. During the winter of 1783-84 William Lee, Mother Ann's brother and "able support," became seriously ill. His decline was probably related to the beatings he received during the evangelistic tour, especially at Harvard. He died on 21 July 1784 at Niskeyuna. Father William's loss was not in itself a heavy blow to the Shakers' chances of survival, for his gifts were primarily liturgical rather than social or theological. But his passing did have an ominous effect on Mother Ann. "Brother William is gone," she lamented, "and it will soon be said of me, that I am gone too." Her prophecy proved accurate, for within weeks Mother Ann "began visibly to decline in bodily strength," and on 8 September 1784, only seven weeks after her brother's death, she, too, passed away at Niskeyuna. There is no evidence that Mother Ann died of infectious or degenerative disease. And since she had not yet established the Shaker center at Harvard, it seems clear that it was not a sense of fulfilled mission that precipitated her decline. Father William was Mother Ann's younger brother, first convert, and most intimate sharer of her spiritual odyssey. The loss of her "constant companion" and principal support seems the likeliest cause of Mother Ann's death. On her deathbed Mother Ann saw a vision of "the opening of the heavens" through which "Brother William [was] coming in a glorious chariot to take me home." In any case, Mother Ann and Father William died as they had lived—together. Within a few short weeks the Shakers were bereft of their founder and her chief companion, left with a widely scattered collection of undisciplined converts and no acknowledged successor.[18]

The most obvious criteria for a new leader were seniority in the faith and charismatic endowment to "protect" the Believers from error. John Hocknell, a highly gifted visionary and healer and the eldest of the English Shakers, was a clear possibility. No New England converts were yet established enough to take over the movement, though Joseph and David Meacham, Calvin Harlow, and several others were acknowledged leaders. But the standards pointed to James Whittaker, who though only thirty-four years old had emerged as the most effective public evangelist and charismatic leader in the New England mission. Whittaker had also been particularly close to Mother Ann and was the only Shaker who had been reared in the faith since early adolescence by the founder herself.

At Mother Ann's funeral all the attending members spoke in remembrance of her power and in exhortation to carry on in her memory. Whittaker spoke "under a great weight of grief and sorrow," then returned home where he addressed the community in a powerful manner. " 'My two friends and Elders are gone! I pray God to help me!' He then called upon all the Brethren and Sisters to help him keep the way of God; and urged the necessity of their being more faithful and watchful than they had been, since those who had the greatest gift for their protection were gone." Whittaker's exhortation was received by the Believers as divine inspiration and moved them to pledge loyalty to him at once. "It was plainly seen and felt that Mother's mantle had fallen upon hin, and that God had anointed him to lead and protect the people. After he had done speaking, Elder Joseph Meacham, Elders Calvin Harlow, John Hocknell, and others came forward and acknowledged him as their Elder, and that the gift of God rested upon him for their protection."[19]

Whittaker's basic strategy for maintaining the movement was to consolidate it through increased discipline, greater exclusivism, and central organization. Father James "felt a deep sense of the danger" presented to the community by Mother Ann's death and by popular hostility to Shaker practices: "He did not cease to warn the people, with tears in his eyes, to be faithful and persevering, and not lose that which they had already gained." Under Father James the Shakers turned increasingly toward spiritual and physical purification, particularly "laboring" against all manifestations of sexuality. The Believers took his instruction to "mortify the flesh" to the point of extended fasting and penitential exercises in hopes of halting the sexual instinct itself. He urged the Shakers "to become eunuchs for the kingdom of heaven's sake" and to accomplish "a total destruction of the nature of generation, both as to the inclination of the spirit and the natural faculties of the body." Whittaker's asceticism was aimed especially at the many Shakers who had been married before their conversion and who continued to live together in celibate households. "The marriage of the flesh is a covenant with death, and an agreement with hell," he wrote. "If you want to marry, you may marry the Lord Jesus Christ."

This rigorous discipline had the inevitable effect of forcing the Shaker gospel into an increasingly elitist mold. "The gospel is without fault," Father James taught, "it is as strait as straitness; it is pure as the heavens; and if you obey it not, you will lose your souls." The community at Niskeyuna began to take on a militantly exclusive quality, urged on by Father James to remove itself from all traffic with the world. "We have an altar whereof no one shall partake," he declared, "but those who rejoice in Christ Jesus, and have no confidence in the flesh; for our altar is God's altar, and the wicked shall not eat thereon or therefrom."

Community of goods continued to be observed at Niskeyuna, and as the sect received gifts of land and farm stock from converts, Father James contemplated the fulfillment of Mother Ann's dream of a permanent communal center for the sect. When David Darrow of New Lebanon, New York, deeded his substantial farm to the Shakers, Whittaker seized the opportunity to establish a new residential base in that Berkshire town. The marginal farming operation at Niskeyuna was temporarily abandoned, and Believers were instructed to purchase land in the New Lebanon area for consolidation into one communal holding. Father James demanded no formal covenants to govern property relationships, however; simple verbal agreements served to maintain a "free table" and all things in common. "The time has come," he declared to the faithful, "for you to give up yourselves and your all to God—your substance, your temporal property—to possess as though you possessed not. We shall have one meeting together [at New Lebanon]," he promised, "which will never break up."[20]

At the new communal village Whittaker began the task of fashioning "an outward visible order" for the Shakers. The chief element of that order, aside from the property arrangements and hierarchy of authority within the sect, was the organization of formal worship. On 15 October 1785 the first Shaker meetinghouse was raised at New Lebanon. At its dedication Whittaker delivered the first set of "gospel orders" to be obeyed scrupulously by Believers on pain of reprimand and public humiliation. The rules were simple guidelines for Sabbath decorum, urging Believers to practice physical separation of the sexes, observe "reverance and godly fear" in worship, and prohibit any secular use of the house.

Father James's rules were the first formal standard of collective behavior for the Shakers, and as such they marked a crucial step toward permanent organization. The detailed instructions, reminiscent of Mother Ann's careful management of the Niskeyuna community, were a critically important precedent in establishing behavioral discipline and formal authority. Shakerism under Whittaker began to assume shape as an ascetic and uniformitarian faith demanding strict conformity to elaborate codes issued by charismatic leadership. Father James completed the internal reorientation of the sect by "closing the testimony" early in 1786. He ordered all public evangelism to cease and directed converts to practice absolute separation from the world. During 1786 and 1787 he continued to consolidate the community, while encouraging those Believers unable to enter the order to make pilgrimage to New Lebanon.

Whittaker's success, however, was largely limited to New Lebanon. Despite intense effort, he was unable to extend discipline to the far-flung Shaker converts throughout New England. He exhorted Believers in person and by letter to share their goods and work their farms with divine zeal. A letter written to Josiah Talcott during the New England mission caught the rigor of Whittaker's discipline of outfamilies. "I write unto thee to warn and stir thee up to thy duty in the things that are needful for the support and comfort of the body. Thou art idle and slothful, thy land lyes unimproved and pretty much waste . . . What mean ye by these cursed ways and works? Will you bring yourself not only to want and poverty but distress those connected with thee in this life?"[21] Father James gave Talcott detailed instructions on planting and repairing his farm and also demanded more sexual discipline from Talcott's family.

Father James personally visited "all the different places in the land where the gospel had been received, and some of them several times."[22] He also dispatched Reuben Rathbun, the Meacham brothers, and other leading converts to outfamilies as his representatives. On these journeys Whittaker continually emphasized his program of purification, penitence, and mortification to build spiritual community.

Early Shaker life demanded discipline, and Father James continued Mother Ann's practice of powerful criticism and charismatic exhortation in his visits. For example, many Shakers were attracted to Shays' Rebellion; "in expressing their sentiments" on that movement they "manifested some party feelings." Whittaker swiftly and curtly struck down such political agitation: "Those who give way to a party spirit, and are influenced by the divisions and contentions of the world, so as to feel for one political party more than another, have no part with me . . . the spirit of party is the spirit of the world, and whoever indulges it, and unites with one evil spirit against the other, is off from Christian ground."[23]

Despite Father James's forceful leadership, the combined forces of politics, economics, and Mother Ann's death took a heavy toll on convert communities in the mid-1780s. The situation at Enfield, New Hampshire, illustrated the insufficiency of Father James's regime. Recruited in 1782 by Zadok Wright, Ebenezer Cooley, and Israel Chauncy, the Enfield Shakers quickly lost cohesion after the missionaries returned to Mother Ann at Harvard. "Living, as they did, in distinct, and in most instances, widely separated families, their union together, as one body, was of necessity very slight, and consequently the strength which they could receive, from each other, was proportionally small."[24] Economic consolidation was difficult; despite "hard and constant labor" the Believers could reap only a "poor and scanty living" from the White Mountains foothills.

Spiritual life at Enfield was poorly disciplined. "Regular, constant, and often long continued meetings" were held "at least once a day, generally twice," but there was "no fixed time or place of holding their evening or morning meetings," necessitating worship in small groups of one or two families. Sabbath meetings were held in "an old dwelling house," but these lacked guidance by any experienced convert or missionary. "They . . . had no particular creed or form of faith, laid down as a standard, or any fixed or particular manner of worship; although this consisted . . . mainly of singing and dancing."[25]

The disarray at Enfield could only be helped by strong leadership from New Lebanon. Between 1784 and 1787 the community was visited several times by Father James and a number of the native New England leaders. At first these infrequent seasons of discipline and exhortation were effective. But soon the Enfield community "came to show or feel but little respect, for any intermediate person, or authority whatsoever." This intransigence combined with the Enfield community's "own high sense, and self esteem, which caused each one to regard himself as equal at least to any of his brethren." This Radical Evangelical egalitarianism ultimately led to a complete breakdown of New Lebanon's authority. "They had but an indefinite idea of submission to any visible lead whatever, and as to authority several times delegated, they could hardly receive it."[26] By 1787 the Enfield community went so far as "to nominate themselves . . . as the proper persons to be the Minister or Elders" rather than rely on the authority of Father James at New Lebanon.

The conditions at Enfield were probably not unique. At other locations where only inexperienced missionaries had evangelized—particularly in southern Maine and central New Hampshire—localism was a constant threat. The tendency toward fragmentation was enhanced by economic problems, geographical isolation, and the tendency of charismatic religion to become idiosyncratic. These factors combined with the questionable leadership of Father James to lead the sect to the brink of dissolution by 1787.

Whittaker's fierce asceticism, personally abusive manner, organizational efforts at New Lebanon, and decision to end public evangelism were guided by an authentic charisma, but his inexperience and youth obviously hampered his leadership efforts. Soon after Father James assumed control of the sect two of the senior British Shakers, John Shepard and John Partington, refused to accept Whittaker's judgments and left the faith. Such defections and the broad disintegration of the movement beyond New Lebanon drove Father James to ever-increasing heights of activity in service of his people, but to no avail. The demands of maintaining the far-flung sect took a heavy physical and emotional toll on Whittaker. Though only thirty-six, he began to decline in health in 1786. Labors at New Lebanon and extensive travels to mission communities forced him into lengthy convalescence in early 1787, and a premature return to the ministry cost him his life. Father James died at Enfield, Connecticut, on 21 July 1787, three years to the day after William Lee.

Whittaker sustained Shakerism through its most critical period. In the face of the most serious difficulties he managed to preserve the sect and rally a core of Believers to the new center at New Lebanon. But Father James was the last of the original British Shaker leaders, and his passing left the sect with only tentative organization and a host of pressing institutional problems. The loss of all three Shaker founders within three years was potentially catastrophic. The future of the sect now lay with an unproven native New England leadership with just seven years of experience in the faith.

In the mid-1780s New England's Radical Evangelical sects were forcibly made aware of the institutional requirements necessary for their long-term success. Each was stunned by the weakness of its leadership. Universalist leaders feuded about doctrine and polity, Freewill Baptists awaited the development of Benjamin Randel's social vision without result, and Shakers mourned the untimely loss of their three principal founders. It was not apparent to either leaders or followers that anything more than the guidance of the Holy Spirit was needed to assure effortless community and the triumph of their gospels. Their experience of evangelism had produced successful initial ad hoc communities, but after the passing of the New Light Stir new mechanisms were needed to unite converts. Essentially charismatically led sects, the three groups faltered when their leaders continued to improvise institutional arrangements based only on Radical Evangelical precedent and evangelistic experience. Yet in this crucial stage of near collapse, the sects began to fashion the practical and conceptual foundations on which they would ultimately erect successful, innovative polities.

7

Gospel Union, Gospel Liberty, Gospel Order

By the late 1780s the Radical Evangelical sects of New England faced an imperative demand for more comprehensive and effective social design. Through the development of new leadership, congregational structures, and interchurch organization, the three sects assumed distinctive social form in the 1790s and early 1800s. The Radical Evangelical heritage continued to inform these new arrangements, but sectarian belief and historical experience transformed the norms of the gathered church into alternative shapes quite beyond the range of eighteenth-century tradition. The crucial step in this process of social design was the employment of self-conscious ecclesiological concepts by sectarian leaders in response to the institutional crisis of their communities. These concepts, created and transmitted orally then manifested in written documents, became the criteria by which the sects understood their social needs and fashioned their institutions. These basic notions — Freewill Baptist "gospel union," Universalist "gospel liberty," and Shaker "gospel order" — synthesized the social experience and religious vision of the sects into workable institutions, new religions for a new society.

In 1791 the attention of the Freewill Baptist Connection was concentrated on the defunct New Durham congregation and its struggling leader, Benjamin Randel. The disintegration was so complete at New Durham that itinerants from other congregations visited the beleaguered community to maintain some kind of order. The most successful peacemaker was Mary Savage of Woolwich, Maine, one of several female exhorters who were widely known and effective evangelists in the sect's early years. Savage took

116

up residence at New Durham for more than a year, during which her sermons had "marked success in reconciling Christians who were at variance" with one another.[1]

The ministry of Mary Savage helped revive Randel's own enthusiasm and leadership. Under his urging the New Durham church took the unprecedented step of recovenanting. This action dismayed many connectional churches because it relativized the sacred character of the original covenant vows. Randel and New Durham seemed to presume that solemn agreements among saints could be dissolved and reformulated with impunity. But the simplicity and candor of the new agreement could not be faulted: "We whose names are under written, having fellowship with each other as brethren of one family, and children of one Father, do now, in the most solemn manner, and in the fear of God, covenant together; and promise to walk together in the ordinances and commandment of our Lord Jesus Christ, as we do or shall understand them."

This sentence embodied a new Randelite rhetoric of familial relation and mutual responsibility that was spelled out in detail by a list of ten duties required of members. Conformity to the world in "customs, fashions, and idle conversation" was prohibited. Unscrupulous business practice and lawsuits between members were also banned, and the golden rule was to be observed in all worldly dealings. An important sanction rejected the bearing of "carnal weapons" for any purpose. The positive moral obligations of the covenant included liberality to the poor, regular secret prayer, family worship, and just family government. Prescribed liturgical ordinances were three in number—adult baptism, the Lord's Supper, and foot-washing.[2]

The New Durham covenant of 1792 provided Freewill Baptists with a new model of community based on moral action and spiritual growth. Randel had redefined the social elements of Christianity to include spiritual intimacy, mutual discipline, and consensual governance, or what he called gospel union. Under the model of the New Durham covenant, this ideal quickly became the institutional norm for the entire connection.

In order to achieve and maintain gospel union, churches met weekly for worship and monthly for discipline and conference. These latter sessions, which Randel called Monthly Meetings in Quaker fashion, became the fundamental unit of Freewill polity. Governed by itinerant teaching elders or local ruling elders, the Monthly Meeting undertook "to inspect into the faith and practices of its members, to Labour with the Burthened; Deal with the unfaithful, admonish the unruly, and in certain cases to reject the refractory."[3]

The key feature of the Monthly Meeting—and the basis for all Freewill order—was the "relation of present standing." This consisted of each member's specific account of his performance of covenant obligations during the preceding month. The relations, delivered before the whole congregation, were evaluated by collective standards of "satisfaction" of covenant vows.

Members were expected to admit all failures in belief or practice, and any saint had the right to challenge or accuse another of errors unconfessed. When such accusations or admissions of error were made, the elder was charged to "labor" publicly with the offender, offering exhortation and moral advice, and if necessary taking testimony from witnesses. The object of this procedure was to produce confessions of guilt "with griefe and a resolution to forsake." When all members had testified to the "satisfaction" of the covenant, the congregation was considered in gospel union, sanctified and empowered by the Holy Spirit to continue its "travel" toward Christian perfection.[4]

The rigor of Monthly Meetings generally served to maintain order, but occasionally an intransigent member or issue would emerge. In such cases Randel specified scrupulous enforcement of the "gospel rule" of Matthew 18:15-20 as "a standing ordinance of the church." According to gospel rule, if direct dealing with an "offender" failed, "the aggrieved Brother or Sister shall . . . define a Select Committee of Males or Females, which shall be granted without any questions being asked." The committee, in the presence of the two conflicting parties, heard accusations and sought to arbitrate the dispute in strict secrecy. If the arbitrators were successful they were to "report reconciliation to the Monthly Meeting without mentioning then or ever afterward, either the Name of the Offender or the Nature of the Offence." If no reconciliation could be obtained, the case was reported in detail to the congregation, which "must forthwith enter into a Labour with the Parties" leading to "satisfaction" and restoration of union. If either party refused to be subject to the public disciplining, they were "cut off from communion, fellowship, and membership."[5]

Randel's 1792 covenant also clarified the structure of congregational polity. He mandated the three traditional offices of teaching elder, ruling elder, and deacon but redefined their functions and relationships. Teaching elders preached and administered ordinances, ruling elders maintained loyalty and monitored covenant obligations, and deacons oversaw the church's material needs and exhorted members. Itinerant teaching elders held primacy and were deferred to in Monthly Meetings; in their absence local ruling elders held authority, and when no elders were present deacons were empowered "to administer the ordinances." Deacons in fact held full ministerial office, were ordained, and carried the responsibility "to improve their gifts in the Church, as helps to the Teaching and Ruling Elders, in exhortation, prayer, and praise." By thus permitting all three officers to perform the ordinances, Randel sought to avoid the problem of ministerial shortage.[6] A roster of secular officers—clerk, treasurer, and wardens—completed the rather complex Freewill local structure. The wardens were especially important in their role as assessors for church fund raising. Monthly Meetings collected funds by specific resolution; percentage shares were determined by the wardens based upon the tax assessment and real property of each member.

Randel's new order of gospel union placed both the material and the spiritual aspects of Freewill churches on solid footing. The plan was immediately successful: At New Durham a revival ensued so intense that by late 1791 the congregation required subdivision. In the spring of 1792 Randel organized separate Monthly Meetings at New Durham, Middleton, Barrington, and Pittsfield, New Hampshire, "all on different days, so that the public gifts [teaching elders] might circulate from branch to branch." In addition, once each quarter a meeting was held at New Durham at which representatives from each congregation reviewed the Monthly Meetings. The entire structure of four Monthly Meetings and the Quarterly Meeting was called "the Church at New Durham," with each congregation labeled a "branch."[7]

On 9 June 1792 Randel completed the Freewill polity by proposing a "method" for the organization of three more Quarterly Meetings at major Freewill centers and the establishment of a plenary session for all clergy and representatives of each Monthly Meeting to gather four times annually. This latter session Randel confusingly termed the Yearly Meeting, because it circulated among the four Quarterly Meeting sites, convening only once a year at each place. The Yearly Meeting held final powers over ministerial discipline, expulsion of members, and all matters referred to it on appeal from the Quarterly Meetings; but in effect it existed to maintain gospel union among the entire connection.[8]

Randel's organizational plan was a hybrid of Quaker, Congregationalist, and Baptist polities, as befit his Radical Evangelical allegiance. His unique vision of church order was drawn from the perspective of the local congregation. Every four months each congregation would have access to all levels of connectional decision making — monthly, quarterly, and yearly meetings — maximizing the extent of consensus and guaranteeing the strictest sort of review for each disciplinary and doctrinal question. All three kinds of meetings dealt with essentially the same problems through the process of review and appeal and at the same time provided occasions for large-scale mass worship and revival.

Randel's initiative through the new polity of 1792 soon achieved its goal of greater order and stability for the Freewill sect. Delinquent churches were disciplined and reorganized. New Quarterly Meetings formed as the sect quickly expanded west and north: Edgecomb and Farmington in eastern Maine in 1795, Gorham and Parsonsfield in western Maine in 1796 and 1798 respectively; Unity in western New Hampshire in 1799; Hardwick and Strafford in Vermont in 1802.[9] Each of these Quarterly Meetings expanded vigorously in the Second Great Awakening. By 1815 additional Quarterly Meetings had been established in each of the three northern New

England states, and each Quarterly Meeting had itself become a flourishing community of twenty to thirty Monthly Meetings.

A good example of how the entire Freewill polity could be brought into a single decision was the case of John Buzzell's placement as a minister. Buzzell, an early Randel convert, was ordained in 1792 at Middleton, New Hampshire. But in 1797 the Edgecomb Quarterly Meeting, after a poll of its constituent Monthly Meetings, issued a call to him as an itinerant "public gift." Buzzell referred the question to a poll of the New Durham Quarterly Meeting—Middleton's superior session—while the Edgecomb Meeting, unsure of the propriety of its request, sought the counsel of the Yearly Meeting. Both the Yearly Meeting and the New Durham Quarterly Meeting replied that the matter was up to Buzzell's discretion. He refused the invitation, but this single act of conscience had required the attention of twenty-six of approximately fifty Monthly Meetings, two of the six Quarterly Meetings, and the whole connection through the yearly Meeting. The popular preacher was called again by both the Farmington and the Parsonsfield Quarterly Meetings in 1798, with similarly elaborate deliberations before Buzzell accepted Parsonsfield's invitation. Despite the obvious complexity of such a decision-making process, there were "many instances of this kind on the record" of the Freewill Connection.[10]

The close community of the 1792 polity gradually developed functional differentiations in later years. The Monthly Meeting remained a session for worship and gospel union where local members were most directly held accountable for their actions. Quarterly Meetings, though still occasions for the ordinances, increasingly took up financial, disciplinary, and clerical concerns. In effect they became the administrative center of the connection, acting as ordaining body, board of appeal, and representative assembly for their constituent churches. The Yearly Meeting consequently tended toward more general matters of policy and theology while assuming the character of mass revival meetings.[11]

In June 1798 the Yearly Meeting at New Durham witnessed the opening manifestation of the Second Great Awakening among the Freewill Baptists. A large crowd gathered at the first day's session and instead of proceeding to business, "the whole assembly appeared to be shocked" by "the power of God." An adolescent exhorter, Hezekiah Buzzell, summoned the crowd to "come, taste, and see that the Lord is good," and suddenly the whole congregation was alive with "a diversity of operations" of the Holy Spirit. "Some of the penitents would cry aloud for mercy; some would fall upon the floor and lay motionless for a considerable time, and then recovering their strength, would shout aloud the praises of God." Others prayed silently, sang, or exhorted. The assembled elders plunged into the crowd and "conversed with, and prayed for, those in distress." Randel, at first apprehensive of the disorder, finally urged the crowd to follow the Spirit in this moment of grace: "Brethren, look not to me," he proclaimed, "but to God, and obey him in all things." The revival went on uninterruptedly for four days, drawing crowds of up to three thousand people with over one hundred professed conversions, and fanned out into the Connection bringing mass conversions from almost every quarter and a new missionary zeal to Vermont and New York.[12]

For almost a decade Yearly Meetings were so heavily attended and so spiritually powerful that little business could be accomplished. This severely jeopardized the gospel union of the ministry in a time of rapid growth and change. To remedy the situation Randel turned to the Elders Conferences that had been convened in Maine since 1794 for "consideration of our standing and the necessity of being uniform" among "our publick speakers, both those who are termed doctrinal gifts and those who are termed exhorters." After 1800 the Elders Conferences rather than the Yearly Meetings became the primary location for gospel union among the sect's ministers.[13]

For more than a decade Randel's polity functioned smoothly, but in the first decade of the nineteenth century the forces of growth and expansion demanded further modification. Responding to the impossibly large agenda of individual disciplinary cases before it, the Strafford, Vermont, Quarterly Meeting in 1803 resolved that Monthly Meetings be empowered to discipline and reject disorderly members without appeal. The Yearly Meeting concurred, authorizing appeal to the Quarterly Meeting only in exceptional cases and turning over to the Monthly Meeting most of the membership functions for which the whole polity had originally been designed.[14] In 1804 the venerable practice of reading and reviewing minutes from Monthly Meetings in Quarterly Meetings was also abandoned. Though such measures were justified on practical grounds, they served to cut off the higher-level church organizations from close interaction with local congregations and, in turn, to increase the authority of local elders. All these shifts opened the way for increased clerical prestige and bureaucratic control at the expense of the sect's original emphasis on intimacy and mutuality.[15]

The death of Benjamin Randel in 1808 furthered the breakdown of gospel union. Randel had been a universally respected leader and arbitrator for almost thirty years. His passing marked the waning of the Revolutionary generation's influence on the Freewill movement. His loss especially affected the Yearly Meeting; his salving influence was missed, and the session's records were "not so full" after his departure as standing clerk. The careful survey of Quarterly Meeting records that he had conducted since 1784 broke down completely after 1812.

By 1815 the Freewill Baptist vision of gospel union had been compromised and its communal intensity weakened. Local congregations slowly abandoned the ideal of undifferentiated community action and were increasingly served by new ministers anxious to pursue social and financial goals commensurate with colleagues in other faiths. Benjamin Randel had consistently opposed "the hireling disposition" of ministers "who will move anywhere and preach for any people where they can get most."[16] But within a decade after Randel's death, John Buzzell—his successor as consensus leader—would insist that each Monthly Meeting consider itself an independent church and look to the liberal support of its ordained ministers.[17]

The Quarterly Meeting continued to examine candidates for ordination and hear disciplinary appeals and increasingly became the locus of ministerial counsel and fellowship. The Yearly Meeting proved unable to manage the growing sect except in matters of general policy, publication, and mission. After 1810 westward expansion put an end to the Yearly Meeting's original character as a circulating plenary session, and in 1827 this last vestige of connectional gospel union was abandoned with the organization of autonomous annual meetings in Maine, New Hampshire, Vermont, New York, Pennsylvania, and Ohio. In place of a mass connectional meeting for revivalistic renewal, the Freewill Baptists in that year established an annual delegated General Conference to run the affairs of what had become a small American denomination.[18]

The Freewill Baptists around 1790 encountered new problems of social and religious order that they had not foreseen in the days of the New Light Stir. Their response to these problems was the concept and institutionalization of gospel union. Drawn from the Radical Evangelical ideal of the gathered church, supplemented by Quaker and Baptist habits of consensual governance and geographical organization, and infused with Benjamin Randel's quest for perpetual revival and spiritual intimacy, Freewill gospel union was a synthesis of the disparate ecclesiological imperatives that were available to rural sectarians of the Revolutionary generation. The issues facing all the sects were those of the age: how to establish community in a rapidly changing environment, how to define the moral and social duties of that community, how to create just and democratic institutions to enforce those community norms. For the Freewill Baptists, the sudden realization that they would have to create social and ideological norms generated a successful quest to render permanent the familial intimacy of revival and mutual discipline and to institutionalize "the unity of the Spirit in the bonds of peace."

New England Universalists reverted to localism after the disbanding of the Oxford Association in 1786. No longer pressed by legal problems and lacking any acknowledged single leader, the sect remained institutionally diffuse. Believing that they were literally the only people who properly understood the gospel's "mystery hid from the ages," universal salvation, they resisted all religious standards of human authorship. Universalism, they believed, did not depend on any one theological norm. Beyond the divine standards of the Ten Commandments and the commands of Christ, Universalists insisted on radical freedom of action, "the liberty wherewith Christ hath made us free." Under the inspiration of the Holy Ghost, each soul appropriated the truth in its own way and exercised the capacity to make correct moral judgments. The Universalists grouped these spiritual rights and moral freedoms under the term gospel liberty.

This stance offered clear if challenging criteria for the structure of Universalist institutions. Any doctrinal covenants would have to be strictly limited to minimal, nonpartisan statements of the essential truths; organizational structures would have to be simple and able to facilitate gospel liberty, not limit it. But after 1786 Universalists possessed no effective unity at all. In 1789 Elhanan Winchester deplored "the unsettled condition we are in—without order, rule, or system" and proposed a national convention in Philadelphia "to unite us into one general church" and to create "one uniform mode of divine worship, one method of ordaining suitable persons to the ministry, one consistent way of administering the Lord's Supper."[19] On 25 May 1790 the Philadelphia Convention opened with a Winchesterite majority, a Murrayite minority, and no Richite delegates at all from rural New England. The convention adopted five minimalist Articles of Faith and a Plan of Church Government that endorsed congregational autonomy, the validity of non-Universalist ordination, and optional observation of the ordinances.[20]

The Philadelphia Articles and Plan were carefully designed to accord with gospel liberty, but they met strong resistance in New England. John Murray was outraged that the convention had refused to endorse Rellyan theology and objected in print to both the doctrinal and the ecclesiological rationales for the new standard. Speaking for rural Universalism Caleb Rich hailed the articles as "more consistent with the liberty of the gospel than any that ever were presented to our view before." But he reported that most hill country congregations still refused to submit to uniform church order. The Egremont, Massachusetts, church, for example, doubted "whether a particular compact can be entered into to satisfy the different members" of its congregation.[21] And leaders like Zephaniah Lathe of Grafton, Massachusetts, continued to object in principle to any human instrument of church governance as a violation of gospel liberty. The outcome of the Philadelphia Convention in New England was increased confusion and conflict over organizational norms. All agreed on the priority of gospel liberty, but neither the theology of the articles nor the structure of the governance plan received wide approval.

Hill country congregations, where formally organized at all, continued to follow their own individualized modes of organization. The church at Langdon, New Hampshire, organized by Zebulon Streeter in 1791, was typical of the Richite rural style. Its covenant included only the doctrinal affirmation of "universal salvation of all men from sin by Jesus Christ" and

"the universal love of God to all mankind through a Redeemer." It also included commitment to the "gospel rule" of discipline and a pledge of mutual
legal aid. The formal organization reflected typical Universalist practice,
naming a prominent local citizen—Ensign Seth Walker—to the lone office
of clerk and an itinerant evangelist—Streeter—as moderator.[22] Thus did
the churches in the New England interior preserve gospel liberty and ecclesiastical order on the basis of local circumstances and advice from itinerants.

Elhanan Winchester, however, continued his efforts to unite the fiercely
independent New England Universalists. Returning to his native Massachusetts, he persuaded reluctant rural leaders to meet at Oxford in September 1794. This first New England General Convention seated delegates and
ministers from seventy-one localities, roughly fifty of them from Richite
churches. With Rich's support, the conclave recommended that the Philadelphia Articles and Plan be "observed by the churches and societies making up this convention," though it did not claim the authority to enforce this
policy. The body then turned to the pressing problem of ministerial supply.
It appointed the first Universalist missionaries, Richites Michael Coffin
and Joab Young, to "preach the everlasting gospel" to the inhabitants of upper New England "for the space of one year." Under Winchester's urging
the convention also assumed the authority to ordain candidates for the
ministry. Without warning Winchester sparked the spontaneous ordination
of Hosea Ballou at the conclusion of a sermon before the convention. "He
took up the Bible, and pressing it against the breast of the young man, he
said, 'Brother Ballou, I press to your heart the written Jehovah!' The effect
upon the congregation was sudden and powerful. After holding the sacred
volume in this manner for a moment, he spoke to Elder Young in an imperative but affectionate tone, saying, 'Brother Young, charge him,' which the
elder proceeded to do."[23]

From 1795 to 1800 the New England General Convention met annually
at different hill country locations. In form and function it closely resembled
the Baptist associations from which most of its members had come. To
carry out its business the convention required only two officers, a clerk and
a moderator, to keep records and compose the circular letter. But before
1800 it was not effective in bringing order to the chaos of gospel liberty.
Zebulon Streeter, moderator of the 1796 convention, acknowledged the
weakening effects of pluralism and besought his colleagues to cease their
theological and ecclesiastical disputes. "We . . . entreat our brethren, that
they would not give themselves over to vain disputations," Streeter wrote,
"and receive all those who are blessed with gifts of edification, however diverse their gifts may be, preferring no man above his fellow man."[24] But
Streeter's appeal revealed precisely the Universalist dilemma by urging as a
solution to the problem the very exercise of gospel liberty that was the
greatest cause of disorder in the sect.

In 1800 the convention meeting at Orange, Massachusetts, at last took constructive action to remedy the sect's disunion. It agreed to keep permanent records, make formal arrangements for ordination councils, and receive written reports from constituent churches. This same session for the first time issued disciplinary directives to congregations and undertook to arbitrate disputes between ministers and congregations. The convention also recommended that local congregations choose delegates four months in advance and report their views on the liturgical ordinances "that uniformity of practice may, if possible, be established." In words quite without precedent in rural Universalist annals, the convention sternly demanded "that those societies who are not in order, be entreated to remember that God is a God of order; and pay particular solemnized attention to regularity and discipline; every member mutually caring for every other member, and holding this truth in memory, that if one member suffer, all the members suffer with it."[25]

In succeeding years the convention established committees to oversee ordination, mission, publication, and charities. But the most significant aspect of Universalist reorganization was the renewal of the movement for a creedal formula. In 1800 Walter Ferriss of Charlotte, Vermont, first proposed a motion to compose a profession of faith. "I considered some measure of this kind necessary," he wrote in his diary, "to prevent confusion, dispel ignorance, and remove the charge . . . against us of being wholly divided amongst ourselves and agreeing in nothing essential."[26] Ferriss's resolution for a "regular approved testimony of those essentials in which we did agree" failed outright in 1800. But two years later, responding to pleas that further delay would "cause our association to fall to pieces," the convention approved a committee to report on the matter the next year at Winchester, New Hampshire.

At the 1803 convention Ferriss presented a brief statement and plan of association to the committee comprising himself, Hosea Ballou, Zebulon Streeter, Zephaniah Lathe, and George Richards of Salem, Massachusetts. They reported favorably on Ferriss's proposal but met the serious objection on the floor "that it would be of no utility, if not of dangerous tendency, to commit, that or any other form of writing as an act of the association."[27] The issue was drawn not over the content of the standard, but over the threat it presented to gospel liberty. Anticreedalists held sway until the committee argued that some minimal accord was needed to support local congregations against legal harassment from state and town governments still able to engage in religious taxation. The case of Christopher Erskine, a New Hampshire Universalist taxed and imprisoned in 1801 for religious dissent, was still vivid in the minds of all delegates, and on such pragmatic grounds — reminiscent of the 1785 Oxford Association — a majority was obtained for what was to be called the Winchester Profession of Faith and Articles of Association.[28]

The profession of faith asserted the authority of scripture; the existence of "one God, whose nature is Love, revealed in one Lord Jesus Christ, by the Holy Spirit of Grace, who will finally restore the whole family of mankind to holiness and happiness"; and the obligation of believers "to maintain order and practice good works." The articles of association were a classic statement of gospel liberty, declaring "that every church possesses within itself all the powers of self-government" and urging that congregations be tolerant of theological minorities in their midst.

The convention also claimed formal power to establish ordination standards, appoint occasional committees, and "adopt all such measures . . . as may tend to the promotion of general order, instruction, and edification." No provisions were made for coercive discipline, however, and the articles emphasized the purely advisory role of the convention in local church affairs.[29] In 1803 as in 1785 and 1794, hill country Universalists reached consensus on the practical demands of legal and political defense and the norms of biblical primitivism and gospel liberty.

The Winchester Profession of Faith did little more than legitimate the anarchy of Universalist practice and formalize ad hoc institutions that had existed for a decade. It did provide a written norm that unified the sect, but it did not significantly improve the lot of local congregations, which were usually served by itinerants from the largest and oldest congregations like Oxford and Richmond. In newer areas of settlement regional organizations were required, and soon after the Winchester Convention, such associations began to form along its model. The first of these was the Eastern Association, founded by Thomas Barnes at New Gloucester, Maine, in 1803; others organized in northern Vermont in 1804 and in upstate New York in 1806. These associations, convened annually by a committee from the New England General Convention, were in effect the first jurisdiction for congregational disputes, and within a few years they became effective in this oversight function. While the convention was in recess, its visiting committee visited the associations in circuit, hearing all grievances and dispensing discipline, then returned to the convention a year later with a detailed report on the status of the whole sect.[30]

For another decade Universalist polity functioned in good order, encouraging gospel liberty with a minimal institutional structure. But before the War of 1812 Universalists, like the Freewill Baptists, showed signs of increasing bureaucratization. In 1811 younger ministers led by Hosea Ballou gathered in a Conference of Ministering Brethren at Gloucester to inquire into "questions or statements" that "have relation to the cause of religion." The impulse for greater clerical fellowship also produced a short-lived periodical, the *Gospel Visitant* (1811-1813), in which minutes and articles from the conferences were published.[31] This clerical initiative was abortive, but by 1815 expansion and ministerial authority combined effectively to end the social model of gospel liberty. The formation of the Genessee Association (1814) in western New York and the Southern Association (1816) in Connecticut diminished the feasibility and effectiveness of the New England General Convention.[32] After 1815 it began to lose its spontaneous, plenary character and to ramify into a bureaucracy similar to that of mainstream American denominations. Between 1815 and 1820 association constitutions were rewritten to provide autonomy in mission and discipline, while the general convention fell into obsolescence.

By 1820 Universalism had become a small American denomination complete with an extensive geographical organization and a clerical bureaucracy. Expansion into the west and the growing concentration of Universalist activities in the urban centers of the east resulted in the speedy decline of rural New England as center of the communion. The sect soon turned toward political and moral issues and concern for its own expansion as chief institutional priorities. Further pressure toward fragmentation came from the Restorationist Controversy, a serious theological dispute between 1817 and 1830 that eventuated in the schism of western Universalists who retained belief in future punishment for sin.[33] The Restorationist Controversy represented a rupture of gospel liberty's vision of radical freedom of belief. The emergence of irreconcilable doctrinal issues and their crystallization into factions combined with geographical growth, ministerial elitism, and bureaucratization to mark the end of classic Universalist gospel liberty.

Consciously designed Shaker institutions were the creation of Joseph Meacham, "father" of the sect after James Whittaker's death on 21 June 1787. For several months during late 1787 Meacham, his brother David, and Calvin Harlow shared the leadership of the Shakers, but by 1788 Elder Joseph had become the primary spiritual virtuoso at New Lebanon. At a worship service in the early spring of 1788, Job Bishop, a leading young convert, received a spiritual "gift" proclaiming Meacham the new leader. In a scene reminiscent of Whittaker's earlier succession to Mother Ann, the assembled Shakers acknowledged Bishop's utterance to be the divine will and immediately pledged their loyalty to Meacham.[34]

Through a series of revelations Meacham formulated a plan to transform Shakerism into a well-organized communitarian movement. His first move was to establish separate lines of authority for men and women. In 1788 he appointed Lucy Wright of Pittsfield, Massachusetts, twenty-eight years old and one of Mother Ann's earliest and most trusted American converts, to head the female order. Meacham insisted that holy celibate community be based on the separate and equal governance of the sexes. "The man cannot gather and build the church of Christ in this day without the woman," he taught, "nor the woman without the man: a just equality in both is necessary." The membership was not easily convinced to support Meacham's dual-authority scheme. Lucy Wright "had great prejudice to overcome, and many erroneous ideas and sentiments to correct, before the correspondent spiritual order . . . could be fully understood, accepted, and made useful in the Church."[35] Father Joseph, however, placed the full authority of his charisma behind Mother Lucy, and before the end of 1788 she had been confirmed in office by the consensus of the membership.

The introduction of separate governance by gender was only the beginning of Meacham's reforms. In vision he saw the Second Temple, described in Ezekiel 40-47, as the divine model for his millennial community. He called on all Believers to gather at New Lebanon to establish this new structure for perfect life, which he termed gospel order. According to Ezekiel's account, the Second Temple was divided into three courts, which Meacham understood as groups of Believers separated by age and function. The "Outer Court" was composed of the oldest persons, the most recent converts, and those most encumbered by worldly experience. Their task, accordingly, was to deal with the outside world in the sale and purchase of crops and manufactures. In the "Middle Court," those people "second in faith and ability" were responsible for production of foods and goods. Their calling was to "chiefly work out as they are able to bear, and as the good of the Church in things temporal may require." The "Inner Court" or "first building" was the most important and most carefully selected group at New Lebanon. "The greatest faith and abilities of all that were prepared, both old and young, should be gathered into the first building." Their goal was to establish the greatest possible spiritual intimacy and communal solidarity. Hence they were confined to the New Lebanon property and charged with the maintenance of domestic arts and crafts. In its earliest form, Meacham's gospel order correlated the assignment of physical tasks with spiritual attainments and status.[36]

On 27 August 1788 Father Joseph ordered construction of a "great house" at New Lebanon for the Outer and Middle Courts, and when it was completed the Inner Court went into isolation, residing in the meetinghouse. Father Joseph and Mother Lucy joined the Inner Court, teaching its members "the order of the Temple of the Lord." For more than two years Meacham and Wright, "the first pillars," supervised all aspects of life in the Inner Court, overseeing performance of chores, assigning economic tasks, teaching doctrine, worship, and sacred dance, and leading their charges to new heights of spiritual perfection and "the power of God." During this intensive experiment, Father Joseph developed the forms of community maintenance and discipline that became the basis for subsequent Shaker social life.

The most important component of gospel order was an elaborate and all-inclusive hierarchy of members based on spiritual merit, termed spiritual relation. Each Believer, according to Father Joseph, occupied a particular place or calling in the community, determined by the increment of his or her successful "travel" toward perfection. This locus on the spiritual hierarchy indicated a specific vocation and role, called a "lot." The higher one's position, the greater the status and responsibility assigned. Thus Meacham and Wright were "the first lot" and held the right to place other members "in order and relation" to each other.

Father Joseph also envisioned spiritual relation in the metaphor of the family. "Christ is revealed in his members according to their order and lots . . . in the relation of Parents and Children, and of elder and younger in grace."[37] The primary form of Shaker community thus became the spiritual family, of which Father Joseph and Mother Lucy were "spiritual parents," and lesser members took on roles of older or younger brothers and sisters. Meacham's genius was to transfer the basic social categories and metaphors of the biological family that Believers had abandoned to the Shaker community itself. As members made the transition from carnal sexuality to spiritual celibacy they gave up the biological family for the holy family of "spiritual relation." Meacham's gospel order in many ways elaborated precedents established by Mother Ann and Father James at Niskeyuna and New Lebanon. But his visionary norms moved quite beyond their ad hoc arrangements to a concrete and determinate social reality.

No area of Shaker life was more important than spiritual and moral discipline, and here too Father Joseph elaborated Mother Ann's practices into formal norms. Her primary mode of authority had been as confessor of sins, and at New Lebanon Father Joseph employed confession as a way of maintaining order. Regularly each member had an interview with his or her spiritual parent. At these sessions, called church privilege, the Believers "opened their minds" by relating their "travel" toward perfection, temptations along the way, and any committed sins. After confession, Father Joseph or Mother Lucy delivered a "gift" of exhortation, advice, reproof, or penance to guide the person until the next "privilege."[38]

Early in the New Lebanon gathering it became clear that the Inner Court or "First Family" would serve not only as a model of community but also as a training ground for future leaders. The First Family existed, Meacham wrote, "that they may not only have a deeper planting of faith in Church Order . . . but also be more able to be helps in the Church, when they are left to keep the way of God for themselves in their own order."[39] The time for such service came quickly. Despite the success of the New Lebanon experiment, by 1790 most Shakers had spent nearly a decade living under ad hoc discipline of local house-churches scattered throughout New England. As members of the Inner Court developed leadership abilities, Meacham ordered Believers who could not come to New Lebanon to purchase land and gather at the old missionary centers of the 1780s. Late in 1790 he tapped the leadership pool at New Lebanon and named Calvin Harlow and Sarah Harrison to gather the faithful at Hancock and Tyringham, Massachusetts, and Enfield, Connecticut, into gospel order. The next year Eleazar Rand and Hannah Kendal were sent "to stand as the immediate parents" of Shakers at Harvard and Shirley, Massachusetts. In 1792 organization at Canterbury and Enfield, New Hampshire, was placed in the care of Job Bishop and Hannah Goodrich, and the next year "gathering into order" was completed by John Barnes and Sarah Kendal at Alfred and New Gloucester, Maine. The communities at Niskeyuna and New Lebanon remained under the direct control of Father Joseph and Mother Lucy.[40]

The teams brought with them detailed organizational instructions from Father Joseph. Members were gathered by affirming the family covenant, at first an oral contract but after 1795 written according to Father Joseph's promulgated model. The covenant's preamble stated the principles of gospel order—equality, unity, and hierarchy—as the basis for Shaker community. "There could be no Church in Complete order, according to the Law of Christ without being gathered into one Joint Interest and Union, that all members might have an equal right and privilege, according to their Calling and needs, in things both Spiritual and Temporal."[41] The covenant, unlike Radical Evangelical precursors, contained no doctrinal statements or standards; it was strictly a contract stipulating the terms of membership and economic arrangements. Signatories affirmed only that they entered the Shaker order "freely and voluntarily as a religious duty."

Community of goods was established by a pledge to contribute all debt-free property "for the use and support of the church, and any other use that the Gospel requires." In return for such a contribution each member, regardless of financial status, received "one Joint Interest, as a religious right" in the material effects of the community, conditioned only upon "obedience to the Order and Government of the Church." The 1795 New Lebanon covenant concluded with a provision that no member "bring debt or blame against the church" and an affirmation that all would contribute "time and talents . . . for the mutual good of one another, and other Charitable uses, according to the order of the church."[42]

Father Joseph permitted variation in degree of commitment in the new Shaker societies as he had at New Lebanon. Societies "gathered into order" typically contained several kinds of families who signed different covenants: the "church" family of elite Believers in full property covenant, other lesser families in full covenant, and "junior" or "novitiate" families that "fitted and prepared" members "for advancement in Shakerism at the will of the candidate."[43] These novitiate communities comprised those "whose circumstances did not immediately admit a joint union and interest in all things." Their estates were "used and improved" by the family but "remained in substance as they were at the time of their coming together."

Responsibility for gospel order in all families rested with the "ministerial lot," elders and deacons charged respectively with oversight in "things spiritual" and "things temporal." Each gender group of the family had two members in the eldership and two in the diaconate appointed by the "gatherers" sent by Father Joseph from New Lebanon. As in all matters of appointment, the nominees were to be ratified by "a spontaneous influence and a mutual concurrence of every other member."[44] The duties of elder brothers and sisters included the establishment and maintenance of "spiritual relations," general oversight of the family, preaching and teaching, and discipline through administration of "church privileges."

Deacons were also fundamental to Shaker order, for the well-being of each family depended on the health of its collective economy. Though most families possessed solid financial underpinnings in contributed goods, cash, and land, the economic enterprise required careful and prudent management. Father Joseph had divided the diaconate at New Lebanon between his brother David, the business manager of the community, and Jonathan Slosson, its construction and maintenance agent. The two men had played these roles since the days of the Harvard mission. In the extension of gospel order Father Joseph preserved this division of labor and, following the precedents of Mother Ann, issued careful instructions on practical matters ranging from animal husbandry and carpentry to general principles of parsimony and efficiency.[45]

Given the critical importance of both the eldership and the diaconate, Father Joseph anticipated the need for careful definition of their relationship. He laid down three rules, the first demanding unanimity between elders and deacons "in all orders which they give or execute." The second specified that the eldership was the highest family office, owing to its greater spirituality. The third protected members against arbitrary government: "All orders" were to be "justly applicable to the occasion, and to the faith and abilities of those unto whom they relate."[46]

Meacham thus demanded a complex network of simultaneous power relationships to govern the family: Officers were to establish union with their peers across gender and with assistants of their own sex before making any major policy decision, while scrupulously following their carefully defined individual tasks and obtaining voluntary consent of members to their actions and instructions. Father Joseph developed this pattern not only to prevent spiritual or material usurpation and authoritarianism. It had a constructive purpose. Meacham's vision was of a community of souls each at a different stage of "travel" to perfection who required discipline and guidance from superiors and who administered their own spiritual counsel to those below them. Community of goods, apostolic union, and equality before God combined with this spiritual meritocracy to bring Believers to full perfection.

Each family of as many as one hundred fifty members functioned independently, much like a congregation. Several families gathered together at one location formed a "society," but each family unit remained administratively and geographically distinct.[47] The very autonomy of families made further organization at the society level necessary. Father Joseph originally set up a conference system between officers of different families to govern society affairs. But as the number of families in the societies grew, Meacham appointed the original "gatherers" to permanent positions of authority. These pairs, along with two assistants, were termed apostles, the bishopric, elder and elderess, or simply the ministry. The ministry followed the same procedures of decision making as family elderships, but it held authority to appoint all family elders and deacons and, after 1798, missionaries and out-family officers as well.

The primary duty of the ministry was to stand as spiritual parents to elder brothers and sisters in each family, offering "church privileges" to them and exhorting them to uniform standards of doctrine and purity. Bishop Ebenezer Cooley of New Lebanon issued a typical "gift" of admonition in 1799 to an elder brother, Benjamin Seth Youngs, who confessed to certain minor irregularities. "There is an entire lack in you," Cooley fumed, "and unless you get hold . . . and are tenfold more zealous, the family will be lost in ye flesh and you with them." Cooley, like all bishops, followed the tradition of Mother Ann and the Elders in demanding close attention to the smallest details of community life and in threatening to remove the offender if improvement was not forthcoming: "If you are not faithful in these things, others will take the lead that are faithful, for there must be a foundation."[48]

In addition to putting this kind of hierarchical pressure on family officers, the ministry, through exhortations in public worship, both articulated the ideas of gospel order and legitimated its own authority. One bishop's sermon made these priorities quite clear: "Those who are sincere in heart and love to walk in God's ways—who believe the work of God through the ministers of Christ, and are obedient to it, they will find peace, and they that are deceitful, and keep their sins covered, may try to get along for a while, but their sins will find them out, and they shall be burned!"[49]

By 1792 gospel order had reached completion at New Lebanon. In that year Father Joseph announced that "the work of gathering and building, as to the establishment of orders, by the Ministry, is chiefly finished in this place at present; each order is equally left to keep the orders of God for themselves." For the "first lot," himself and Mother Lucy, "the chief that remains to be done . . . is to oversee the whole, and counsel the Elders of each order, as they may need."[50] To that end they created an elaborate system of visitation. They conducted inspection tours of every family once a year and also required all bishops to visit New Lebanon annually to receive "church privilege" from them. At the local level, elder brothers and sisters often visited their counterparts in other families, and delegations of officers traveled to other societies within their bishopric. New Lebanon, of course, remained a pilgrimage site for all members of the sect, though the journey could be made only with approval of the ministry. This face-to-face leadership network kept information, economic advice, doctrinal pronouncements, and ritual developments circulating through the entire sect and eliminated the need for plenary conventions or written instruction.

Joseph Meacham died in 1796, but before his passing the institutional structure of Shakerism had become a working social reality. From "first lot" through bishops, family elders, and deacons to the membership, the Shakers had constructed a religious order that united spiritual growth and physical labor, equality and authority, heaven and earth. With Meacham's death, supreme authority was vested in Mother Lucy until her own passing in 1821. Though several men served as elder in the "first lot" at New Lebanon, none of them ever approached Mother Lucy in influence and seniority. Wright did not make any major changes in Meacham's system of gospel order during her tenure; rather she served, like Mother Ann, as inspirational leader, counselor, and liturgical guide. She was "incessantly devoted to support and maintain the System, in all its orders and principles in their Primitive purity. She was also assiduous and untiring in her endeavors to cause the System to supply every need, and to render it agreeable and happifying to all. She was very fervent in her labors to have the meetings for sacred worship rendered beautiful and edifying."[51]

Mother Lucy's most important decision was to reopen Shaker evangelism in 1798 after a twelve-year hiatus. The first stirrings of the Second Great Awakening convinced her that a new dispensation of the gospel was at hand, and the Shaker missionaries proved her correct. Their most spectacular success occurred in the West, where through the efforts of John Meacham, Benjamin Seth Youngs, and Issachar Bates, five societies were organized in Ohio and Kentucky between 1805 and 1811. But gains were also made in New England. Mission Families were organized at Pittsford, Guilford, and Lyndon, Vermont; Tuftonboro, New Hampshire; Gorham, Maine; Savoy, Massachusetts; and elsewhere. Each society, moreover, organized a "gathering order" under the church family elders to instruct new converts in the way of perfection.[52]

This new growth and the passing of the Revolutionary generation, however, spelled an end to the social development of Shakerism. After 1815 Shaker energies primarily were devoted to the maintenance of gospel order rather than its elaboration. The hierarchy of authority became increasingly well defined and routinized. Mother Lucy had been one of the youngest and earliest Shaker converts; when she died in 1821, few active members of her generation remained. The future of Shakerism fell to persons who had been raised in its institutions and who were dedicated to establishing bureaucratic and publicly articulated standards for it. By Wright's death the oral culture of Shakerism had already given way to printed forms of hymnody, theology, and history. Just six months after her passing, the New Lebanon ministry drew up a code of "millennial laws" drawn largely from

Father Joseph's writings and Mother Lucy's pronouncements. Mother Lucy had explicitly opposed such a compilation, "believing that conditions would necessitate a constant change of content."[53] But the appearance of the Millennial Laws in codified form was an appropriate symbol for the end of Shakerism's protean period.

The Shakers created the most detailed and ambitious social system of all the New England sects. Because of the Shaker hope that their gospel order would become the norm for all human society, the sect has been classified by most sociologists as utopian. But in fact all the sectarians held this hope. Rather, the genius of Shaker social structure was its articulation of the need for order per se in community life and its employment of the biological family as a design concept to provide that order. The Shakers acknowledged that freedom was meaningless without strong institutions to shape it into human good. For them, the goal of life was spiritual and physical perfection; confession of sins and conversion were but the first steps toward that end. The attainment of perfection depended upon obedience to divinely constituted parental authority and faultless performance of shared obligations to the community. The hallmark of successful "travel" to perfection was the effortless functioning of the spiritual family, egalitarian in constitution, hierarchic in structure, uniform in intention. To their hill country contemporaries, the Shakers offered a totally rationalized religious lifestyle, in which individual rights, autonomy of gender, collective responsibility, and the attainment of spiritual perfection were made available in the gospel order of Christ's Second Appearing.

In the late 1780s and early 1790s the New England sects developed comprehensive social institutions that continued to flourish for more than two decades. After almost ten years of experiment and improvisation, the Freewill Baptists, Universalists, and Shakers achieved a rationalized social order that combined elements of the Radical Evangelical tradition with the communal implications of their beliefs and the realities of rural New England life. The sects had begun the task of institutionalization guided by the simple principles of the gathered church. As preached by Whitefield and embodied by Separates, Baptists, and New Lights, the gathered church included spiritually guided decision making, discipline by the gospel rule, covenantal specification of religious and moral duties, and a simple organization of elders and deacons. Most of these patterns were transferred into the sectarian polities as an initial basis of organizational order.

But from this base each sect developed innovative norms that followed the logic of its doctrines and the vicissitudes of its history. Freewill Baptists focused on the tribal union of consensus and mutual criticism. In covenanted communities Freewillers carried out a life of partial withdrawal from secular society. Eschewing normal practices of business, legal, and political life, they sought to construct an all-sufficient social and moral existence within the horizon of the local congregation. Living in but not of the world, they centered their community around procedures that required doctrinal, moral, and spiritual union. Superimposed on this local order was a complex system of traveling connectional meetings designed to make the zeal of revivalism permanent. Their system of overlapping geographical meetings buttressed by painstaking discipline, gospel union, and mass revivalism was the unique product of the sect's voluntaristic world view and schismatic origins.

Universalists early and permanently resisted any infringement of the individualism and freedom they believed implicit in the doctrine of universal salvation. Their tenets of gospel liberty and apostolic imitation combined with the social circumstances of small, far-flung country congregations to create a persistent Universalist distrust of all creedal and institutional norms. Making a virtue out of this necessity, the sect followed a unique mode of governance rooted in absolute congregational autonomy, a constantly circulating itinerant ministry, and the briefest of formal instruments.

The Shakers combined the logic of perfectionist asceticism and the social experience of the family in their polity of gospel order. Father Joseph Meacham developed the communal discipline of Mother Ann and Father James into permanent form at New Lebanon. But he went much further than his predecessors in giving structure to Shaker gospel order. Sexual equality, rigorous and all-encompassing discipline, charismatic hierarchy in the mode of familial social relationships, and a millennial vision of a complete social world of regenerate saints informed Meacham's design for gospel order.

The Freewill Baptists, Universalists, and Shakers of rural New England created new models for religious and social life that embodied the cultural ferment of the Revolutionary era. For these radical dissenters, allegiance to the good news of their faith required nothing less than the fabrication of new styles of life independent from the norms of received religious tradition and the secular pressures of a revolutionary society. Following the imperatives of their heterodox beliefs, the sectarians created new social structures that proved lasting and effective. Each sectarian social design was different, a distinctive transformation of Radical Evangelical tradition in light of doctrinal innovation and social circumstances. But each accomplished the same vital task: the construction of a social reality grounded in new beliefs that withstood and indeed reintegrated the enormous forces of social, political, and religious change abroad in the land.

8

The History of Redemption

The focal point of sectarian religious culture was theology. In the 1780s the sects had emerged preaching radical anti-Calvinist doctrines of universal salvation, freedom of the will, and celibate perfectionism. Through the 1790s and into the nineteenth century, sectarian thinkers molded these theological axioms into systematic belief structures. The context of sectarian theology was governed principally by internal influences. The development of permanent church structures demanded coherent theological rationales and uniform standards of belief and practice. Evangelism continued to bring new members who, along with older adherents, carried on intensive oral development of major tenets and biblical interpretation. In the hands of a new generation of converts, the teachings of the founders were supplied with scripture proofs, logical and typological extension, and a systematic form. Congregationalists and Baptists mounted a belated but telling attack on the rising heterodox faiths from pulpit and press. And though the sects engaged in little disputation with their detractors, the Evangelical Calvinist critique underscored their intellectual vulnerability.[1] By 1815, however, Freewill Baptists, Universalists, and Shakers had created comprehensive theological positions that stated their worldview in the language of New England religious thought.

The core of sectarian theology was a counterargument to Evangelical Calvinism. As classically formulated by Jonathan Edwards and embraced by succeeding generations of New Light Congregationalists, Separates, and Baptists, Evangelical Calvinism argued for four distinctive and interlocking beliefs: the absolute sovereignty of God, the innate depravity of human beings, the limited substitutionary atonement of Jesus Christ, and the predestination and election of souls. Evangelical theories of religious sensation, original sin, virtue, and freedom of the will all derived from the demands and constraints of this deterministic and elitist model of the cosmos.[2]

Calvinism depicted God as the supreme lawgiver and righteous judge whose creation exhibited His awful power and arbitrary will as well as order, justice, and mercy. Human beings, perfectly cre ted by God, were equipped with knowledge of divine law, the capacity to obey or disobey, and responsibility for the consequences. The disobedience of Adam and Eve violated God's law, for which the irrevocable and just sentence was physical death and eternal punishment. In addition, sin genetically flawed the intellectual and spiritual powers of mankind so that every human volition and act committed evil and rebellion against God.

The good news of Calvinism was that God through Christ, the second person of the Trinity, displayed mercy and forgiveness to some of these depraved humans. In order to satisfy divine retribution for sin, Christ took human form, endured death by crucifixion, and employed this suffering as a substitute penalty for sinners. Christ's atoning sacrifice, however, was applied only to those whom God, in a separate act of sovereign will, had chosen "before the foundation of the world." These elect, whose salvation depended solely on the unmerited grace of God through Christ, were regenerated and sanctified—but not perfected or restored to the Adamic state—by the Holy Spirit in this life and would persevere to live and reign with Christ eternally. The reprobate, also destined by divine fiat, died in their sins and awaited the Last Judgment and a just sentence of eternal damnation.

The sectarians created their theologies in order to deny the moral, metaphysical, and scriptural arguments of this economy of grace and to present others that propounded a benevolent God, human perfectability, universal nonpenal atonement, and free grace for all believers. The mature sectarian theologies moved beyond defiance of Calvinism on particular doctrines to construction of alternative systems that circumvented and invalidated its internal logic.

The sectarians were thus often doctrinally allied with liberal Arminians of the Revolutionary generation like Charles Chauncy and Henry Ware. There were, however, crucial differences between these two parties of anti-Calvinists. The Arminians, writing from New England urban centers, rested their case on the logic of "supernatural rationalism," the claim that God's conduct of the universe proceeded from reasonable principles intelligible to and observable by the human mind. This premise led to rationalism, the conclusion that true religion itself consisted of reasoned, empirical judgment of scriptural and doctrinal evidence and not, as Edwards had argued, "principally of holy affections or emotions."[3] Above all, Arminians rejected the necessity of the New Birth and Edwards's investment of the emotions as the principal medium of saving grace. Rationalism was unacceptable to sectarians, who shared with Evangelical Calvinists an experiential imperative in religious epistemology. Although both the sects and the Arminians endorsed a number of anti-Calvinist correctives, the former could not follow the rationalist critique of religious experience and scriptural revelation. The sectarians thus represented a third stream of post-Revolutionary religious thought in New England, rooted in Evangelical Calvinism yet categorically opposed to some of its major tenets, apparently Arminian in teaching yet unambiguous in rejecting rationalism.

The distinguishing mark of sectarian theology lay in its hermeneutic, the epistemological stance from which it interpreted scripture, reason, and religious experience. In contrast with Arminian rationalism and Evangelical emotionalism, the sectarians located the source of religious truth in the direct contact of the human soul with the spirit of God. The sectarians agreed with Edwards that true religion was experiential. But Evangelical Calvinists were careful to place moral and doctrinal qualifications on the testimony of holy emotions and spiritual sensations, whereas the sectarians interpreted religious experience as the gift of the Holy Spirit, a self-validating manifestation of divine wisdom, power, or will. From this position they could be much more sanguine about the significance of charisma than Edwards and elevate it to primacy as "the key to knowledge" of saving faith. By the same token this spiritual hermeneutic provided a substantive counter to Arminian reliance on human reason in sacred affairs. Sectarian insistence on the primacy of transcendent spirit provided a fundamental assumption from which they derived definitions of divine and human nature and an economy of grace neither Calvinist nor Arminian.

In creating a theological system, the sectarians thus did not lack for method or substance. What they did not possess was a formal structure to organize their beliefs. The task of sectarian theology was to articulate the truth of charismatic teaching through scriptural exegesis. To accomplish this, the sectarians turned to the oral tradition of Radical Evangelicalism and to the dramatic form of popular theology that Edwards labeled "the history of redemption." George Whitefield had pioneered the proclamation of a gospel focused on dramatic episodes of biblical history, particularly the Fall and the Atonement. Evangelicals of all varieties promulgated this style of popular theology throughout rural society in the late eighteenth century, but it was Jonathan Edwards who raised it to a systematic doctrinal framework.

In 1739 Edwards "planned a body of divinity, in a new method . . . for the instruction and improvement of ordinary Christians." His aim was to show "how the most remarkable events, in all ages from the fall to the present times . . . were adapted to promote the work of redemption."[4] To organize this cosmic history, Edwards outlined three periods or dispensations of grace — from the Fall to the Incarnation, from the Incarnation to the Resurrection, and from the Resurrection to the end of the world. Each dispensation carried with it a corresponding roster of doctrinal considerations.

The first dispensation taught creation, fall, and the Law; the second treated Christ's nature and atonement; and the third dealt with regeneration, ecclesiology, and eschatology.[5] Using scripture, Calvinist doctrine, and historical scholarship Edwards sought in the history of redemption to assemble divine activity and human experience into a single dramatic narrative.

Edwards did not live to complete his new theological scheme, but the 1739 plan did eventuate in a series of sermons posthumously published in 1782 as *A History of the Work of Redemption,* which enjoyed wide popularity. More important, Edwards transmitted his model of theology as historical narrative to an entire generation of colleagues and students. Samuel Hopkins, for example, employed the history of redemption to organize his *System of Doctrines* (1793), the most influential New England Calvinist theological work of the late eighteenth century. Baptist divines, including Samuel Stillman, Thomas Baldwin, and Caleb Blood, also employed the dispensational scheme to condemn "infant sprinkling."[6]

From the Revolution to the Second Great Awakening the history of redemption was a staple format of Evangelical Calvinist preaching and theological writing that powerfully shaped popular religious thought. It is not surprising that the sectarians also seized on the dispensational model as an explanatory medium for their heterodox beliefs. As heirs to the Whitefieldian tradition and representatives of rural religious culture, the sectarians tended to cast their spiritual exegesis of scripture in this same narrative mode. The major episodes of the history of redemption served as the expository framework for sectarian doctrines and provided the rationale for the elaboration of those doctrines into a comprehensive system. When the sectarians at the turn of the nineteenth century finally articulated their spiritual hermeneutic, radical doctrines, and scriptural exegesis, it was the epic cycle of the history of redemption — creation and fall, law and grace, atonement and regeneration — that gave form to their utterance.

Freewill Baptist theology before 1815 was influenced by the writings of Henry Alline. From his first encounter with Alline in 1783, Benjamin Randel adopted the Nova Scotia revivalist's highly speculative doctrines of creation and atonement. Randel's only published work, an 1803 funeral sermon, followed Alline on all major points. A year later Randel published an edition of Alline's treatise *Two Mites on Some of the Most Important and Much Disputed Points of Divinity,* a history of redemption containing his most coherent and systematic thought. The other major Freewill theological resource was *A Religious Magazine,* the quarterly serial published by John Buzzell in 1811–12 and 1820–21. Buzzell like Randel was a follower of Alline, and in occasional essays he vigorously attacked Calvinism with arguments and doctrines drawn from *Two Mites* and Randel's own teachings.[7]

The Freewill Baptist version of the history of redemption began with the divine perfections. Henry Alline depicted God as omniscient, omnipotent, omnipresent, and immutable, existing in what he called "the Eternal Now," a realm of constant duration unaffected by time or flux. The Trinity conjointly formed the physical universe to operate by uniform laws that mirrored the essential constancy and regularity of the Godhead. The creation of human beings was motivated by "God's electing love," a divine willingness that all nature work for good and happiness. According to Alline, the creation process consisted of two acts. First, God created male and female images, named Adam and Eve, in a "holy, free, and innocent" state. These two beings were not part of physical nature; rather they consisted of "an immortal Mind clothed with a spiritual and immortal body." At this point Adam and Eve did not possess life, but by the second creative act of breathing into the "immortal mind," God gave life not only to Adam and Eve but also to all human souls ever to live. These other souls were not bodily present, since only the two "spiritual bodies" of Adam and Eve had yet been created. But all human posterity were "seminally" present in Adam's "loins" and shared in a conjoint or "federal" relationship to the first parents a perfect "union with the Immutable."[8]

The Freewill Baptists denied the Calvinist teaching that God had decreed the salvation or reprobation of human souls before creation. The destiny of humanity, rather, depended upon the "bent of the free will or voluntary turn of mind." Endowed with "an information of the dreadful consequence of turning away from God," the federal Adam had the ability to abide by or break the bond of spiritual union. The cosmogonic or creation episode of the Freewill history of redemption thus postulated the sect's primary doctrine, volitional freedom, as the fundamental quality of human and divine nature before the Fall.[9]

In this condition of freedom and innocence, all humanity sinned through Adam by succumbing to carnal desires for the fruit of the tree of knowledge. The error of aspiring after an object other than the Creator affected "man" both physically and spiritually. "When he fell," wrote Henry Alline, "his immortal mind was immediately imprisoned in the immortal body, which . . . by its fall, has become related to an animal world, whereby it assumes an animal body."[10] The abuse of free will by Adam and Eve violated the immutability of creation. "They broke the law of innocence," Randel wrote "and were seminally exposed to everlasting ruin and destruction, and would have eternally sunk, for aught man or angels could have done."[11]

As humanity descended toward extinction, however, Christ interposed to restore equilibrium to the cosmos. "Unmerited, self-moved, spontaneous love, immediately broke forth in pursuit of the rebel! . . . God immediately appeared in the character of a Mediator! a Jesus! a Saviour! and entered into the law place and stead of the sinner."[12] For Freewill Baptists, Christ began his redemptive role at the moment of original sin, reversing the lethal effects of humanity's disobedience and freely enforcing God's will that His creatures be saved. All souls, seminally present in Adam and Eve, were rescued from the generic effects of original sin at the very outset of human history.[13] This creation and fall episode was crucial to Freewill theology. It replaced Calvinism's doctrine of predestination and election of souls with a notion of divine sustenance of human freedom despite original sin. Freewill Baptists thus worked their fundamental tenet into the creation story to show that the essence of the soul was its ability to obey or disobey God's laws and that its destiny rested on the exercise of that ability.

As a consequence of Christ's action, humans were placed in a new state of probation. Saved from annihilation, they appeared in the natural world still endowed with the "ruins" of their original spiritual nature. Their freedom rendered them able to choose to sin further or to find the way of salvation by faith in Christ. The history of human probation, as recorded in the Old Testament, was only of secondary interest to Freewill Baptists. The biblical chronicle of Israel was valuable because it taught the nature of sin and the repeated failure of even God's own chosen people to live in obedience to divine law. The promises of salvation given to the Israelites were similarly instructive, pointing in veiled ways to the true means of salvation to come.

But for Freewill Baptists the decisive event of human history was the incarnation of Christ in the man Jesus. Their picture of human capacities and divine initiative concentrated around the figure of Jesus and the need for his atoning mission. The necessity of incarnation was to them self-evident. Although human souls were actually saved already from the penalty of original sin, they were still incapable of full reunion with God because they continued to commit volitional sin as a consequence of their fallen state. To provide a "legal door" for the forgiveness of this kind of sin, the Freewillers reasoned, Christ had to take human form, to "be like man and become capable of suffering and death for them."[14] Full participation in the fallen state was necessary to qualify Christ to act for and in behalf of humanity.

The Freewill theologians emphasized that Jesus did not undertake atonement to pay a penalty to a wrathful Calvinist God for human sin. Christ's death was not "to appease vindictive wrath, or satisfy any incensed justice in the Deity," wrote Alline.[15] Rather it was motivated by Christ's love, graciousness, and willingness to restore the broken union of humans and God. Jesus' total obedience to the divine law and his suffering and death were later accepted by God for the forgiveness of human sin, but the atoning sacrifice itself was voluntary.

Christ's atonement on the cross was as universal as his intervention for humanity had been at the Fall. Both were manifestations of God's will that "all should come to the knowledge of the truth and be saved." But in the crucial matter of salvation, as in all other central points of Freewill theology, the human soul's power of choice was determinative. The human condition remained probationary after Christ's earthly career; human souls were still endowed with a free yet corruptible will. To preserve the dignity and responsibility of human moral agency, Christ gave all persons a "second chance" to follow the law of love and regain union with God through belief in Jesus as savior. The distribution of salvific grace thus depended on each sinner's conscious choice. Faith in Christ brought eternal life and sanctification; rejection of salvation was "the second death," absolute and eternal separation from God.

Alline, Randel, and Buzzell, however, all rejected the idea that salvation could result from a sinner's unassisted personal ability to believe the gospel. The fallen and corrupt nature of human will required further gracious initiative from God to guide the soul to truth. "A carnal mind doth not delight in God," said Randel, "for none can love sin and holiness at the same time."[16] To assist sinners, Christ sent the Holy Spirit to teach the truth to all souls in this life. Every soul, Freewill thinkers claimed, has "a day of grace." Such testimony could come in many forms, but every soul would at some point be presented with a clear and conscious choice between true faith and fatal eror. "The rational powers and faculties of the soul" were offered the opportunity to cooperate with "the operations of the spirit of God" in the quest for salvation. Once the chance was offered and rejected, however, there was no guarantee that it would ever be renewed.[17]

Those who chose to cooperate with the Holy Spirit underwent a process of regeneration that Randel described in terms reminiscent of his own Radical Evangelical conversion. The first fruit of the Spirit was contrition and repentance, followed by the "weaning or working out" of sin from the soul. With proper weaning, "the power of God has got such possession of the soul that [it] is constrained to fall down and yield up all." This yielding leads to the embrace of the gospel and the request that Jesus "take possession" of the soul. "Then the light, life, and love of God breaks into the soul, subdues the fear, removes the guilt and condemnation, takes out the state of sin, brings the soul to the liberty of the sons of God."[18] This crucial act of self-surrender was not simply a fruit of contrition before a predestinating God; it was a voluntary exercise of the free will regarding an empirical choice of destiny.

The result of true conversion, Freewill Baptists believed, was the forgiveness of all committed sin and the restoration of the Adamic nature to the soul. When "a soul [is] converted to God," Randel declared, "his sins are all blotted out . . . When once he has been forgiven, he will never come into condemnation for what is past."[19] The Freewill saint thus began a new spiritual career utterly free of any pollution from sin in the eyes of God. Furthermore, salvation brought with it the indwelling of the Holy Spirit that restored the soul to its original purity and innocence. "The soul of every true believer is purified," wrote John Buzzell, "and made clean through the sanctifying influence of the divine spirit, by washing of regeneration, and so freed from the love, act, guilt, and dominion of sin."[20]

Freewill Baptists were gradualists in their perfectionism, believing that growth in grace occurred only in and through community discipline. The gospel union of the saints, they held, was a social fruit of the Holy Spirit, the visible sign of voluntary commitment to Christ. "It is [Christ's] divine nature, that unites all believers to God, and to one another, originated in him, and they receive it all from him."[21] Only within the sacred community could the Spirit be magnified and individual souls grow in their "travel" toward holiness. Thus the voluntarism and consensual style of Freewill institutions received an explicit theological rationale in their history of redemption.

The influence of carnal nature could, however, overtake even a sincere believer. Freewill theology was especially sensitive to this possibility of backsliding because of the enormous consequences attached to it. If a regenerated soul sinned again, it must have done so by willful error, since it was aware of the volitional basis of moral and spiritual acts. By backsliding, a soul recapitulated the Adamic sin and became again liable to damnation. If such an end befell a backslider, "it will be his own fault; — God's throne will be clear — the soul will have none to blame, neither men nor devils, but himself."[22] A sinning believer, however, was not automatically condemned to eternal punishment by God. The formula "repent and forsake" was still available, if contrition were truly sincere and resolution sure.

In Freewill theology those who chose to follow Christ, though sanctified in this life, would return to their primal created union with God only after Christ's second coming in power and glory. "All whose will has been turned, or inward creature redeemed," Alline taught, will be "again united to the infinite and eternal spirit" of God. Those who rejected the universal offer of salvation through Christ "will sink forever, both inward and outward creature in its own hell."[23]

The Freewill Baptists thus lived in a cosmos governed by divine and human volition. Their theological structures remained elementary; their speculation, governed by the principle of radical free will, was largely restricted to novel explanations of human nature and the economy of grace. Indeed, they consciously resisted liberal or Wesleyan labels. Alline and Buzzell both denied being "refined Arminians" and documented their claim by rejecting any ascription of salvation to "personal ability" of human beings. They argued that the power of choice itself was divine in origin and must be divinely assisted to operate correctly for redemption. They also denied the doctrines of perseverance and punctiliar sanctification, the Wesleyan hallmarks, and pictured the saints as embarked on a perilous path of growth toward full sanctification, liable to backsliding and even loss of salvation.

Their mode of theologizing functioned at the more popular though not necessarily simpler level of the history of redemption. In effect, they fabricated the history of redemption into one vast metaphor expressing the meaning of human will and divine design. The entire framework of Freewill beliefs rested on the role of human and divine freedom in establishing the spiritual realities of the cosmos. Each crucial dimension of their redemptive history—creation, fall, atonement, conversion, sanctification, and final judgemnt—was accompanied by the voluntary actions of the participants. The Freewill gospel was a message of salvation available to all persons willing to exercise free choice and resolved to seek after godliness, expressed through a unique hybrid of Evangelical Calvinism, revivalistic voluntarism, and spiritual exegesis.

Universalist theology was far more diverse than Freewill Baptist thought, owing to the disparate origins of the sect. The writings of John Murray and Elhanan Winchester were strongly influenced by British and Continental thought and did not clearly reflect native New England beliefs. Caleb Rich did not commit his influential scriptural exposition to writing, but his convert Hosea Ballou emerged around 1800 as the principal spokesman for rural Universalism.

Ballou's correspondence with Calvinist Joel Foster of New Salem, New Hampshire, published in 1799 without his consent, was the first major statement of hill country Universalism. Ballou soon produced some anti-Calvinist sermons and pamphlets, but his major works followed the ratification of the Winchester Profession of Faith in 1803. *Notes on the Parables of the New Testament* (1804) was an immediate success, exhibiting an appealing combination of Richite exegesis and commonsense argument. Ballou's *Treatise on Atonement* (1805), however, was the masterwork of early New England Universalism, containing a comprehensive statement of the history of redemption in distinctive sectarian terms. Other rural theologians also contributed to the Universalist synthesis, notably Walter Ferriss and Abner Kneeland, both of whom published significant sermon collections before 1812. Despite occasional differences in detail, Ballou, Ferriss, and Kneeland—all products of Radical Evangelicalism and heavily indebted to Caleb Rich's thought—created a powerful indigenous theology for Universalism.

The Universalist history of redemption began with a picture of God that emphasized infinite goodness almost to the exclusion of any other attribute. All other aspects of divine being and action were subsumed under God's character as a "benevolent Deity." God's love brought into existence a universe that was intentional in nature and determinate in operation. His moral purpose in the act of creation was happiness, to be achieved through the operation of natural laws. God's initiating action was to create a spiritual self-image, "a dependent being" second only to Godhead, who was Christ. "Christ is said to be the image of the invisible God, and the first born of every creature," explained Hosea Ballou. "His being the first born of every creature, agrees with his being the beginning of the creation of God. It is plain to me, from scripture, that the Mediator is the first human soul which was created."[24]

Christ in turn became the source and pattern for all visible creation, especially for human beings, who were originally created as purely spiritual entities: "As man stood in his created character, which is Christ, the heavenly man, he was not, at that time, formed of the dust of the ground, was not of the earth earthy."[25] Only after this spiritual creation did God through Christ's agency "form" the physical bodies of Adam and Eve out of matter and complete the creation of humans as composite creatures. The primal pair stood in perfect innocence, combining Christ's spiritual nature with the untested powers of physicality. In order to guide Adam and Eve, Christ "shadowed forth" a law into their minds that taught them the need to obey the divine First Cause and to fear the lethal effects of disobedience.

Armed with the knowledge that they should "yield not to the passions and powers of the flesh," yet also necessarily "made subject to vanity and temptation" by their carnal nature, Adam and Eve sought to live in total dependence on God. "But immediately the powerful vibrations of fleshly nature absorbed" the heavenly mind of Adam and Eve. They "sought to the carnal man for food, ate, and died."[26] The cause of original sin was the necessary exercise of "fleshly appetite." The primal pair did not sin by the rebellion of their free will or in defiance of divine moral injunction. Rather their sin was simply a violation of God's law brought on by human "imbecility of nature and weakness of judgment," according to Abner Kneeland.[27] Moreover, original sin was a *felix culpa*, a fortunate fall perpetrated by humans acting under the "overruling and superintending" determination of God. Thus Ballou epitomized the human condition in two aphorisms: "1st. Man is dependent, in all his volitions, and he moves by necessity. 2nd. The Almighty has a good intention, in every volition of man."[28]

Therefore the consequences of sin were finite and were intended, like creation itself, to achieve the "glorious purposes" of God's "grand design." Hosea Ballou explained the finitude of sin as a simple example of the law of cause and effect: "As no finite cause can produce an infinite effect, no finite creature can commit an infinite sin."[29] Sin did indeed produce immense misery for Adam and Eve and ultimately resulted in fleshly lust, jealousy, idolatry, political chauvinism, conflict, and above all spiritual death and separation from God. Yet these effects were strictly limited by God in a way commensurate with their cause: Finite sin begat only finite punishment.

Moreover, God shaped history to reveal His extraordinary benevolence and paternal love toward His creation.[30] The first clear indication of God's intentions for humanity after the Fall was the divine promise that through Abraham's progeny all nations and persons would be blessed. According to Universalist exegesis, this "Abrahamic faith" constituted the first dispensation of the gospel of universal salvation, an "everlasting covenant" of union between God and humanity. The Mosaic Law constituted a second increment in saving knowledge. The enumeration of sin by the Law illustrated the finitude of human evil; God's willingness to honor the Law reflected His disposition to save.

The Abrahamic covenant and the Mosaic Law enhanced human consciousness of sin and underlined the need for faith. But despite God's gracious care, two fundamental errors of "unbelief and darkness" remained "in the mind of Adam," according to Ballou. "The first was, he believed God to be his enemy, in consequence of disobedience; and secondly, that he could reconcile his Maker, by works of his own."[31] These errors led souls to the two false conclusions that God was the unreconciled party in the Fall and that He required retributive punishment of sinners. In reality God, unchangeable in His love, was not the unreconciled party; humanity was by separating from its spiritual union with the Creator. And since humans were unable to restore this primal union, God provided an atonement "to renew man's love to his creator." "The atonement by Christ was the effect, not the cause, of God's love to man," Ballou taught.[32]

Christ, "the first human soul" and the "immediate cause" of human existence, performed this atonement by manifesting the ultimacy of God's "spirit of love" in the man Jesus. But it was not the incarnational or sacrificial aspects of Jesus' ministry that produced the reconciliation of humanity with God. Rather it was Jesus' factual demonstration that the divine "spirit of love" was "stronger than death, that it hath power to remove the moral maladies of mankind, and to make us free from the law of sin and death" that opened the hidden truth of God's salvific plan to the human soul.[33] Through the example of Jesus, the ultimate primacy of love over sin, life over death, and spirit over law was revealed. Jesus empirically demonstrated the availability of the Adamic nature to humans in the probationary state. His own death and resurrection were simply a metaphor for the greater fact of human liberation from the bondage of sin and the Law.[34]

With the Atonement Christ established a new dispensation and a "second covenant" that revealed the unconditional restoration of alienated human nature to union with God. Universal salvation thus was not a matter of choice or even of faith by contingent creatures. It was determined, as Abner Kneeland put it, "wholly on the will, purpose and wise council of God, antecedent to any act or acts of finite beings."[35] The truth of universal salvation existed independent of human faith in it. "Faith," said Hosea Ballou, "does not make a fact any more true than it was before it was believed."

Yet one element remained incomplete in this economy of salvation: "Rebellious creatures . . . are not willing subjects of [God's] moral government, they are not his obedient subjects in the law of love."[36] To induce such obedience God provided "a gift of divine light and grace" to all humans. "The word which is nigh us, even in our hearts and mouths," wrote Walter Ferriss, "is everywhere, operating, in some degree, in all hearts."[37] And though "the degree of manifestation" was different in each soul, all persons possessed a moral conscience capable of comprehending the ultimacy of goodness, happiness, and final salvation through Christ.

Conversion and sanctification thus did find a place in Universalist theology. Through the "atoning grace" of Christ and the witness of scripture, the mind discovered the "truth as it is in Jesus." This knowledge "brings the mind from under the power and constitution of the earthly Adam, to live by faith on the son of God, and to be ruled and governed, even in this life, in a great measure, by the law of the Spirit of life in Christ Jesus."[38] This cognitive transformation also generated moral imperatives as the regenerate mind came to understand Jesus' death and suffering as a model for human action in union with God.

Universalists believed that suffering was a necessary punishment and antedote to committed sin in this life. Moreover, in order to gain union with God, according to Ballou, "it is evident that the creature must . . . give up everything of a temporal nature."[39] The Holy Spirit assisted the mind in "being weaned from the world, and united . . . to those unseen things which God hath prepared for them that love him." The unleashing of the Spirit curbed the will to sin; and as the finite but awful consequences of sin became more comprehensible and abhorrent, the spiritual nature in turn gained greater control over carnal nature, until the soul became effectively free from sinful will and behavior. Complete sanctification was not attainable in the finite state, but progressive perfection and gradual recovery of the Adamic powers were necessary concomitants of "the Abrahamic faith."

The task of Universalist saints was to actualize the potential for perfection made available to humans by Christ the creator, former, and restorer. Each soul received its own unique form of the truth and individually grew toward sanctification.[40] The communion of saints, therefore, did not exist to provide a means of grace or a standard of authority. Rather, it was a pilgrim community that enabled those who knew the truth to identify one another in gospel liberty and to aid one another in the travel toward sanctity.

Universalist theology culminated in an eschatological vision of the final restoration of all souls to the paradise state. The saints who already had discovered the truth would "immediately pass into the enjoyment of rest" in the general resurrection. Those souls who had not been restored through faith would attain salvation eventually through means known only to God. Universalists disagreed on the scriptural evidence for punishment. Hosea Ballou denied that punishment occurred after death, whereas Walter Ferriss believed that punishment for sins now committed may extend beyond the temporal realm as instruction and purification for the erring soul. The manner of restoration for unbelievers would, like all aspects of divine knowledge, follow the operations of the universal natural laws designed for precisely that purpose. But regardless of the means, at the moment of universal restoration God's grand design and purpose in creation would finally be achieved, and "all that ever mourned shall be comforted; and through all the wide creation of God, not one voice shall be heard to complain."[41]

The Universalists molded the history of redemption to their own doctrinal needs. The assertion of final salvation for all souls demanded that sacred history be determinate and uniform. The Universalists therefore rendered the dispensations of history into necessary and contingent effects of God's will and cosmic laws. Beginning from the postulate of God's infinite benevolence and power, they depicted a divine economy of regular order, each part of which depended on the necessary action of prior law. God alone was infinite; even Christ was less than divine, though so constituted as to be the source and pattern for all human life. The created condition of Adam and Eve was similarly structured to require sin as a finite and ultimately beneficial element in God's plan. The source of salvation for sinners in this world was simply the knowledge of these truths, the appropriation of a determinate cosmos through the agency of the Holy Spirit. In the hands of the Universalists, the history of redemption became the vehicle of holy wisdom the impact of which brought perfection to the soul, enlightenment to the mind, and true virtue to the will.

Like the other rural New England sects, the Shakers before 1820 produced theological texts few in number but rich in content. James Whittaker served as primary theologian and exegete in the early years, and Mother Ann's oral tradition remained vital. But the shaper of Shaker theology was Joseph Meacham. His only published work, *A Concise Statement of the Principles of the Only True Church*, appeared at Bennington, Vermont, in 1790. This short treatise outlined a dispensational history of redemption based on Old Testament exegesis. Father Joseph also composed manuscript sermons and treatises for the community that served as reference points to his extensive oral teachings. A second generation of Shaker thinkers appeared after 1800, most prominently Benjamin Seth Youngs and Calvin Green, both of whom were directly influenced by Father Joseph at New Lebanon. Youngs was a trusted family elder at New Lebanon and a pioneer missionary to the West. In 1806 Youngs sent an outline for a "statement of faith" to the New Lebanon Ministry for approval as a printed standard for use in evangelism. Mother Lucy Wright accepted the outline, which was published in full form in 1808 at Lebanon, Ohio, as *The Testimony of Christ's Second Appearing*. Green, a young believer literally born in the faith who became elder of New Lebanon's Church Family at the age of twenty-five, was also at work on a dispensational scheme during this period. His manuscript "Treatise upon the Work of God in Different Ages" (1806) held a slightly different perspective than Young's *Testimony*. At the direction of Mother Lucy, Green undertook to prepare a "corrected and improved" version of the *Testimony*, which was published at Albany in 1810 and became the definitive work of Shaker theology for the post-Revolutionary generation.[42]

Shakers depicted God as the "Great First Cause," "a being of infinite perfections — eternal and unchangeable" whose "nature and purpose" was revealed in the natural law. One of these laws, the complimentarity of gender, supplied evidence that the Deity was divided into two modes, "the Father, who was everlasting before all worlds, and . . . the Mother, who was with him that was everlasting."[43] The Father was the divine modality of power and creation, the Mother of spirit and wisdom. Visible creation, the Shakers believed, came into existence gradually, developing through a hierarchy of forms generated by the evolutionary effect of natural laws "in one harmonious concert with the first moving cause.[44]

Human beings were "the head and most noble part of the creation." They possessed "animal faculties, or bodily sensations" combined with a living soul that was uniquely "capable of dictating and ordering every faculty and sensation of the natural body aright." God crowned the creation of this primal human by dividing it into two complementary parts, first male then female, in the image of divine nature. Only when functioning together in thought and deed were Adam and Eve truly alive and exercising their created purpose. "These two, as to their local situation were different," wrote Meacham, "but in point of nature and union, they were one, and formed but the one entire man, complete in his manhood."[45]

Yet the primal soul of Adam and Eve, though "superior to the instinct of . . . earthly nature," was also linked to the "animal sensations and natural desires" of the physical body. This wedding of earthly and spiritual natures constituted a "state of trial" for "the primordial man . . . and placed him, as it were, between two worlds." God's prohibition against consuming the fruit of the tree of knowledge tested the obedience of human creation. But the spirit of animal nature, in the form of a serpent, tempted the female part of "the man," since it was second and hence weaker in the order of creation. The serpent's deception caused envy and "the influence of an inferior attraction . . . to take root in her animal nature." Hoping for "something more delightful . . . than the order and counsel of God," Eve ate the fruit and gave it to Adam, who did likewise, thereby completing the act of disobedience. By this "subversion of the true order of God," sin "took possession and government of all those faculties and affections of body and mind, which had constituted man a noble creature in his state of innocence."[46]

The Fall did not involve a physical change of state; rather, Adam and Eve experienced an alteration of which they were ignorant, whereby their spiritual powers were transformed into their opposites. The deceitfulness of sin consisted precisely in the beguiling of Adam and Eve into "believing that to be LOVE, which in truth is nothing but LUST." Thus when Adam and Eve after the Fall sought to obey God's command to be fruitful and multiply, they did so by lustful sexual intercourse instead of using "a perfect law of nature" which God would have shown them for spiritual generation. Far from establishing union with God, intercourse consummated the union of "the serpent's nature" with the human body and loosed the consequences of sin on generations yet unborn. The sin of disobedience transformed fruitfulness into concupiscence, and "the man of innocence" became "the man of sin."[47]

Extinction was the necessary penalty for violating the order of creation.

But God, "for wise purposes," determined to prolong the life of the "first parents," though He condemned them to a life of pain and travail in a corrupted nature. At the expulsion from the Garden of Eden God explicitly cursed "the man's" genitals. "It does not appear that God took any notice of the hand, or the mouth," in pronouncing the curse that they had merited "but laid it on the same part which they covered, and of which they were ashamed."[48] Further, Adam and Eve experienced physical death for their carnal disobedience and saw the evil consequences of their lust in Cain's murder of Abel. Thus human history began, dominated by the corruption of love into lust and ruled from "the principal seat of depravity."

The Shakers read the Old Testament as an account of the evil effects of lust and God's attempts to show sinners their error. The monstrous consequences of unbridled carnality became so great that God destroyed all humans in the Flood except Noah, who by his five hundred years of sexual continence and obedience to immediate revelation was found worthy to reconstitute the human race.[49] But even his progeny could not free themselves from the curse of lust. The first dispensation of grace in Shaker theology began with Abraham who, according to Joseph Meacham, "was received into covenant relation with God" and obtained a promise of salvation "to be fulfilled in a future time." As a sign of the true nature of sin and as a test of obedience, God commanded Abraham and all his progeny in the Old Covenant to perform circumcision. This act explicitly identified "the principal seat of human depravity" and also was "a sign of the mortification and destruction of the flesh by the gospel in a future day."[50]

God gave a "further measure of light" through the Law of Moses. In this code Israel received a set of outward regulations that established "a line of obedience" whereby they could be blessed. In the Shaker view the Law "pointedly condemned every fleshly gratification" and dealt particularly with the lustful essence of sin. "Almost all the ceremonies and Sacraments of the Law, centered in this very thing, that is, the outward purification and cleansing of the People from the Nature and works of Natural generation."[51] Father Joseph's exegesis of the history of Israel from the Exodus to the Second Temple also emphasized the imperatives of purification and obedience to divine order.

Yet despite observation of the "outward law" and complete faith in the covenant of promise, the Shakers declared, even Noah, Abraham, and Moses, the "elect witnesses" of God, "did not attain that salvation which was promised in the gospel."[52] In order for salvation to become accessible to humans, the Shakers claimed, it was necessary that the means of grace appear immanently in the created order: "As sin entered into the world by the first man's disobedience, and all his posterity, in the same nature of rebellion, continued to follow his example, it required a life and example directly contrary to theirs, in order to their recovery."[53] That "life and example" was provided by the man Jesus, a created dependent being "who took upon him the same nature and enmity, and thereby became united to the fallen race, that he might crucify that nature, and slay the enmity." Though he shared in the carnal body of humans, Jesus was not the product of cursed natural generation. His body and soul were "begotten by the eternal word of the Father, in the Holy Ghost, through the medium of a woman, who with the rest of mankind, was under the law of a corrupt nature." Thus Jesus initiated yet a third dispensation, "an entire new order of things, properly called the adjusting of a new age, or a new creation."[54]

As the offspring of divinity in fleshly form, Jesus enjoyed precisely the same status as did Adam in innocence and was endowed with the same capabilities and purpose. This restored "second Adam" reestablished the union of the human soul with God by obeying the laws that the first Adam had broken. In Shaker theology, Jesus' achievement was to break the influence of sexual attraction and natural generation. "His flesh saw no corruption by reason of sin." By becoming "the first that travelled out of that lost nature," Jesus demonstrated the primacy of the spiritual over the physical. He endured crucifixion and death in order to exhibit "the power of resurrection" over his own purified body. At the same time Jesus also fulfilled all the promises and conditions of the Old Covenant, and with his resurrection restored spiritual life to the souls of those who had lived during the first and second dispensations.[55]

The successful completion of Jesus' ministry ushered in a new dispensation of full salvation for all who followed his model of perfect life. His true disciples received the gift of the Holy Ghost "with which Jesus himself was annointed . . . to lead them to truth, and which brought to their remembrance whatever he had taught them, either by precept or example." The Spirit also brought gifts of tongues, interpretation, prophecy, and healing, and it bound the early church into a perfect spiritual union "of one heart and of one soul." Above all, however, Jesus' disciples were required to destroy their carnal corruption. "All his real followers without exception, took up their cross, and denied themselves of every carnal gratification of the flesh."[56] Salvation was to be obtained only by duplicating the actual achievement of Christ in "travelling through" carnality to activate the pure spiritual nature of human beings.

The few apostles who actually bore the cross of mortification did attain "the resurrection state" in this life. Soon after the death of the apostles, however, a decline began in the primitive church, humanity rejected the true gospel, believers were scattered, and the reign of the Antichrist began. According to the Shakers not all the church was lost in this apostasy. As He had done in the earlier dispensations, God elected a number of witnesses to the truth during the reign of the Antichrist, including "Marcionites, Manicheans, Bogomilians, Cathari, Beghards, Picards, Waldenses, Albigenses, Anabaptists, and Quakers."[57]

The witness of Jesus had been rejected, but "the mystery of God was not finished . . . there was another day, prophesied of, called the second appearing of Christ, or final and last display of God's grace to a lost world."[58] This completion of divine purposes, following the immutable law of complementary gender, was to occur in "the line of the female." "As the order in the foundation of the old creation could not be complete by the first man without the first woman; so the order in the foundation of the new creation could not be complete in the man alone: for the man is not without the woman in the Lord, nor the woman without the man."[59] "Christ" in this theology was manifested in male and female form just as "God" and "Man" had been originally, for by Christ the Shakers understood not a person or a being, but a condition of endowment "with the spiritual unction or anointing power of the Holy Ghost."

The Shakers believed that in the eighteenth century, "the same spirit and word of power, which created man at the beginning—which spake by all the prophets—which dwelt in the man Jesus—was revealed in a woman . . . That woman, who was anointed and chosen of God, to reveal the mystery of iniquity, to stand as the first in her order, to accomplish the purpose of God in the restoration of that which was lost by the transgression of the first woman, and to finish the work of man's final redemption, was ANN LEE."[60] Mother Ann, "the second Eve," initiated the fourth and final dispensation that completed the cycle of history by providing a second efficacious appearance of salvation to parallel the two dispensations of promise under Abraham and Moses. Mother Ann's ministry was of the same order as Jesus', but in one crucial aspect it surpassed his work. By rooting out sin as a human being "conceived in sin, and lost in the fullness of man's fall," she established spiritual dominion over an imperfect body. Jesus had restored spiritual perfection, Mother Ann physical perfection to human nature, thereby completing the reunion of humanity with God.[61]

But even the definitive appearance o Christ in Jesus and in Mother Ann did not create an easy or automatic path to salvation. Jesus had demanded that his followers "undergo the ame sufferings he suffered, and to die the death that he died."[62] Mother Ann taught the same truth. Sinners must "feel tribulation and darkness that they may be humbled" and realize the magnitude of sin. To aid them, the church provided leaders who would hear confession of sins and recommend spiritual remedies. But ultimately salvation depended on each person performing the same "travel" that Jesus and Mother Ann had. "Everyone in order to become children of God," wrote Calvin Green echoing Father Joseph, "must labor out of that nature by which they are separated from God, and then they will be leavened into the nature of Christ, and will be of Christ, and in Christ, as Christ is in God."[63]

Through confession, celibacy, pain, and suffering it was possible, the Shakers affirmed, to join Jesus and Mother Ann in the attainment of sinless perfection through "the power of resurrection." Father Joseph proclaimed:

"When man ceases from man, whose breath is in his nostrils; when he dies to himself and lives to God alone; when he ceases from his own works and does the work of God; when he renounces the will of the flesh, and is subject to the will of the Spirit; then he is raised from a death of sin to a life of righteousness; and this is his resurrection."[64] Proper "travel" restored the Adamic nature of the saints, evidenced by revival of "proper spiritual sensations" and triumph over sins of mind and body. Those who did not complete their travel in this life would attain resurrection after death "according to their faith and order." The souls of the dead who were "elect witnesses" during the period of the Antichrist were restored to union with God by Mother Ann, just as those who had believed in the covenant of promise had been raised to heaven by Jesus at his resurrection.

Thus Jesus and Mother Ann ruled a spiritual order that was accessible to human beings and to the souls of the dead. On earth, the cosmic governance of these "first parents" was mirrored in the organization of the true church into gospel order. On the metaphysical plane, the salvation of the souls of the dead continued as Jesus and Mother Ann exercised the power of resurrection over those who had rejected the gospel while alive. Ultimately, the Shakers believed, all human souls would be restored to their original spiritual nature through this gradual working out of salvation in heaven and on earth. Jesus and Mother Ann would finally redeem all souls of previous dispensations, and the millennial church would become a "blessing to all the nations" as the medium for salvation in the Last Days. The ultimate vision of Shakerism was of a universal kingdom of spiritual beings reunited with the power and wisdom of the Creator, ruled jointly by Jesus and Mother Ann, and differentiated into male and female hierarchies of faith and order. This spiritual kingdom was the new creation, the messianic banquet, the actualization of God's orignal intention in the old creation, "the perfect day" of eternal union and order in the Spirit.

The Shakers, like the Freewill Baptists and Universalists, employed the history of redemption as the basic metaphor of their religious thought. In the Shaker variant, the principal doctrines of sexual sin, perfectionism, and dual hierarchy were elaborated through a dispensational scheme that linked Believers with the entire cosmic process. Understanding themselves to be at the end of time, the Shakers surveyed the dispensations and moral teaching of salvation history from the perspective of perfect beings restored to the Adamic state through their union with Jesus and Mother Ann.

Sectarian theology constitutes an important and little-studied episode in the evolution of New England religious thought. It was a late-blooming variety of theological discourse engendered by the radical wing of the Great Awakening. Sectarian thought was rooted not in the sophisticated philosophic disputations of Evangelical Calvinism and Arminianism, but in the oral tradition of the history of redemption preached by Anglo-American itinerants since the 1730s. The relationship of the sects to Whitefield was particularly intimate and substantive. Ann Lee, Benjamin Randel, and John Murray were all at one time converts or adherents of the Grand Itinerant. Joseph Meacham, Caleb Rich, Hosea Ballou, Elhanan Winchester, and Henry Alline were products of Whitefield's Radical Evangelical constituency. In the New Light Stir, these sectarian prophets broke up the Radical Evangelical consensus on Calvinism. They and their followers seized on the lineaments of the history of redemption to provide a schema for their new revelations and spiritual exegesis of scripture. After a generation of intense oral development, these salvation narratives emerged as a family of indigenous theologies distinctive in their spiritualism and perfectionism.

The characteristics of these new theologies may be summarized around the four major episodes of the history of redemption: creation, fall, atonement, and regeneration. First, the sectarians challenged the judgmental and arbitrary God of Calvinism, defining the Deity as immutable, benevolent, and bound by natural law. Such a God, they taught, could have created the universe only for a good purpose, which was embodied in a spiritual and natural cosmos governed by absolute and benign laws. Second, each sect formulated an anthropology in which humans were originally created as spiritual minds and bodies in perfect union with God. The amalgamation of animal nature with spiritual essence produced inherent instability in the human condition that eventuated in the Fall. But in sectarian theology God issued no predestinating decrees of eternal damnation, nor were Adam and Eve guilty of infinite genetic sin. Freewill Baptists, Universalists, and Shakers all held a doctrine of the fortunate fall that denied Calvinist innate depravity. Whether defined as finite, forgiven, or surmountable, original sin in sectarian theology was limited in its effect, leaving human beings innocent of genetic penalty or able to overcome its consequences in this life.

The sectarian economy of grace concentrated therefore more on committed volitional sin than on original sin. This orientation placed the doctrine of the Atonement in a new context. The Christ of sectarian theology was not an expiational sacrifice nor were the effects of the Atonement limited. Rather, Christ was preeminently the Restorer of spiritual essence to humans, the Second Adam whose example again made the perfections of the created state available to all. Shakers and Universalists removed Christ from the Godhead altogether; Freewill Baptists divided the Atonement into separate modes for original and volitional sin and applied its effects to all souls. The sectarians underscored the spiritual solidarity of Christ with humans and pointed to Christ's wisdom, goodwill, or life — rather than sacrifice — as the source of efficacious spiritual power.[*]

Finally, the sectarians rejected Calvinist ideas of the regenerate state. The liabilities of sin and physical temptation, they claimed, could be overcome in this life. Perfection not only was possible, it was the reasonable and revealed terminus of human existence. Freewill Baptists defined the regenerate state largely in moral terms; for Universalists it consisted in the possesion of holy wisdom; and Shakers pursued spiritual and physical perfection through charismatic gifts and ascetic discipline. But the sects agreed on the fundamental position that the very Spirit of God had removed the scales of carnal blindness from their eyes and revealed new truth that irrevocably altered human destiny. This new gospel, communicated to all souls by the Holy Spirit, empowered humans to reclaim their Adamic legacy, to live a life of perfect love and union, and to experience here and now "the glorious liberty of the sons of God."

9

The Language of the Soul

The New England sects completed their construction of religious cultures by creating new systems of ritual expression. The Radical Evangelical tradition mandated only a limited range of liturgical actions: scripture teaching, exhortation, prayer, praise, and the ordinances of baptism, the Lord's Supper, and ordination. The sects preserved much of this tradition, but they also made major innovations, particularly with respect to the ordinances. The Freewill Baptists practiced foot-washing as an ordinance, claiming scriptural authority from John 13:1-20 and regarding the rite as an act of apostolic humility and union. Universalists abandoned all liturgical standards, believing the ordinances simply to be educational devices for the exercise of the enlightened mind, subject to personal discretion in gospel liberty. The Shakers rejected the ordinances altogether as irrelevant to souls already in "the resurrection state." Rather they drew on the example of Mother Ann, the instruction of Father Joseph, and biblical argument from both Testaments to create a unique form of liturgical dance that expressed the spirituality and ascetic discipline of the sect.[1]

Each of these reforms occurred early in sectarian development and were part of the movements' initial self-identification. By 1800, however, new liturgical functions were demanded by the increasingly complex social and intellectual structures of the sects. Along with a measure of success and stability had come needs for uniformity and a convincing defense of sectarian peculiarities. Sheer size and geographical scope mandated the standardization of worship, the primal act of sectarian identity. The rise of systematic theologies placed a burden of doctrinal orthodoxy on sectarians that could best be borne through the collective experience of worship. And when the

Second Great Awakening presented the sects with heightened demands for public articulation of their faith, they turned especially to hymnody to create a comprehensive symbolic and ritual vocabulary.

In Radical Evangelical tradition the hymn was understood as the language of the regenerate soul, the inevitable burst of praise issuing from redeemed intelligent creatures to their Creator. It was Isaac Watts, the great English Independent hymnist, who set the pattern for Evangelical hymnody with his confessional and meditative verse of the early eighteenth century. After 1735 a new generation of poets including Charles Wesley, Phillip Doddridge, Samuel Stennett, Augustus Toplady, Anne Steele, John Newton, and William Cowper translated the imperatives of the New Birth into a pietistic poetic saturated with emotion, biblical metaphor, and theological implication.[2]

In New England, Congregationalists and Baptists imitated this style of hymnic composition. Typical of indigenous verse was the hymn "O, When Shall I See Jesus," written about 1805 by John Leland, a Baptist elder at Cheshire, Massachusetts. The composition, among the most popular American hymns of the early nineteenth century, exemplified the distinctive Evangelical blending of emotion, otherworldliness, militancy, biblicism, and millennial expectation.

> O when shall I see Jesus and dwell with him above,
> And from the flowing fountain drink everlasting love?
> When shall I be delivered from this vain world of sin,
> And with my blessed Jesus drink endless pleasures in?
>
> Whene'er you meet with troubles and trials upon your way,
> Then cast your cares on Jesus and don't forget to pray.
> Gird on the gospel armor of faith and hope and love,
> And when the combat's ended, He'll carry you above.
>
> Our eyes shall then with rapture, the Saviour's face behold;
> Our feet, no more diverted, shall walk the streets of gold,
> Our ears shall hear with transport the hosts celestial sing;
> Our tongues shall chant the glories of our immortal King.[3]

Hymnody occupied a central place in the development of the Evangelical tradition. Isaac Watts conceived his spiritual songs as edifying aids to private meditation. Many ministers and lay people in New England followed his example, noting in diaries and memoirs their versed renderings of "the beauty of holiness" in their souls. George Whitefield and the Wesleys transformed the spiritual song into performative language, using hymns as a strategic element in revivalism.[4] In the Great Awakening and all subsequent revivals, public song became a principal medium of spiritual invocation and a badge of regeneration. In the schismatic aftermath of the Great Awakening, hymnody took on a more partisan character. Competing itinerants and ecclesiastical parties published hymnals each designed, as John

Wesley put it, to be "a little body of practical and experimental divinity."[5]

In New England, hymn singing in worship itself became a hotly debated issue as Evangelicals sought to enliven the spirit of local congregations by including "Watts and select" hymns in the order of service. By 1770 the new hymnody had begun to replace the Psalter in many churches. This development in turn gave impetus to musical experimentation in the form of congregational part singing and new tunes for the new texts. The years between 1775 and 1815 were "the golden age" of New England hymnody, during which William Billings, Jeremiah Ingalls, Daniel Read, and other Yankee singing masters developed a vigorous indigenous musical style based on folk and popular tunes and simple choral effects.[6]

By 1800 hymnody had become a popular, potent, and complex dimension of Evangelical worship, rivaled in importance only by preaching. Indeed it could be argued that hymnody was liturgically more essential to the Evangelical manner. For whereas prayer and preaching were matters of extemporaneous spiritual effusion by congregational leaders, hymnody was fixed in form, a body of oral and written tradition that provided regularity and group participation in an otherwise passive ritual mode. More than any other medium, hymnody constructed a common symbolic language for Evangelicalism. Whether employed as a device in private meditation, as a vehicle for family devotions, or as a unifying frame for congregational worship, hymnody supplied an indispensable structure for the articulation of Evangelical faith.

The New England sects were inevitably informed by this habit of hymn writing and singing. From the beginning the sects sang their new faiths and did so within the norms of Evangelical style. The Freewill Baptists and Universalists embraced the musical style of the Yankee singing masters, while the Shakers produced an enormous repertory of original spiritual songs and hymn tunes. The sects' hymnody quickly developed into nothing less than the expression of their entire religious culture: spiritual experience, evangelism, church order, doctrine, and worship. In the early nineteenth century the Freewill Baptists, Universalists, and Shakers each produced a standard volume of hymns, a comprehensive body of ritual texts that rehearsed and objectified sectarian identity through a distinctive sacred language.

Freewill Baptists began composing their own hymns as soon as the movement emerged from the New Light Stir. The Freewill church records kept by Benjamin Randel from 1779 on were punctuated with short verses composed at Monthly, Quarterly, and Yearly Meetings and sung on the spot. In 1783 Randel came under the influence of Henry Alline's hymnic style. Alline had published "one little Pamphlet containing twenty-two of his short Hymns" sometime before 1782. A much larger collection titled *Hymns and Spiritual Songs* appeared posthumously at Boston in 1786. Second and third editions, enlarged and edited by Randel, were published by the Freewill Baptists in 1795 and 1797. Alline's output of 488 hymns easily claimed for him the title of "most prolific American hymn writer of his day" and left a lasting mark on Freewill hymnody.[7]

After Randel's death in 1808, the Freewill Baptists apparently explored a wide range of Congregationalist, Baptist, and Methodist hymnody. But the definitive hymnal of the sect, John Buzzell's *Psalms, Hymns, and Spiritual Songs,* did not appear until 1823. Buzzell's collection was an eclectic grouping of lyrics drawn almost entirely from Evangelical tradition. The proximity of Freewill song to Evangelical roots was indicated by the inclusion of many hymns by Watts, Doddridge, Steele, and Toplady. Buzzell, however, also acknowledged the esoteric spirituality of the sect by adding verses from the Moravian Joseph Hart, the Swedenborgian Joseph Proud, and Henry Alline. Alline was Buzzell's favorite contemporary author, appearing in the collection more often than any poet except Watts. *Psalms, Hymns, and Spiritual Songs* also contained roughly thirty-five hymns written by Freewill clergy and laity, most of them attributable to Randel or Buzzell.[8]

Freewill Baptist hymnody gave liturgical expression to all dimensions of the movement's religious culture. Especially prominent were hymns of origin and doctrinal peculiarity. Freewill Baptists sang a song that aggressively proclaimed their Radical Evangelical beginnings. "Come all who are New-Lights indeed, / Who are from sin and bondage freed; / From Egypt's land we've took our flight, / For God has giv'n us a New-Light." The hymn also proclaimed militancy and otherworldliness in the face of cultural dispossession: "Though by the world we are disdain'd, / And have our names cast out by men; / Yet Christ our captain for us fights, / Nor death, nor hell, can hurt New-Lights." The hymn concluded with a confident assertion of God's protection of the sect: "Thus guarded by the Lord we stand, / Safe in the hollow of his hand; / Nor do we scorn the New-Light's name, / The saints are all New-Lights, Amen."[9] Such hymns stated the ecclesiastical and social rootage of the Freewill community. They functioned as statements of public identity, anthems calling worshipers to awareness of their particular background and pietistic style.

Doctrine also received extensive hymnic treatment. The poems of Henry Alline were particularly effective expressions of the drama of free will and free grace. For example, one of his most popular hymns presented the gospel through a dramatic personification of Christ's call to sinners: "Amazing sight: The savior stands, / And knocks at every door; / Ten thousand blessings in his hands, / For to supply the poor." Alline explicitly stated the doctrine of universal atonement from the infinity of God's love in these words of Christ; "Not to condemn your guilty race, / Have I in judgment come; / But to display unbounded grace, / And bring lost sinners home." The hymn ended with an evangelistic appeal that stressed the importance of free will: "Though long you have his grace abus'd, / And all his calls of love refus'd; / Yet even now, he will forgive, / O sinners, hear his voice and live."[10]

The most eloquent and intense Freewill hymns, however, were those that recalled personal religious experience. Hymnists were especially concerned with recreating in poetic terms the core experiences of conversion and sanctification. John Buzzell's 1812 hymn is an exemplary spiritual autobiography of a Freewill Baptist:

> Once I was going on in sin,
> All filled with pride and unbelief!
> Refus'd to let the Savior in,
> And often did his spirit grieve.
>
> But O! At length, my state I saw,
> And felt a load of guilt within;
> I found I'd broke God's righteous law,
> And lay expos'd to hell by sin.
>
> At last I smote upon my breast,
> And did to God for mercy cry;
> And soon he answered my request,
> I found his pardoning mercy nigh.
>
> From dark to light, from hate to love,
> From death to life, he rais'd my soul;
> He placed my mind on things above,
> And all the powers of sin controll'd.[11]

Buzzell's poem followed the classic Freewill morphology of conversion, moving from worldliness to conviction, from conviction to conversion, and from conversion to sanctification. The Whitefieldian rhetoric of the narrative line underscored essential Freewill beliefs in human ability and perfectionism while sustaining the emotional intensity of the converison experience.

The Freewill Baptist model of Christian life also acknowledged backsliding and the struggle to maintain perfection, giving rise to a genre of penitential hymns. A song titled "Ask, and It Shall Be Given You" from *Psalms, Hymns, and Spiritual Songs* presented this more somber experience of the saint in sin: "My soul, take courage from the Lord; / Believe and plead his holy word; / To him alone do thou complain, / Nor shalt thou seek his face in vain." In response to backsliding, the hymn invoked the Freewill theology of redemption as mutual commitment between believer and divinity: "Faithful, Jehovah must remain." The saint, therefore, should "pray and wait at mercy's door" for spiritual power to overcome sin and persevere in the knowledge that "God will explain" the mysteries of sin at the Last Judgment.[12]

The most extreme sort of experiential poetry in the Freewill tradition depicted the rapt contemplation of Christ by the converted soul. Benjamin

Randel's hymns focused on this dimension of spirituality, particularly the soul's "submission to Christ" and its wondering encounter with love.

> O Jesus, my saviour, to thee I submit,
> With joy and thanksgiving fall down at thy feet;
> In sacrifice offer my soul flesh and blood,
> Thou art my redeemer, my Lord, and my God.
>
> I love thee, I love thee, I love thee, my love;
> I love thee, my Saviour, I love thee, my dove;
> I love thee, I love thee, and that thou dost know;
> But how much I love thee I never shall show.
>
> All human expressions are empty and vain,
> They cannot unriddle this heavenly flame;
> I'm sure if the tongue of an angel were mine,
> I could not this mystery completely define.[13]

The overwhelming emotional and sensual impact of Freewill conversion was nowhere better expressed than in this hymn. The poem moves from the conscious act of voluntary submission to Christ to the explication of the obedient soul's experience of love, joy, pleasure, and praise so transporting that even speech fails to describe it. The hymn is a perfect verbalization of the elevated religious affections that were the foundation of Freewill faith.

Of no less importance to the sect's hymnody were songs of church order and gospel union. Another of Randel's hymns identified love as the unifying source of sectarian life: "Love, love, pure love fulfills the law, / Love purifies the heart; / Love will us into union draw; / Love will not let us part." For Randel, the bond of mutual spiritual affection was the hallmark of Christian community — "In love, O! be entire."[14] Freewill lyrics also depicted gospel union through biblical images, especially Paul's metaphor of the church as the body of Christ: "When joined to thee, our vital head, / Our virtues grow and thrive; / From thee divided, each is dead, / Though it may seem alive." Through spiritual union, in Christ, "The body's one in mutual love, / And thou our common Lord."[15]

The culminating expression of collective sacred experience, however, appeared in hymns for beginning and ending worship and for special ritual occasions. These lyrics articulated the status of believers as the angelic choir praising God or as saints engaged in apostolic imitation. In baptismal hymns, the most important liturgical verse of the Freewill Baptists, the act of immersion became charged with experiential, doctrinal, and social meanings. In a hymnic treatment probably written by Randel, baptism became a sacred mimetic action by the pilgrim community in compliance with Christ's explicit command.

> In pleasure sweet, here we do meet,
>   Down by the water side,
> And here we stand, by Christ's command,

> To wait upon his bride.
>
> Here we do bid the world, "farewell,"
> To practice his command,
> It is the road that leads to God,
> The way to Canaan's land.

The hymn then abruptly shifts focus to the unconverted who are witnessing the baptism and urges them to join the apostolic life: "Come sinners, all, obey the call, / 'Repent and be baptiz'd,' / Forsake your sins, and follow him, / Till you in glory rise." The pilgrim motif returns to reiterate the church's testimony of faith and life-style. "We've found the road that leads to God, / The way of holiness; / We'll follow him, where he has been, / For all his paths are peace."[16]

Freewill Baptist hymnody was the least developed sacred song of the New England sects. Yet the works of Alline, Randel, and Buzzell succeeded in sketching the outlines of a systematic ritual language for the movement. *Psalms, Hymns, and Spiritual Songs* provided a detailed interpretation of Freewill origin, belief, evangelism, church order, and liturgical practice through the medium of the sung word. The achievement of such a hymnody reflected not only the maturation of the Freewill Baptists as a religious culture but also the centrality of hymnic expression in maintaining and transmitting that new religion.

The earliest authorized Universalist hymnal was *Hymns Composed by Different Authors,* prepared at the request of the New England General Convention and published in 1808. During the late eighteenth century New England Universalists had sung from James and John Relly's popular *Christian Hymns, Poems, and Spiritual Songs* and from Silas Ballou's *New Hymns on Various Subjects,* the first original American Universalist hymnal. But *Hymns Composed by Different Authors* was the definitive expression of rural Universalist hymnody. The book was planned as a collection of Evangelical hymns appropriate to Universalist belief and practice. But the hymnal committee, comprising Hosea Ballou, Abner Kneeland, and Edward Turner, determined that Evangelical hymnody, especially the lyrics of Watts, was too pervasively Calvinist for use in Universalist congregations. "Dr. Isaac Watts," they wrote in the preface of *Hymns Composed by Different Authors,* "has, in almost every instance extended the idea of punishment of sin infinitely beyond the design of the inspired authors; and has thereby sorely wounded the divine theme of devotional Psalmody."[17] They decided instead to compose an original hymnal, incorporating into it only some of Silas Ballou's poems written in 1785. The result was a hymnal uneven in quality and derivative in form, but quite comprehensive in its articulation of rural Universalism.

Hymns Composed by Different Authors contained several poems that attacked religious "superstition" and viewed the rise of Universalism as a historic breakthrough to the sacred. Hosea Ballou's "Errors Detected" invited singers to reflect on the doctrinal follies of the past. "Turn ye the page of hist'ry o'er, / Learn all the wisdom of the world; / Their present creeds and those before, / Are all in endless error hurl'd." Calvinism was singled out for several more stanzas of polemic: "To bound the God of boundless grace, / Has been the aim of Pharisees; / Arm God against the human race, / Measure and fix his firm decrees." The hymn concluded with an exhortation that identified the gospel of universal salvation as the true revelation of God.[18]

Doctrinal hymns abounded in the 1808 collection. Typically these lyrics were far more propositional and systemic in tone than their Freewill parallels. Universalist emphasis on the rational consistency of doctrine carried over into their hymnody, producing efforts like Ballou's "God, in Each Attribute, Is Love."

> God, in each attribute, is love;
>   Justice and mercy, too,
> By its eternal goodness move,
>   And have no other view.
>
> Knowledge and wisdom both agree,
>   In all its gracious plan,
> To set from death, and bondage free,
>   The helpless creature, man.[19]

Even homiletic tactics of rhetorical question, paradox, and satire were included in Universalist doctrinal hymns. Abner Kneeland's rhymed explanation of the finitude of sin and the fortunate fall is representative of this sort of hymnic theologizing.

> What is the cause of moral death?
>   Of misery and pain?
> Is it not sin, which only hath
>   Rewards of guilt and shame?
>
> But what is sin? — my soul inquires,
>   Producing all this wo?
> Is it not want of holiness?
>   O tell me! you that know.
>
> I next inquire, can God produce
>   An end without a mean?
> Or can his nature, which is love,
>   Join in effect with sin?
>
> If not — can God admit of pain,
>   Without th' immediate cause?
> Or will he say that man's to blame,
>   Obeying nature's laws?[20]

This rehearsal of Universalist arguments against Calvinism concluded with Kneeland's affirmation of God's redemptive purpose in all things. "O now the mystery I see —/ God all for good controls;/ The guilt in us, in him may be/ Designed for good of souls."

Despite the crude didactic qualities of such verse, Universalist hymnists were capable of more evocative poetry for evangelistic purposes. Kneeland's "Invitation to the Gospel," for example, employed the metaphor of the messianic banquet or "gospel feast" in a sensuous plea to the sinner.

> Hear ye that starve for food,
> By feeding on the wind,
> Or vainly strive with earthly good,
> To fill an empty mind.
>
> The Lord of love has made,
> A soul reviving feast,
> And lets the world, of every grade,
> To rich provision taste.[21]

Even more intense and appealing was Hosea Ballou's rendering of the biblical image of Christ at the door. "Jesus is knocking at the door,/ His locks are wet with dew;/ He brings salvation to the poor;/ Sinners, there's life for you."[22]

Universalism's Evangelical background manifested itself most clearly in songs of spiritual autobiography. Hosea Ballou's working of the symbol of light into a rousing hymn of personal conversion echoes the conversionist rhetoric of Watts:

> I shall no more in darkness roam,
> Nor walk in gloomy night;
> The Lord my God, he makes my noon,
> And Jesus is my Light!
>
> What great deliverance I have found,
> 'Twas by Jehovah's might;
> He hath my soul with mercy crowned,
> And JESUS is my Light!
>
> No more shall doubts and darkness rise,
> To put my hope to flight;
> The Lord hath opened both my eyes,
> And JESUS is my Light![23]

In Universalist as in Freewill hymnody, this type of exalted witness accompanied other more penitential and devotional meditations on the soul's labor against temptation. Abner Kneeland's lines on 1 Corinthians 9:27, titled "I Keep My Body Under," spoke of the need for saintly discipline. "My body under I must keep,/ Subjected to my mind;/ Lest, like a lost and wand'ring sheep,/ Destruction's road I find." Kneeland's asceticism was essentially intellectual; the rationality of divine truth was for him the decisive element in religious discipline: "My railing passions, lust, and pride,/ To reason must resign;/ My carnal mind must be deny'd,/ If I the truth would find."[24]

In the realm of church order and community life, Universalist hymnists celebrated the benefits of gospel liberty and spiritual union. One of the sect's earliest social hymns was Silas Ballou's "Love and Harmony," composed in 1785 and reprinted in *Hymns Composed of Different Authors.*

> How pleasing is the lovely sight!
> O, how it does my soul delight!
> To see the sons of light agree,
> And live in social harmony!
>
> Faith is thy gift, almighty Lord,
> From faith in thy sure promis'd word,
> And from the hope of heaven'ly things,
> This social love and union springs.[25]

In "The Union of Souls," Hosea Ballou substituted his characteristically sensuous rhetoric for his cousin Silas's more restrained encomiums to the effects of community: "So th' honey of love in the mind/ Makes it flow in desires far abroad;/ 'Till to others, by love, it is join'd,/ In its journey of faith to its God."[26]

Universalists, like other sectarians, composed hymns for specific occasions of worship. Lacking a sacramental norm or a dramatic initiation like baptism, Universalists focused on singing itself as a subject for liturgical hymns. Their favorite image was the classic Christian one of the angelic choir. In Kneeland's lyric "Heavenly Joy on Earth" the very act of singing became both the manifestation of corporate religious identity and a medium for the reception of sacred knowledge.

> Come all ye saints, who love the Lord,
> With melody divine,
> Tune every harp in sweet accord,
> And all in concert join.
>
> Proclaim abroad your sacred joy,
> To earth's remotest bounds;
> In heavenly notes, your tongues employ.
> In symphony of sounds.
>
> Let ev'ry doubt and slavish fear,
> Be banished from the mind;
> While joyful songs our spirits cheer,
> We'll trust the Lord is kind.[27]

Universalist hymnody, like its Freewill Baptist counterpart, performed a crucial role in providing symbolic definition for an emerging religious culture. Distinctive elements of Universalism, particularly its theological notions, rationalistic style, and libertarian morality, found a badly needed normative statement through the new hymnody. To a sect imbued with an individualism of anarchistic proportions and distrustful of the speculative niceties of even its own theologians, the creation of a systematic oral tradition through sacred song was indispensable. At the same time, hill country Universalists preserved and developed the Evangelical style of hymn writing that was their New Light heritage. In songs of conversion, testimony, community, and praise Universalist hymnists imitated and modified the spiritual rhetoric of Watts and Wesley, revealing in form and content the synthesis of Evangelical tradition and theological radicalism that defined their religious identity.

Music and singing were central elements of Shaker worship from the earliest days. Mother Ann and the Elders sang tunes that were unworded or syllabic as part of the improvised charismatic worship at Niskeyuna. Father Joseph introduced "solemn songs" and "laboring songs" at New Lebanon. The former were wordless tunes sung in worship to attain spiritual union and the latter, wordless tunes for the performance of "the square order shuffle," the first regular form of Shaker dance, which facilitated charismatic states and symbolized the union of the Believers. A substantial body of Shaker spiritual ballads had also been composed by Believers before 1800. But the full flowering of Shaker hymnody began only with the increased zeal and mission of the Second Great Awakening and the perceived need for doctrinal clarification and devotional discipline that accompanied the sect's expansion after 1805. The tempo of Shaker singing increased to accommodate the faster "skipping manner" of dance that appeared first in the western mission. Mother Lucy introduced mimetic gestures to Shaker songs and marching into the dance repertory. The habit of composing lyrics and tunes spread throughout the New England societies.

In this context the first published Shaker hymnal, *Millennial Praises*, appeared at Hancock, Massachusetts, in 1812. The collection, probably compiled by Seth Youngs Wells of New Lebanon, contained 140 hymns for the opening and closing of worship "composed by Believers of different places, and which have met the general approbation of the Ministry and Elders of the church." The preface to *Millennial Praises* explained the significance of hymnody for the Shakers. In singing, "true Believers can feel their spirits assimilated to saints and angels in the world of spirits, where the highest praise and thanksgiving is poured forth in the blessed gift of song." Precisely because it was a charismatic experience, "the gift of song" was regarded by the Shakers as developmental. Hymns "must be limited to the period of their usefulness: for no gift or order of God can be binding on Believers for a longer term of time than it can be profitable to their travel in the gospel." Thus *Millennial Praises* was designed as a compendium of hymnody "conformable to the present faith and testimony of Believers," for the purpose of sharing "the gift of song" in common and inspiring further composition of hymns and tunes. As the first printed hymnal, however, it also served as a public standard for a hymnic expression; and in its comprehensive treatment of Shaker belief and practice it provided a guidebook in song to classic Shakerism.[28]

Like the other New England sects, Shakers produced a hymnody expressive of Evangelical tradition and radical innovation. Poetically the Shakers placed their history in a more millennial framework than the Freewill Baptists or Universalists. One of the most striking of such hymns, titled simply "The Shakers," played on the sect's name to call up an image from the Book of Revelation of the saved remnant at the dawn of the apocalypse.

> Now the flame begins to run,
> Now the shaking is begun;
> He that gave creation birth,
> Shakes the heavens and the earth.
>
> We'll be shaken to and fro,
> Till we let old Adam go;
> When our souls are born again,
> We unshaken all remain.
>
> Some will boldly try to stand,
> But the Lord will shake the Land;
> Sinners who shall dare rebel,
> Will be shaken into hell.[29]

More historically oriented was "Christ's Second Appearance," a verse from New Gloucester, Maine, that recounted the early New England career of the sect.

> With Mother, the Elders like angels did stand,
> With her crossed the ocean, and came to this land,
> They gave us the gospel, which stained our pride,
> And for us those saviours all suffered and died.
>
> Then our Father Joseph, whom God did prepare,
> By faith and obedience became the true heir.
> Our Blessed Mother's mantle did cover his soul,
> And a faithful elder he was to the whole.
>
> Then our Mother Lucy who now is our guard,
> Became a true helper to him in the Lord.
> A Father and Mother we children have found,
> From fleshly relation our souls they unbound.[30]

Doctrinal hymns played a prominent role in Shaker hymnody. The intensity of Shaker worship and dance sustained hymns of exceptional length, permitting poets to explicate virtually the entire Shaker history of redemption. One such verse, from *Millennial Praises,* "The Restoration," described Mother Ann's renewal of the paradise state among Believers. "The first Eve was tempted and led into sin,/ The second, more faithful, was led out again;/ With firm resolution, (her word was a sword)/ She fought her way through, and creation restor'd." The hymn pointed out that through Mother Ann humans are "made free from the curse" of original sin, thus "Adam's probation is brought down to us." The Shaker hymnist pressed the necessity of reversing Adam's choice in these latter days. "Since such a probation is given to all,/ Let none cast reflection on old Adam's fall;/ To chuse or refuse is now free for each one,/ And old Adam's trial no mortal can shun."[31]

Despite the erratic evangelism of the sect, a number of invitation hymns were produced before 1815. One particularly effective song was a variant of Joseph Hart's popular lyric "Come, Ye Sinners, Poor and Needy." This version was being used in the New England societies when *Millennial Praises* was published. It gives clear voice to Shakerism's ascetic millennialism:

> Come ye sinners poor and needy,
>   Try the cross as we have done.
> You will find the yoke is easy,
>   If you'll only put it on.
>
> But if you pursue your pleasure,
>   Till the spirit's grieved away,
> You will find you'll have no treasure,
>   That will stand the judgment day.[32]

In these hymns of origin, belief, and evangelism the Shakers exhibited their pervasive concern with concrete detail and personal experience in presenting their gospel. The most notable expressions of Shaker emotionalism, however, occurred in devotional and meditational lyrics. A manuscript hymn composed around 1805 called "Fervent Meditation" represented the interior reflection of the Shaker convert. "I love thee, I thank thee, my saviour my King,/ I bless thee, and now I thy praises will sing,/ I love the pure gospel, and I bless the day,/ My soul was obedient to this holy way." The hymn then turned to the subject of the holy community: "I'll walk with thy people the straight narrow road/ That leads me to peace, joy, and comfort in God." Its climax was a vision of Shakerism's worldwide triumph. "Thro the male and the female united in one,/ Shall the glory of God and his kingdom be known,/ And the new creation spread over the earth."[33]

More indicative of ecstatic Shaker contemplation is "My Feelings" from *Millennial Praises*. The hymn is essentially a litany of spiritual virtues and desiderata. The cumulative effect renders an epitome of Shaker perfectionism.

> How joyful, how thankful, how loving I feel,
> And still I want more love, yes more love and zeal:
> I want my love perfect, I want my love pure,
> That I may with patience all things well endure.
>
> I want to feel little, more simple, more mild,
> More like our blest parents, and more like a child,
> More thankful, more humble, more lowly in mind,
> More watchful, more prayerful, more loving and kind.
>
> In duty enduring, in bearing believe,
> Forgiving if any my spirit should grieve:
> Remembering at all times as Mother did say,
> To set out anew and begin evry day.[34]

The crucial importance of gospel order in Shakerism made songs of collective experience a much-worked hymnic genre. Several poems in *Millennial Praises* expressed the ideal of loving union. "See beauty, love, and union join/ and form a triple band:/ May all these graces in us shine,/ and lead us hand in hand."[35] But beyond these general calls to union, Shakers articulated their central concept of "spiritual relation" as the model for the community of saints. The hymn titled "Natural and Spiritual Relations" asserted the ultimacy of the Shaker family in this world and the next.

> To live in obedience is heaven's employ,
> And faithful believers will count it their joy,
> To honor their parents, on whom they depend,
> With filial affection that never can end:
>
> Come let us, dear brethren, our privilege prize,
> And kind loving sister, be faithful and wise;
> How precious our calling: How glorious the day;
> What blessings are given to those who obey:
>
> Since the gospel relations encircle us round,
> Let praise and thanksgiving forever abound;
> Our humble dependence can never decrease,
> And feelings of gratitude never will cease;
>
> When heavens of heavens shall be our abode,
> And all our relations shall center on God,
> While ages of ages continue to roll,
> Eternal thanksgiving will live in the soul.[36]

Shaker liturgical hymnody took special note, of course, of sacred dance. To Shakers, dancing and singing were manifestations of the holy: "For dancing is a sweet employ,/ It fills the soul with heavenly joy,/ It makes our love and union flow,/ While round and round and round we go."[37] A pre-1800 manuscript hymn from New Gloucester, Maine, expressed the same attitude that song and dance were external responses to the ecstatic internal music of the sanctified soul.

> Let music rowl through every soul,
> And everyone that hears the sound,
> With heart and hand may join the band,
> And let their voices echo round.
>
> Let none refuse, but all may chuse,
> A saviour now in Zion stands:
> Now in this day, all who obey
> May shout and dance and clap their hands.[38]

Shaker liturgical hymnody reached the same culminating image as did Freewill Baptist and Universalist songs of worship, namely the angelic choir. In Shaker hymns, Believers were preeminently those souls who would reign eternally with God in heaven. At the same time through acts of worship they already experienced on earth a full measure of heavenly bliss. Thus, symbolically, as they sang and danced like angels, they became more angelic in spirit and emotion. This combination of identity and experience found definitive expression in the Shaker hymn "The Joyful Worship," in which song and dance were portrayed as the medium and type of angelic praise:

> Come let our worship now begin,
> And though we dance, rejoice, and sing,
> Tis all in praise of Zion's king,
> For grace we have received.
>
> We love to sing and dance we will,
> Because we surely surely feel,
> It does our thankful spirits fill
> With heavenly joy and pleasure.
>
> Then let our love and zeal increase,
> And let us dance in love and peace,
> And sing that song which cannot cease,
> We shall be saved forever.[39]

Each of the New England folk religions thus created a hymnody that preserved the major stylistic characteristics of Evangelical sacred song yet employed that style toward distinctively sectarian purposes. The sects used the sensuous imagery, subjectivism, and bibilical paraphrase of Evangelical hymnody to create songs for their religious life-styles. The hymn became an indispensable medium for sectarian self-expression and self-reflection. Through hymns, sectarian congregations shared collective experiences and individuals articulated their faith. Hymn writing in the sects had begun as a spontaneous mode of ordering the disarray of intense, even ecstatic worship. But by 1815 the composition of sacred poetry had become a mental habit of sectarians lay and ordained, and in the publication of formal hymnals the folk religions promulgated detailed symbolizations of all aspects of their identity and experience.

The creation of a public hymnody was a crucial step in the shaping of New England folk religion. It marked the full emergence of sectarian self-awareness by providing an objective, uniform, and replicable set of symbols consciously designed to express collective identity and experience. Virtually no aspect of religious life was left untouched by hymnic treatment. Sectarian history, evangelism, and the history of redemption — the major elements of the sects' public identity — were given versed form to be sung by congregations of the faithful in worship. Conversion, the life of holy community, and worship itself also found symbolic expression in sectarian hymns of experience. Hymnody gave each sect a medium through which to render its distinctive beliefs, practices, and institutions into objective symbolic form.

The medium itself was part of the Evangelical heritage shared by all sects, and the folk religions did not stray far from the poetic style of the Evangelical hymnists. Sectarian hymns were for the most part derivative and imitative; the sects did not contribute anything to poetic art by their hymns. Their creativity lay in giving the hymn new content, based on their distinctive religiousness. As that religiousness developed clear-cut social forms and theological claims, the sects came to possess unique vocabularies and characteristic modes of reflection. It was these vocabularies and intellectual styles, expressive of sectarian spirituality, social design, and theology, that filled the Evangelical lyric with enough new content to create new languages of the soul.

Conclusion

A Revolution of the Spirit

The radical sects of Revolutionary New England unleashed a potent and permanent force in the history of American civilization, the creation of indigenous religious cultures. That force first took shape in the Great Awakening which, from the perspective of the study, represents British North America's initial break with Old World religious traditions. The consequence of the Great Awakening in New England and elsewhere was the reorientation of religious organizations and popular piety away from received forms and scholastic interpretation toward a demand for indubitable personal religious experience and a concomitant ecclesiastical order grounded in the sharing and amplification of that experience among members. Before the Revolution, however, this reorientation remained muted and ambiguous. Despite the schism of Congregationalism, the objective of the revivalists was not to overthrow Calvinist tradition but to repristinate it through the experience of the New Birth. Yet the Awakening did create a large new consistuency of Radical Evangelicals — Separates and Baptists — who began to polarize Calvinist culture from within.

The most radical implications of the Great Awakening, however, remained latent until the multiple crises of the era of revolution created a new context for religious change. The political revolution of 1776 weakened the governmental structures upon which the Congregationalist establishment depended and opened the possibility for Radical Evangelicals to achieve their principal political goals of toleration and freedom of conscience. At a more fundamental religious level, the Revolution presented them with an unavoidable choice between the city of man and the city of God. The fabric

172

of material, social, and economic life also underwent simultaneous change as New Englanders, many of them Radical Evangelicals, embarked on the settlement of the Republic's first transmontane frontier. The new New England of the 1780s was, like its successor frontiers to the south and west, a social world more egalitarian, culturally diverse, and tribal than its parent society. It was less controlled by the political and religious institutions of the Puritan Commonwealths; indeed the mere maintenance of civil order and religious conformity proved impossible, and the new settlements sought and attained autonomy in affairs of church and state.

The decisive factor in the causal context of the new religions was the return of revival. Stimulated not only by the alarms of war and ecclesiastical destitution but also by the continuing activity of native and British itinerants, the New Light Stir of 1778-1782 fused the emerging religious, political, and social identities of the hill country into a sweeping movement of spiritual quickening. The New Light Stir was a pivotal episode in New England — and American — religious history. It sustained the momentum of the Great Awakening and pointed to the paroxysm of revival that greeted the nineteenth century. It indicated that revivalism in America would be cyclical and episodic, not a once-and-for-all explosion of popular piety. And it conclusively demonstrated that the cultural formation of the Republic would occur not only at the forge of democratic revolution but also in the crucible of religious revival.

The religious message of the Stir pressed beyond the Calvinism of Whitefield and Edwards to a new focus of millennial and perfectionist expectation. The fact of war recalled the apocalyptic vision of the Book of Revelation; the achievement of independence signaled a new beginning of history; the possession of a new land betokened unlimited possibilities to create heaven on earth. The revivalists of the New Light Stir synthesized these new cultural realities with the classic Evangelical imperative of the New Birth and urged their hearers to strive for the sinlessness and charismatic powers reserved for the saved remnant in the Last Days. From this situation emerged the potential for a religious stance at once critical of Calvinism and expressive of a new indigenous culture. In rural New England during the 1780s the distinctive American concatenation of democracy, frontier, and revival first attained coherence and began to define the parameters of cultural development. And among the first fruits of this new identify were the radical indigenous religious cultures of the Shakers, Universalists, and Freewill Baptists.

What the radical sects of rural New England achieved was more than a set of novel beliefs or a successful mode of social control. It was nothing less than the creation of alternative cultures, complete models for human life structured by religious priorities and fabricated by a native constituency intent on finding ultimate meaning amid rapid and violent change. The sects constituted an alternative trajectory whereby obscure yet representative members of the generation of 1776 brought order and significance to their lives.

At the heart of the new religions were ideas, notions of the divine and the human that seemed intellectually credible to rural Radical Evangelicals and had the capacity to interpret their revolutionary world and to define a new role for them in it. These ideas possessed such power because they struck down the Calvinism that, far more than British Crown, had first failed and then oppressed many Radical Evangelicals. Mother Ann Lee's vision of celibate perfection, Caleb Rich's gospel of universal salvation, and Benjamin Randel's evangel of free grace and free will liberated Radical Evangelicals from a Calvinist faith that denied them the very assurance of salvation and spiritual power they sought in the New Light Stir. Tested and tried by the spirit and the letter, these prophets and their messages fulfilled the hopes of hill country folk for a faith that was intellectually satisfying and charismatically certified.

As hundreds of converts joined the sectarian movements they introduced a new agenda for organization and discipline. For almost a decade the nascent sects struggled to bring institutional order out of revivalistic chaos. And through a labyrinthine process of dialogue, improvisation, and consensus, they brought forth effective constitutional norms. Each sect generated its own form of experimental self-government rooted in the ideals of the gathered church of apostolic saints. Out of the dialectical process of idea and social experience emerged concepts of community as innovative as the theological notions upon which they were grounded.

The sectarian polities were precise and comprehensive, manifesting in different ways the encounter of charismatic religion with the complex reality of democratic society. For the Shakers holy community was one of absolute sexual and material equality administered by spiritual hierarchs through the metaphor of the biological family. The Freewill Baptists envisioned a direct democracy of the saints founded on mass consensus and mutual discipline. Universalists embraced a polity of anarchy in which the knowledge of the truth liberated every person to pursue it as he or she saw fit. Oligarchy, direct democracy, and anarchy were principles of order not taken by the political revolution but embraced by the radical sects as the foundations for their new religions. Upon these foundations they built edifices of moral injunctions and behavioral rules that described in detail the style of life implied by radical religious commitment. In both oral and written form, sectarian social designs brought under purview the entire range of rural life, familial, economic, legal, political, and—especially in the Shaker case—material. Through these instruments the sects defined themselves over against secular society. Into the nineteenth century they continued to oppose religious establishments, to refuse to bear arms, to shun unscrupulous commerce and litigation. But even more important than this rejection of secularity was the sectarian acceptance of the challenge to create alternative cultures, patterns of life inspired by radical religious insights and embodied in the forms of gospel union, gospel liberty, and gospel order.

The success of sectarian institutionalization generated new needs for public defense and the instruction of converts, which could only be met by the development of formal ideologies. This culminating phase of sectarian development produced systematic theologies and distinctive ritual expressions, especially hymnodies. In the arena of theological disputation the sects seized upon the most accessible form of doctrinal explication — the history of redemption — as a vehicle for articulating and justifying their tenets and practices. Through a spiritual exegesis of scripture the sectarians reinterpreted the dispensational scheme of popular Calvinism in light of their radical doctrines of universal salvation, free will, and celibate perfectionism. Their luxuriant speculations issued in a thorough rejection of the essential positions of Calvinism on the nature of God, predestination and election of souls, the divinity of Jesus Christ, limited substitutionary atonement, the innate depravity of human beings, and the limits of regeneration. In place of these traditional truths the sectarians presented alternative visions of cosmic history grounded in a benevolent and immutable God, the regular operation of divine laws, the dependent status of Jesus, universal atonement, the spiritual essence of human nature, and the restoration of the Adamic state in this life.

Sectarian hymnody developed in a similar way. The sects appropriated the rhetoric and style of Evangelical hymnody pioneered by Isaac Watts. In the manner of this emotive and didactic verse they created extensive collections of hymns that treated every dimension of sectarian religious culture: doctrine, ecclesiology, morality, liturgy, history, and above all religious experience. Through the medium of sacred song they produced a complex and all-embracing symbolic language that celebrated and objectified the new religious cultures they had made.

The Shakers, the Universalists, and the Freewill Baptists were the first American communions to complete the cycle of indigenous religious development. From the appearance of the radical prophets through the genesis of new social structures to the creation of systematic ideological and ritual forms, they demonstrated the furious creativity and potential for religious change latent in revivalism. Their history taught that in America the flood tide of spiritual renewal could not be contained by the confines of tradition and that, once released, the power of religious innovation would not cease until it had thoroughly transformed the materials of inherited faith into unique native religions. The New England sects initiated a process that has continued wherever mass revival has struck. Their most direct successors were the Christian Connection and the Mormons, indigenous religions of the Second Great Awakening. But for American saints the process of creat-ting new faiths has not been restricted to the North or to the antebellum period. Communions as diverse as Disciples of Christ, Republican Methodists, Adventists, Christian Scientists, and the Church of God have all arisen in response to much the same forces that brought the New England sects into being. America has been a great laboratory of religious experiment and innovation; the profusion of its indigenous sects is a distinguishing mark of its character as a civilization. The fountainhead of this native religiousness is to be found in the rise of the Shakers, the Universalists, and the Freewill Baptists in rural New England.

The radical sects of the hill country provided an unanticipated response to the new nation's quest for identity. Even before the Revolution had ended, the sectarians served notice that for significant numbers of citizens in the emergent regions of the United States, new religions of their own making would become the vital center and guiding norm of culture. Such native faiths would be radical not only in their rejection of tradition but also in their demand that religious truth be the sole arbiter of collective life. Shakers, Universalists, and Freewill Baptists gave first voice to the many for whom life in America must always proclaim a revolution of the spirit.

Notes
Bibliography
Index

Notes

1. RADICAL EVANGELICALISM

1. The indispensable works on the rise of Radical Evangelicalism are C. C. Goen, *Revivalism and Separatism in New England, 1740–1800* (New Haven: Yale University Press, 1962); William G. McLoughlin, *New England Dissent, 1630–1833* (Cambridge, Mass.: Harvard University Press, 1971); and Alan Heimert, *Religion and the American Mind* (Cambridge, Mass: Harvard University Press, 1966).

2. David McClure and Elijah Parish, *Memoirs of the Rev. Eleazar Wheelock, D. D.* (Newburyport, Mass., 1811), pp. 214–215.

3. *New Hampshire Gazette,* 12 October 1770, p. 1.

4. Norman Pettit, *The Heart Prepared: Grace and Conversion in Puritan Spiritual Life* (New Haven: Yale University Press, 1966). See also Solomon Stoddard, *A Guide to Christ* (Boston, 1714) for a representative example of pre-Awakening morphologies of grace.

5. George Whitefield, *Eighteen Sermons* (London, 1771), p. 22.

6. See Whitefield's sermon "The Indwelling of the Spirit," in John Gillies, *Memoirs of the Rev. George Whitefield* (Middletown, Conn., 1829), pp. 423–433.

7. Quoted in Stuart Henry, *George Whitefield, Wayfaring Witness* (New York: Abingdon, 1957), p. 152. The standard biography.

8. On the Pietist and Puritan background to the concept of the gathered church see Donald F. Durnbaugh, *The Believers' Church* (New York: Macmillan, 1968), and Edmund S. Morgan, *Visible Saints: The History of a Puritan Idea* (New York: New York University Press, 1963).

9. George Whitefield, *George Whitefield's Journals, 1737–1741,* ed. William V. Davis (Gainesville: Scholars' Facsimiles and Reprints, 1969), pp. 474–475. ·

10. James Downey, *The Eighteenth Century Pulpit* (Oxford: Clarendon Press, 1970), p. 168.

11. Gillies, *Memoirs,* p. 38.

12. Richard Hofstadter, *America at 1750: A Social Portrait* (New York: Knopf, 1971), p. 244.

13. On Whitefield's sermon style see Downey, *The Eighteenth Century Pulpit,* and Horton Davies, *Worship and Theology in England from Watts to Maurice, 1690–1850* (Princeton: Princeton University Press, 1961).

14. Quoted in Downey, *The Eighteenth Century Pulpit,* p. 170.

15. George Whitefield, "The Holy Spirit Convincing the World of Sin," in Gillies, *Memoirs,* pp. 400–401.

16. Goen, *Revivalism and Separatism,* p. 27.

17. Compare Whitefield's and Davenport's itineraries: Whitefield, *Journals,* pp. 452–484, and Goen, *Revivalism and Separatism,* pp. 19–26.

18. *Diary of Joshua Hempstead of New London, Connecticut* (New London, 1901), p. 380.

19. Ibid., p. 379.

20. Richard L. Bushman, *From Puritan to Yankee: Character and the Social Order in Connecticut, 1690–1765* (Cambridge, Mass.: Harvard University Press, 1967), p. 193.

21. James Davenport, *The Reverend Mr. James Davenport's Confession and Retractions* (Boston, 1744).

22. Goen, *Revivalism and Separatism,* chap. 3, pp. 68–114.

23. Ebenezer Frothingham, *Articles of Faith and Practice* (Newport, R.I., 1750), p. 152.

24. Ibid., p. 47.

25. Ibid., pp. 179–183.

26. See McLoughlin, *New England Dissent,* chaps. 23–31, for a detailed account of Baptist development from 1740 to 1776. The basic primary source for New England Baptist history of this period is Isaac Backus, *A History of New England, with Particular Reference to the Denomination of Christians Called Baptists* (Boston, 1777–1796); see also "The Baptist Confession of 1688 (The Philadelphia Confession)," in Philip Schaff, comp., *The Creeds of Christendom,* vol. 3 (New York, 1878), p. 741.

27. See McLoughlin, *New England Dissent,* chaps. 27 and 31.

28. Ibid., pp. 702–704.

29. Ibid., pp. 428–430.

30. Thomas Baldwin, *The Baptism of Believers Only,* 2d ed. (Boston, 1806), p. 37.

31. Daniel Chessman, *Memoir of Rev. Thomas Baldwin, D.D.* (Boston, 1826); McLoughlin, *New England Dissent,* pp. 501–502; and John Gill, *A Body of Doctrinal Divinity* (London, 1769).

32. William G. McLoughlin, ed., *Isaac Backus on Church, State, and Calvinism* (Cambridge, Mass.: Harvard University Press, 1968), p. 44.

33. Phillips Payson, *A Sermon Preached before the Honorable Council and the Honorable House of Representatives* (Boston, 1778) in John Wingate Thornton, ed., *The Pulpit of the American Revolution* (Boston, 1860), p. 340.

34. Samuel Stillman, *The Duty of Magistrates* (Boston, 1779), p. 14.

35. Richard F. Upton, *Revolutionary New Hampshire* (Hanover, N.H.: Dartmouth College Publications, 1936), pp. 68–71; Clarence W. Bowen, *The History of Woodstock, Connecticut* (Norwood, Mass.: Plimpton Press, 1926), p. 305.

2. THE NEW SETTLEMENTS

1. George A. Rawlyk, *Nova Scotia's Massachusetts* (Montreal: McGill-Queen's University Press, 1973), p. 219.

2. Ibid., p. 220.

3. John Bartlet Brebner, *The Neutral Yankees of Nova Scotia* (New York: Columbia

University Press, 1937), p. 29.

4. Ibid., pp. 172-206.

5. J. M. Bumsted, *Henry Alline, 1748-1784* (Toronto: University of Toronto Press, 1971), pp. 42-44.

6. H. Fisher Wilson, *The Hill Country of Northern New England* (New York: Columbia University Press, 1936), pp. 5-6.

7. On Benning Wentworth and the New Hampshire Grants, see Jere R. Daniell, *Experiment in Republicanism* (Cambridge, Mass.: Harvard University Press, 1970).

8. See Ronald F. Banks, *Maine Becomes a State* (Middletown, Conn.: Wesleyan University Press, 1970).

9. United States Bureau of the Census, *A Century of Population Growth from the First Census of the United States to the Twelfth, 1790-1900* (Washington, D.C.: U.S. Government Printing Office, 1909), pp. 4-5, 9.

10. Hamilton Child, *Gazetteer of Grafton County, N.H., 1709-1886* (Syracuse, 1886), passim.

11. Child, *Gazetteer,* pp. 524-547.

12. *A Century of Population Growth,* pp. 153, 155-156.

13. For an excellent treatment of stable New England towns of the mid-eighteenth century, see Michael Zuckerman, *Peaceable Kingdoms: New England Towns in the Eighteenth Century* (New York: Knopf, 1970).

14. Nathan Perkins, *A Narrative of a Tour through the State of Vermont* (Woodstock, Vt.: Elm Tree Press, 1920), p. 2.

15. Ibid., p. 5.

16. Wilson, *Hill Country,* p. 22.

17. Jeremy Belknap, *History of New Hampshire,* vol. 3 (Boston, 1792), p. 194.

18. Samuel Williams, *The Natural and Civil History of New Hampshire* (Walpole, N.H., 1794), p. 163.

19. Wilson, *Hill Country,* pp. 19-26.

20. Jackson Turner Main, *The Social Structure of Revolutionary America* (Princeton: Princeton University Press, 1965), pp.11-23.

21. James Henretta, *The Evolution of American Society, 1750-1815: An Interdisciplinary Analysis* (Lexington, Mass.: D. C. Heath, 1973), pp. 213-214.

22. James Henretta, "Families and Farms: Mentalité in Pre-Industrial America," *William and Mary Quarterly,* 3rd ser., 35 (January 1978): 26.

23. Belknap, *History of New Hampshire,* 3: 197.

24. Henretta, "Families and Farms," p. 32.

25. See John Shy, *A People Numerous and Armed: Reflections on the Military Struggle for American Independence* (New York: Oxford Universiy Press, 1976), chaps. 7-9 for local military and political circumstances.

26. Williams, *Natural and Civil History,* pp. 162-168; Gordon S. Wood, *The Creation of the American Republic, 1776-1787* (Chapel Hill: University of North Carolina Press, 1969), p. 229.

27. Belknap, *History of New Hampshire,* vol. 2 (Boston, 1791), pp. 346-347.

28. Williams, *Natural and Civil History,* p. 200.

29. Ibid., p. 196.

30. Zadok Thompson, *History of the State of Vermont* (Burlington, Vt., 1833), p. 182.

31. Banks, *Maine Becomes a State,* p. 10.

32. Ibid., p. 6.

33. The major contemporary account is George Richards Minot, *A History of the Insurrections in Massachusetts* (Boston, 1788).

34. Jeremy Belknap, *The History of New Hampshire,* 2: 354 and 358.

35. John M. Comstock, *The Congregational Churches of Vermont* (St. Johnsbury, Vt.:

Cowles Press, 1942), p. 14; McClure and Parish, *Memoirs of Rev. Eleazar Wheelock.*

36. Sydney E. Ahlstrom, *A Religious History of the American People* (New Haven: Yale University Press, 1972), p. 365.

37. Ezra Stiles, *The Literary Diary of Ezra Stiles,* ed. Franklin Bowditch Dexter vol. 2 (New York: Scribner's, 1901), p. 412.

38. Comstock, *Congregational Churches of Vermont,* passim.

39. General Association of Connecticut, *The Records of the General Association of ye Colony of Connecticut* (Hartford, 1888), passim.

40. Ibid.

41. For Congregationalist development in the hill country see Joseph S. Clark, *A Historical Sketch of the Congregational Churches in Massachusetts* (Boston, 1858); Henry A. Hazen, *The Congregational and Presbyterian Ministry and Churches of New Hampshire* (Boston, 1875); and Comstock, *Congregational Churches of Vermont.*

42. Ethan Allen, *Reason the Only Oracle of Man* (Bennington, Vt., 1784).

3.THE NEW LIGHT STIR

1. Bumsted, *Henry Alline,* p. 49.

2. Perry Miller, "From Covenant to Revival," in James W. Smith and A. Leland Jamison, eds., *The Shaping of American Religion,* (Princeton: Princeton University Press, 1961), pp. 322–368; Nathan O. Hatch, *The Sacred Cause of Liberty: Republican Thought and the Millennium in Revolutionary New England* (New Haven: Yale University Press, 1977).

3. Bumsted, *Henry Alline,* pp. 1–28. Maurice W. Armstrong's *The Great Awakening in Nova Scotia, 1776–1809* (Hartford: American Society of Church History, 1948) is the standard account.

4. Armstrong, *Great Awakening,* p. 38.

5. Ibid., p. 53.

6. Ibid., pp. 49–53.

7. Ibid., p. 87.

8. Rawlyk, *Nova Scotia's Massachusetts,* p. 250; also Bumsted, *Henry Alline,* pp. 64–68, and 100.

9. Goen, *Revivalism and Separatism,* p. 20.

10. David Sands, *Journal of the Life and Gospel Labors of David Sands* (New York, 1848), pp. 9 and 20.

11. Ibid., pp. 30–45.

12. Ibid., p. 39.

13. Ibid., *Journal,* p. 5.

14. In 1778 churches were established in Norwich and East Hawley, Massachusetts; Alstead, Bath, Croydon, and Conway, New Hampshire; and Halifax and Windsor, Vermont. In 1779: Otis, Berlin, West Hampton, Cummington, Foxboro, and Alford, Massachusetts; Hebron, New Hampshire; and Dummerston and Hartland, Vermont. In 1780: Goshen and Lee, Massachusetts; Jaffrey, Mount Vernon, Orange, Meredith, Thornton, and Camden, New Hampshire; Wells and Poultney, Vermont; and Alfred, Maine. In 1781: Carlisle, Newton, Granville, and Rowe, Massachusetts; Cornish, Lemster, and Nelson, New Hampshire; Springfield, Wilmington, and Woodstock, Vermont; and Acton, Maine.

15. Marshall (1731–1813) was a Separate exhorter and eccentric who itinerated the Green Mountain-Berkshire region during the Revolutionary period, "respected for his piety and wondered at for his eccentricity." From 1779 until his death, Mar-

shall was based in Starksborough, Vermont, from where he traveled widely exhibiting "some of the extreme emotional flights of which the more enthusiastic Separates were capable." Extreme doctrinal positions, "a powerful excitement of the passions," and a "conscience tremblingly alive to every impression" characterized his radical itinerancy in the New Light Stir and afterward. William Grow, an irregular Baptist itinerant, traveled widely in Vermont, agitating for extreme Calvinist theology and separatism during the 1780s and 1790s. The eccentric Grow was dismissed from his pastorate at Hampton, Connecticut, in 1783. Grow's radicalism and obnoxious pulpit style helped precipitate an important Universalist-Calvinist controversy in Woodstock, Vermont, as late as 1798. See Stephen Delano, *Miscellaneous Thoughts on the Doctrine of Limited Election and Reprobation* (Windsor, Vt., 1799), p. 29. On Marshall, see Goen, *Revivalism and Separatism*, pp. 143-148; on Grow, see Elias Smith, *The Life, Conversion, Preaching, Travels, and Sufferings of Elias Smith* (Portsmouth, N.H., 1816), pp. 21-24.

16. David Benedict's *A General History of the Baptist Denomination in America*, 2d ed, (New York, 1848), p. 501, describes Blood's letter. Quotation from Warren Baptist Association, *Minutes . . . 1779* (n.p., 1779), p. 3.

17. Warren Baptist Association, *Minutes . . . 1779*, p. 6.

18. The churches were Guilford, Westminster, and Woodstock, Vermont; Marlow, Croydon, and Newport, New Hampshire. Benedict, *General History*, p. 501, and Henry Crocker, *History of the Baptists in Vermont* (Bellows Falls, Vt.: P. H. Gobie, 1913), p. 621.

19. William Buell Sprague, *Annals of the American Pulpit*, vol. 6 (New York, 1860), p. 136.

20. Warren Baptist Association, *Minutes . . . 1780* (n.p., 1780), p. 2, and *Minutes . . . 1781* (Providence, 1781), p. 2.

21. Stephen Wright, *History of the Shaftesbury Baptist Association* (Troy, N.Y., 1853), pp. 13-17.

22. Ibid., p. 21.

23. Backus, *History of New England*, pp. 306-307; Benedict, *General History*, pp. 487-489, 502-503, and 513.

24. Ezra Stiles, *The United States Elevated to Glory and Honor* (New Haven, 1783), pp. 3-4.

25. Ezra Stiles, *Literary Diary*, 2: 424.

26. Ibid., pp. 430-431.

27. The meteorological explanation of the Dark Day seems to have been a stationary front that resulted in stagnating air over New England. But according to Stiles, the darkness resulted from forest fires caused by extensive droughts and by settlers "clearing land and burning brush." "The woods about Ticonderoga & all through the [New Hampshire] Grants, and Eastwards over to New Hampshire, & Westward into York government and the Jersies," Stiles reported, "were all on fire for a week or more before this Darkness and the Smoke in the Wilderness almost to Suffocation." Ibid., p. 433.

28. Warren Baptist Association, *Minutes . . . 1782* (Providence, 1782), p. 7.

29. Harold Wisbey, *Frontier Prophetess: The Life of Jemima Wilkinson* (Ithaca: Cornell University Press, 1963), p. 10. The major contemporary account is David Hudson, *History of Jemima Wilkinson* (Geneva, N.Y.: S. P. Hull, 1821).

30. Wisbey, *Frontier Prophetess*, p. 12.

31. Ibid., p. 59.

32. Ibid., pp. 27-30.

33. Ibid., p. 52.

34. Ezra Stiles, *Literary Diary*, 2: 380-381.

35. Wisbey, *Frontier Prophetess*, p. 68.

36. Goen, *Revivalism and Separatism,* p. 201; also Clara Endicott Sears, *Gleanings from Old Shaker Journals* (Boston: Houghton Mifflin, 1916), pp. 1-5 for an account of Ireland.

37. McLoughlin, *New England Dissent,* pp. 738-739.

38. Backus, *History of New England,* p. 462.

39. Hugh D. McLellan, *History of Gorham, Maine* (Portland, Me.: Smith and Sale, 1903), p. 200.

40. Ibid., p. 201.

41. Calvin Green, "Biographical Account of Father Joseph Meacham," *Shaker Quarterly,* 10, no. 1-3 (1970): 20-32. 51-68, 92-102.

42. Seth Y. Wells, comp., "Unpublisht Testimonies of Mother's First-Born Children in America," Shaker Manuscripts, VI, B-42, Shaker Collection of the Western Reserve Historical Society, Cleveland, p. 171. This important collection of forty-five spiritual autobiographies testifies to a regular pattern of Shaker conversions from Baptist and Separate origins. The Shaker Collection is also available on microfilm from the Microfilming Corporation of America, Glen Rock, N.J.

43. Ibid.

44. Edwin Emery, *The History of Sanford, Maine* (Fall River, Mass.: Salem Press, 1901), pp. 72-83. passim.

45. John Parker Lee, *Uncommon Vermont* (Rutland, Vt.: Vermont Historical Society, 1926), p. 196.

46. Ibid., p. 196.

47. Benjamin Seth Youngs, "Journey to the East," Emma B. King Memorial Library, Old Chatham, N.Y.

48. Lee, *Uncommon Vermont,* p. 190.

49. James Frisbee, *The History of Middletown, Vermont* (Rutland, Vt., 1867), p. 57.

50. Ibid., pp. 60-61.

51. I. D. Stewart, *The History of the Freewill Baptists* (Dover, N.H., 1862), p. 58; Lee, *Uncommon Vermont,* pp. 197-199; William Bullard, *A Union Prescribed and Recommended* (Windsor, Vt., 1804); Thomas Fessenden, *A Theoretic Explanation of the Science of Sanctity* (Brattleboro, Vt., 1804).

52. Valentine Rathbun, *Some Brief Hints of a Religious Scheme* (Hartford, 1783), pp. 71-72.

53. Samuel Elsworth, *Solemn Predictions of Future Events* (Bennington, Vt., 1787), pp. 7-8.

4. GIFTS OF THE SPIRIT

1. John Buzzell, *The Life of Elder Benjamin Randel* (Limerick, Me., 1827). pp. 16-19. This is the principal source on Randel, compiled from "documents written by Eld. Randel himself" by a colleague of twenty-five years.

2. Ibid., pp. 27-31.

3. Ibid., pp. 38-48.

4. Ibid., pp. 58-70.

5. Ibid., p. 86.

6. Ibid., pp. 87-88.

7. Ibid.

8. Ibid., p. 89.

9. Ibid.

10. Stewart, *History of the Freewill Baptists,* pp. 46-53.

11. Ibid., pp. 80-81.

12. John Murray, *Records of The Life of the Rev. John Murray* (Boston, 1816), p. 22.

13. *Dictionary of National Biography*, S.V. "Relly, James"; also James Relly, *Union: Or a Treatise on the Consanguinity and Affinity between Christ and His Church* (Boston, 1779), pp. 22-23.

14. Murray, *Life*, p. 107.

15. Ibid., pp. 137-138.

16. Ibid., p. 183.

17. Richard D. Eddy, *Universalism in America: A History*, vol. 1 (Boston: Universalist Publishing House, 1886), pp. 212-215.

18. Ibid., pp. 220-226. The standard biography of Winchester is still Edwin Martin Stone's *Biography of Elhanan Winchester* (Boston, 1836). Winchester, a representative religious figure of the revolutionary generation, deserves reexamination and reassessment.

19. Eddy, *Universalism in Amrica*,1:227-237.

20. Ibid., pp. 237-238.

21. Ibid., pp. 239-257, 429-479.

22. Isaac Davis, *What Love Jesus Christ Has for Sinners* (Somers, Conn., n.d.), pp. 11-20.

23. Ibid., p. 24.

24. Eddy, *Universalism in America*, 1:200-206.

25. Caleb Rich, "A Narrative of Elder Caleb Rich," *Candid Examiner*, 2 (April 30-June 18, 1827): 179. This spiritual autobiography is the principal source on Rich's life.

26. Ibid., pp. 180-181.

27. Ibid., p. 185.

28. Ibid., pp. 186-187.

29. Ibid., pp. 189-190.

30. Ibid., pp. 191-194.

31. Ibid., p. 196.

32. Ibid., pp. 205-208.

33. Edward D. Andrews, *The People Called Shakers* 2d ed. (New York: Dover, 1963), p. 6. For background on the French Prophets, see Henri Desroche, *The American Shakers from Neo-Christianity to Presocialism* (Amherst: University of Massachusetts Press, 1971), chap. 1.

34. Rufus Bishop and Seth Y. Wells, eds., *Testimonies of the Life, Character, Revelations, and Doctrines of our Ever Blessed Mother Ann Lee, and the Elders with Her* (Hancock, Mass.: J. Tallcott and J. Deming, Jr., 1816), p. 64.

35. Nardi Reeder Campion, *Ann the Word: The Life of Mother Ann Lee, Founder of the Shakers* (Boston: Little, Brown, 1976), pp. 14-20.

36. Andrews, *The People Called Shakers*, p. 7.

37. Ibid., p. 41.

38. Ibid., p. 47.

39. Ibid., pp. 8-16.

40. Amos Taylor, *A Narrative of the Strange Principles, Conduct and Character of the People Known by the Name of Shakers* (Worcester, 1782), pp. 7-8.

41. Ibid.; see also Reuben Rathbun, *Reasons for Leaving the Shakers* (Pittsfield, Mass., 1800).

42. Bishop, *Testimonies*, pp. 21-22.

43. Valentine Rathbun, *Some Brief Hints of a Religious Scheme* (Hartford, 1783), pp. 20-21.

44. Wells, "Unpublisht Testimonies," pp. 102, 172.

45. Fr. Dan Charette, ed., "A Historical Narrative of the Rise and Progress of

the United Society of Shakers in Enfield, N.H.," Library of the LaSalette Seminary, Enfield, N.H.

5. EVANGELISM AND COMMUNITY

1. Frederick Wiley, *The Life and Influence of the Rev. Benjamin Randel, Founder of the Freewill Baptist Denomination* (Philadelphia: American Baptist Publication Society, 1915), p. 94.

2. Rich, "Narrative," p. 201.

3. Bishop, *Testimonies*, pp. 92–93. See also: Benjamin Randel, *A Sermon . . . at the Interment of Murmoth Fortune Herrick* (Limerick, Me., 1827), pp. 3–5.

4. Stewart, *History of the Freewill Baptists*, p. 63.

5. Thomas Whittmore, *Life of Hosea Ballou* (Boston, 1854–1856), 1: 46.

6. W. S. Balch, "Caleb Rich," *Universalist Quarterly and General Review*, n.s. 9 (1872): 66–67.

7. Levisa Buck, *Memoir of Thomas Barnes* (Portland, Me., 1856), p. 38.

8. Ibid., p. 40.

9. See also Hosea Ballou's conversion, stimulated by discussions with his brothers in 1793, in Whittemore, *Life of Hosea Ballou*, 1: 42–68.

10. Buck, *Memoir of Thomas Barnes*, p. 41.

11. Ibid., p. 45.

12. Ephraim Stinchfield, *Some Memoirs of the Life, Experience, and Labors of Elder Ephraim Stinchfield* (Portland, Me., 1819), p. 20; and Wiley, *Life of Benjamin Randel*, p. 81.

13. Stewart, *History of the Freewill Baptists*, p. 64.

14. Ibid., p. 94.

15. John Buzzell, *A Religious Magazine*, vol. 1 (1811–12), p. 96. This work, issued quarterly at Portland, was the first historical account of the Freewill Baptists. It was authored completely by John Buzzell and carried running pagination. Buzzell issued a second volume with titled articles in 1820–21.

16. Ibid., pp. 100–101.

17. Stewart, *History of the Freewill Baptists*, pp. 62–63.

18. Buzzell, *Religious Magazine*, 1: 101.

19. The dramatic appeal of baptism was recorded in diaries, memoirs, and minutes until after 1815. See especially John Peak, *The Memoirs of Elder John Peak* (Boston, 1832), and the accounts in the *Massachusetts Baptist Missionary Magazine*, 1803–1816.

20. Stewart, *History of the Freewill Baptists*, pp. 473–479; Bowdoinham Baptist Association, *Minutes . . . 1801* (Portland, Me., 1801).

21. Rathbun, *Some Brief Hints of a Religious Scheme*, p. 19.

22. Bishop, *Testimonies*, pp. 20–43.

23. Ibid.

24. Ibid., pp. 25–26.

25. Ibid., p. 83.

26. Ibid., p. 85.

27. Ibid., p. 224.

28. Ibid., p. 297.

29. Ibid, pp. 292–308.

30. Ibid, p. 86.

31. Roxalana L. Grosvenor, comp., "Incidents Related by Jemima Blanchard of

Her Experience and Intercourse with Mother Ann and Our First Parents," pp. 1-4, Berkshire Atheneum, Pittsfield, Mass.

32. Ibid., pp. 4-5.

33. Bishop, *Testimonies,* pp. 111-126.

34. Sectarian estimates are based on information about churches and membership in Stewart, *History of the Freewill Baptists;* Eddy, *Universalism in America;* and Andrews, *The People Called Shakers.* Congregationalist estimate developed from Clark, *A Historical Sketch of the Congregational Churches in Massachusetts;* Hazen, *The Congregational and Presbyterian Ministry and Churches of New Hampshire;* and Comstock, *Congregational Churches of Vermont.* Baptist estimate derived from statistics in David Benedict, *A General History of the Baptist Denomination in America* (Boston, 1813), pp. 497-505.

35. H. Richard Niebuhr, *The Social Sources of Denominationalism* (New York: Holt, 1929) is a classic expression of this view.

36. Jackson Turner Main, *The Social Structure of Revolutionary America* (Princeton: Princeton University Press, 1965), p. 12.

37. "Harvard Shaker Church Record Book," American Antiquarian Society Library, Worcester, Mass.; and Harvard, Massachusetts, Town Records, vol. 2, pp. 420-431, Massachusetts Archives, State House, Boston.

38. New Durham, New Hampshire, Town Records, 1759-1803, vol. 1, pp. 23-35, microfilm, New Hampshire State Library, Concord.

39. Ibid., pp. 56-63.

40. Frank B. Kingsbury, *Historical and Genealogical Register of the Town of Langdon, Sullivan County, New Hampshire* (White River Jct., Vt.: Right Printing Co., 1932), pp. 84-89.

41. Langdon, New Hampshire, Town Records, vol. 1, pp. 279-287, microfilm, New Hampshire State Library, Concord.

42. Adin Ballou, *The Ballous in America* (Providence, 1888), pp. 125-142.

43. Ibid., p. 143.

44. Stewart, *History of the Freewill Baptists,* pp. 473-479.

45. This information was developed from an inventory of the Index Nominum of the Library of the United Society of Shakers, Sabbathday Lake, Maine.

46. Otis Sawyer, comp., "A Record of the Appointments and Removals in Regular Succession of the Elders, Deacons, and Trustees of the Church and United Society of Believers in New Gloucester and Poland, Cumberland County, State of Maine," Library of the United Society of Shakers, Sabbathday Lake, Maine.

6. IMPROVISATION AND CRISIS

1. John Buzzell, *Life of Randel,* p. 82.

2. Stewart, *History of the Freewill Baptists,* p. 54.

3. "Record of Church in Loudon and Chichester, 1780-1782," New Hampshire Historical Society, Concord, N.H.

4. Stewart, *History of the Freewill Baptists,* p. 75.

5. Ibid., p. 80.

6. "Record of the New Durham Quarterly Meeting," New Hampshire Historical Society, Concord, N.H.

7. Stewart, *History of the Freewill Baptists,* p. 84.

8. Buzzell, *Religious Magazine,* 1: 16.

9. Ibid., p. 54.

10. Stewart, *History of the Freewill Baptists,* p. 110.

11. Buzzell, *Religious Magazine,* 1: 60.
12. Eddy, *Universalism in America,* 1: 178.
13. Ibid.
14. Ibid.
15. Ibid., p. 204.
16. Ibid., pp. 205-206.
17. "Oxford Universalist Society Records," p. 5, Universalist Historical Society, Andover-Harvard Library, Cambridge, Mass.
18. Bishop, *Testimonies,* pp. 333 and 351.
19. Ibid., pp. 355-356.
20. Andrews, *The People Called Shakers,* p. 48.
21. James Whittaker, *The Shaker Shaken* (New Haven: Bibliographical Press, 1938).
22. Bishop, *Testimonies,* p. 377.
23. Ibid., pp. 371-372.
24. Charette, "A Historical Narrative," p. 35.
25. Ibid., p. 47.
26. Ibid., p. 35.

7. GOSPEL UNION, GOSPEL LIBERTY, GOSPEL ORDER

1. Stewart, *History of the Freewill Baptists,* p. 191.
2. Buzzell, *Life of Randel,* p. 135; Stewart, *History of the Freewill Baptists,* p. 111.
3. Benjamin Randel, "A Summary of the Order and Disciplines of the Church of New Durham," p. 1, William S. Babcock Papers, American Antiquarian Society Library, Worcester, Mass.
4. Hosea Quinby, "History of the Freewill Baptists," *Freewill Baptist Quarterly* 2 (September 1840), p. 192. See also "Record of the New Durham Quarterly Meeting."
5. Randel, "A Summary of Order," p. 1.
6. Some congregations extended their reliance on the Spirit's guidance to selection of officers by lot. See "A Record of the First Monthly Meeting of Freewill Baptist Church of Christ in Edgecomb, Maine," American Baptist Historical Society, Rochester, N.Y.
7. Buzzell, *Religious Magazine,* 1: 90-91.
8. Stewart, *History of the Freewill Baptists,* pp. 114-115; also *Minutes of the General Conference of the Freewill Baptist Connection* (Dover, N.H., 1859), pp. 6-7.
9. Stewart, *History of the Freewill Baptists,* p. 472.
10. Ibid., p. 179.
11. "Record of the New Durham Monthly Meeting," New Durham, New Hampshire Public Library.
12. Stewart, *History of the Freewill Baptists,* p. 150.
13. Benjamin Randel to Aaron Buzzell, 9 September 1793, American Baptist Historical Society, Rochester; also the Freewill Baptist Connection's "Elders Conference Records," p. 6, New Hampshire Historical Society, Concord.
14. Buzzell, *Religious Magazine,* 1: 235.
15. Ibid., p. 336.
16. Benjamin Randel to Aaron Buzzell, 19 November 1800, American Baptist Historical Society, Rochester, N.Y.
17. Buzzell, *Religious Magazine,* 1: 95.
18. *Minutes of the . . . Freewill Baptist Connection,* pp. 13-16.

19. Eddy, *Universalism in America,* 1: 295.

20. *Articles of Faith and Plan of Church Government* (Philadelphia, 1790), pp. 8-9.

21. Eddy, *Universalism in America,* 1: 248.

22. "Records of the Langdon, New Hampshire Universalist Church," Universalist Historical Society, Andover-Harvard Theological Library, Cambridge, Mass.

23. Eddy, *Universalism in America,* 1: 434.

24. "Records of the General Convention of Universalists," Universalist Historical Society, Andover-Harvard Theological Library, Cambridge, Mass.

25. Ibid., p. 24.

26. Walter Ferriss, "Walter Ferriss's Book," p. 95, Universalist Historical Society, Andover-Harvard Theological Library, Cambridge, Mass.

27. Ibid., p. 96.

28. See account of the case of Christopher Erskine for an example of Universalist resistance to compulsory religious taxes in New Hampshire in Eddy, *Universalism in America,* 2: 19-36.

29. Ibid., p. 50.

30. Buck, *Memoir of Thomas Barnes,* intro.; also "Records of the Western Universalist Association," pp. 1-26, Universalist Historical Society, Andover-Harvard Theological Library, Cambridge, Mass.

31. Edward Turner, "Notebook," Universalist Historical Society, Andover-Harvard Theological Library, Cambridge, Mass.

32. Eddy, *Universalism in America,* 2: 190; also "Records of the Western Universalist Association," pp. 35-40.

33. Eddy, *Universalism in America,* 2: 250-265.

34. Joseph Meacham, "A Collection of the Writings of Father Joseph Meacham Concerning Church Order and Government; Evidently Intended for Way-marks, for All Who Are or Should Be Called in Spiritual or Temporal Care, in the Church," ed. Rufus Bishop, Shaker Manuscripts, VII, B-59, p. 26, Shaker Collection of the Western Reserve Historical Society, Cleveland. This collection is the most important single source for the "gospel order" of Shakerism. Though written in Father Joseph's biblical rhetoric, it contains the only detailed statements of ecclesiology and polity from the crucial period of "gathering into order." See also Andrews, *The People Called Shakers,* p. 55.

35. Calvin Green, "Biographic Memoir of the Life, Character, and Important Events in the Ministration of Mother Lucy Wright," Shaker Manuscripts, VI, B-27, p. 17, Shaker Collection of the Western Reserve Historical Society, Cleveland.

36. Meacham, "Collection of the Writings," pp. 26, 65.

37. Ibid., p. 1.

38. See Benjamin Seth Youngs, "Diary, 1794-1804," Emma B. King Memorial Library, Old Chatham, N.Y., passim, for an extensive account of spiritual relations as practiced at New Lebanon.

39. Meacham, "Collection of the Writings," p. 29.

40. Andrews, *The People Called Shakers,* pp. 61-62.

41. Ibid., p. 61.

42. Ibid., p. 62.

43. "Harvard, Massachusetts, Shaker Church Record Book," p. 24, American Antiquarian Society Library, Worcester, Mass.

44. Benjamin Seth Youngs and Calvin Green, eds., *The Testimony of Christ's Second Appearing,* 2d ed. (Albany, 1810), p. 509.

45. Meacham, "Collection of the Writings," pp. 35-41; also Calvin Green, "Biographical Account of the Life, Character, and Ministry of Father Joseph Meacham," *Shaker Quarterly* 10 (Summer 1970), pp. 62-68 and (Fall 1970), pp. 92-94.

46. Meacham, "Collection of the Writings," pp. 21-22.

47. Charette, "A Historical Narrative," pp. 16–19.

48. Youngs, "Diary, 1794-1804," p. 31.

49. Ibid., pp. 24-25.

50. Meacham, "Collection of the Writings," p. 27.

51. Green, "Biographic Memoir of . . . Mother Lucy Wright," p. 51.

52. See Elisha Pote, "Letters to Tuftonboro," Library of the United Society of Shakers, Sabbathday Lake, Me.

53. Andrews, *The People Called Shakers*, p. 243.

8. THE HISTORY OF REDEMPTION

1. The volume of such polemical literature varied from sect to sect. Universalists came under the direct attack, though most of it was aimed at John Murray and Elhanan Winchester rather than Richite theology. See especially Ariel Kendrick, *A Brief Reply to a Pamphlet Lately Published by S. Delanoe . . . in favour of Universalism* (Hanover, N.H., 1798); Samuel Shepard, *The Principle of Universal Salvation Examined and Tried* (Exeter, N.H., 1798); Samuel Worcester, *Six Sermons on the Doctrine of Future Punishment* (Worcester, Mass., 1800); Lemuel Haynes, *Universal Salvation, A Very Ancient Doctrine: With Some Account of the Life and Character of its Author* (New Haven, 1806); John Peck, *A Poem, Containing a Descant on the Universal Plan* (Keene, N.H., 1801). These popular condemnations concentrated on the argument that Universalism entailed moral anarchy and violation of the Scriptures; their tone ranged from righteous outrage to supercilious parody. Anti-Freewill Baptist publications were largely restricted to the *Minutes* of New England Baptist associations, especially Woodstock, Bowdoinham, and Warren. After the flurry of anti-Shaker publications in the early 1780s only a few public attacks appeared. More serious criticism surfaced after the reopening of the Shaker Testimony in 1798 in the form of autobiographical accounts by apostates. The most famous and effective of these during the period was Thomas Brown, *An Account of the People Called Shakers* (Troy, N.Y., 1812).

2. Evanglical Calvinism is notable for its critique of Puritan scholasticism and its embrace of the logic of Calvin's own writings, most notably *The Institutes of the Christian Religion*. See John T. McNeill, *The History and Character of Calvinism* (New York: Oxford University Press, 1957); Ola E. Winslow, *Jonathan Edwards, 1703–1758: A Biography* (New York: Macmillan, 1940); Frank Hugh Foster, *A Genetic History of the New England Theology* (Chicago: University of Chicago Press, 1907); and Joseph Haroutunian, *Piety Versus Moralism* (New York: Holt, 1932).

3. Conrad Wright, *The Beginnings of Unitarianism in America* (Boston: Starr King Press, 1955) is the best account of "supernatural rationalism" and its theological uses.

4. Jonathan Edwards, *The Works of President Edwards*, vol. 2 (Worcester, Mass., 1808–09), preface.

5. Ibid., p. 23.

6. Samuel Hopkins, *The System of Doctrines* (Boston, 1793) and *A Treatise on the Millennium* (Boston, 1793); Joseph Bellamy, *An Essay on the Nature and Glory of the Gospel* (Boston, 1762); Caleb Blood, *A Concise View of the Principal Points of Difference between the Baptists and Pedobaptists* (Boston, 1815).

7. Randel, *Sermon . . . at the Interment of Murmoth Fortune Herrick;* Buzzell, *A Religious Magazine*, vols. 1 and 2 (1811–12, 1820–21).

8. Henry Alline, *Two Mites, Cast into the Offering of God, for the Benefit of Mankind; with Some Amendments by Benjamin Randel* (Dover, N.H., 1804), p. 20.

9. Randel, *Sermon*, p. 7.

10. Alline, *Two Mites*, p. 64.

11. Randel, *Sermon*, p. 6.

12. Ibid.
13. Ibid., p. 8.
14. Alline, *Two Mites*, p. 24.
15. Ibid., p. 105.
16. Randel, *Sermon*, p. 10.
17. Ibid., p. 7
18. Ibid., p. 13.
19. Ibid.
20. Ibid., pp. 13-14.
21. Buzzell, *Religious Magazine*, 2:286.
22. Randel, *Sermon*, p. 15.
23. Alline, *Two Mites*, pp. 303-304.
24. Hosea Ballou, *A Treatise on Atonement* (Randolph, Vt., 1805), p. 119.
25. Ibid., p. 31.
26. Ibid., p. 33.
27. Abner Kneeland, *A Sermon Delivered Before the Northern Association of Universalists
. . . upon the Two Covenants* (Walpole, N.H., 1807), p. 20.
28. Ballou, *Atonement*, p. 59.
29. Ibid., p. 64.
30. Walter Ferriss, *Five Sermons on the Following Subjects, viz. I. The Love of God to
His Creatures. II. The Christian's Evidence of His Having Passed from Death into Life. III.
The Finite Nature of Things Unseen. IV. God's Love to Zion. V. The Lamb of God Which
Taketh Away the Sin of the World* (Randolph, Vt., 1807), p. 62.
31. Ballou, *Atonement*, p. 105.
32. Ibid., p. 106.
33. Ibid., p. 128.
34. Ibid., p. 127,
35. Kneeland, *A Sermon*, p. 17.
36. Ferriss, *Five Sermons*, p. 81.
37. Ibid., p. 80.
38. Ballou, *Atonement*, p. 140.
39. Ibid., pp. 42 and 55.
40. Ibid., p. 220.
41. Ferriss, *Five Sermons*, p. 20.
42. Benjamin Seth Youngs and Calvin Green, *The Testimony of Christ's Second Appearing*, 2d ed. (Albany, 1810).
43. Ibid., p. 553.
44. Ibid., p. 1.
45. Ibid., p. 9.
46. Ibid., p. 15.
47. Ibid., p. 11.
48. Ibid., p. 45.
49. Joseph Meacham, *A Concise Statement of the Principles of the Only True Church* (Bennington, Vt., 1790), p. 3.
50. Ibid.
51. Calvin Green, "A Treatise upon the Work of God in Different Ages" (1806), Library of the United Society of Shakers, Sabbathday Lake, Me. Green (1780-1852), in addition to editing *The Testimony of Christ's Second Appearing* for the New Lebanon ministry, was a leading religious thinker of the Shakers in his own right. Green is a neglected figure of New England folk religion whose works compare in volume and scope to those of Hosea Ballou, John Buzzell, or Elias Smith. See also Calvin Green, "Biographic Memoir of the Life and Experience of Calvin Green," Shaker Manuscripts, VI, B-28, Western Reserve Historical Society, Cleveland.

52. Youngs and Green, *Christ's Second Appearing*, p. 87.
53. Ibid., p. 93.
54. Ibid., p. 96.
55. Green, "The Work of God," p. 200.
56. Youngs and Green, *Christ's Second Appearing*, p. 110.
57. Ibid., p. 365.
58. Meacham, "Collection of the Writings," p. 78.
59. Ibid., p. 79.
60. Youngs and Green, *Christ's Second Appearing*, p. 439.
61. Ibid., p. 432.
62. Ibid., p. 577.
63. Green, "The Work of God," p. 201.
64. Youngs and Green, *Christ's Second Appearing*, p. 591.

9. THE LANGUAGE OF THE SOUL

1. The definitive study of Shaker music and liturgy is Daniel W. Patterson's *The Shaker Spiritual* (Princeton: Princeton University Press, 1979). See also Edward D. Andrews, *The Gift to Be Simple* (New York: J. J. Augustin, 1940). Freewill liturgical practice is stated in "A Summary of the Order and Disciplines of the Church of New Durham," William S. Babcock Papers, American Antiquarian Society, Worcester, Mass. Universalist diversity in worship is indicated in chap. 7 above.
2. On the hymnody of Watts and other Evangelicals see Davies, *Worship and Theology in England*, Harry Escott, *Isaac Watts, Hymnographer* (London: Independent Press, 1962), and Bernard L. Manning, *The Hymns of Wesley and Watts* (London: Epworth Press, 1942).
3. Quoted in George Pullen Jackson, ed., *Spiritual Folk-Songs of Early America* (New York: J. J. Augustin, 1937) as the most popular American hymn of the nineteenth century.
4. See numerous examples in Whitefield, *Journals, 1737-1741*.
5. John Wesley, *A Collection of Hymns for the Use of the People Called Methodists* (London, 1780), preface.
6. The best study of the emergence of an indigenous hymnic style is Alan Beuchner's "Yankee Singing Schools and the Golden Age of Choral Music in New England, 1760-1800" (Ph.D. diss., Harvard University, 1960).
7. Henry Alline, *Hymns and Spiritual Songs* (Boston, 1786), also editions at Dover, N.H., 1795 and 1797; and Stonington, Conn., 1802. It is most probable that Alline's hymnal served as the main hymnbook for Freewill Baptists before Buzzell's *Psalms, Hymns, and Spiritual Songs*.
8. John Buzzell, comp., *Psalms, Hymns, and Spiritual Songs* (Kennebunk, Me., 1823).
9. Ibid., pp. 250-252.
10. Ibid., p. 148.
11. Buzzell, *Religious Magazine*, 1: 141-142.
12. Buzzell, *Psalms*, p. 58.
13. Ibid., pp. 257-259.
14. Ibid., pp. 125-126.
15. Ibid., p. 103.
16. Ibid., p. 169.
17. Hosea Ballou, Abner Kneeland, and Edward Turner, *Hymns Composed by Different Authors* (Walpole, N.H., 1808), preface; James Relly and John Relly, *Chris-*

tian Hymns, Poems, and Spiritual Songs (London, 1758), also editions at Burlington, Vt., 1776; London, 1777; Portsmough, N.H., 1782; and London, 1791; Silas Ballou, *New Hymns on Various Subjects* (Worcester, Mass., 1785).

18. Ballou et al., *Hymns Composed by Different Authors*, p. 272.

19. Ibid., p. 12.

20. Ibid., p. 160.

21. Ibid., p. 80.

22. Ibid., p. 98.

23. Ibid., p. 34.

24. Ibid., p. 157.

25. Ibid., p. 194.

26. Ibid., p. 185.

27. Ibid., p. 208.

28. Seth Y. Wells, Comp., *Millennial Praises* (Hancock, Mass., 1812), preface.

29. Ibid., p. 239.

30. Dorothy Pote, "Hymnal" (1810), Library of the United Society of Shakers, Sabbathday Lake, Me.

31. Wells, *Millennial Praises*, pp. 20-22.

32. Pote, "Hymnal."

33. "Shaker Music," vol. 398 (ca. 1805), Shaker Manuscripts, Shaker Collection of the Western Reserve Historical Society, Cleveland.

34. Wells, *Millennial Praises*, pp. 65-66.

35. Ibid., p. 139.

36. Ibid., pp. 189-192.

37. Ibid., p. 69.

38. Stitilia Moore, "Hymnal" (ca. 1815), Library of the United Society of Shakers, Sabbathday Lake, Me.

39. Wells, *Millennial Praises*, pp. 212-213.

Bibliography

PRIMARY SOURCES

Allen, Ethan. *Reason the Only Oracle of Man, or A Compenduous System of Natural Religion.* Bennington, Vt.: Haswell and Russell, 1784.

Alline, Henry. *Hymns and Spiritual Songs.* Dover, N.H.: Samuel Bragg, 1797

———— *Life and Journal of the Rev. Mr. Henry Alline.* Boston: Gilbert and Dean, 1806.

———— *Two Mites on Some of the Most Important and Much Disputed Points of Divinity.* Halifax: A. Henry, 1781.

———— *Two Mites, Cast into the Offering of God, for the Benefit of Mankind; with Some Amendments by Benjamin Randel,* ed. Benjamin Randel. Dover, N.H.: Samuel Bragg, 1804

Articles of Faith and Plan of Church Government, Composed and Adopted by the Churches Believing in the Salvation of All Men Met in Philadelphia on the 25th of May, 1790. Philadelphia: Th. Dobson, 1790

Avery, David. *The Lord Is to Be Praised for the Triumphs of His Power.* Norwich, Conn.: Green and Spooner, 1778.

Backus, Isaac. *Government and Liberty Described, and Ecclesiastical Tyranny Exposed.* Boston: Powers and Willis, 1778.

———— *History of New England, with Particular Reference to the Denomination of Christians Called Baptists.* Boston: Draper for Freeman, 1779–1796.

———— *True Faith Will Produce Good Works.* Boston: D. Kneeland, 1767.

Baldwin, Thomas. *The Baptism of Believers Only.* Boston: Manning and Loring, 1806.

———— *A Brief Vindication of the Particular Communion of Baptist Churches.* Boston: Manning and Loring, 1794

———— *Open Communion Examined: Or a Brief Defence of the Practice of Close Communionists.* Windsor, Vt.: Alden Spooner, 1789.

Ballou, Hosea. *A Discourse Delivered at Salem, June 22d, 1809.* Salem, Mass.: Pool and Palfray, 1809.

———— *Notes on the Parables of the New Testament.* Randolph, Vt.: Sereno Wright, 1804.

———— *A Sermon Delivered at Langdon, New Hampshire, on the 30th of October 1805 at the*

Ordination of the Rev. Abner Kneeland. Randolph, Vt.: Sereno Wright, 1806.

———— *A Treatise on Atonement; in Which the Finite Nature of Sin Is Argued, Its Causes and Consequences as Such; the Necessity and Nature of Atonement, and Its Glorious Consequences in the Final Reconciliation of All Men to Holiness and Happiness.* Randolph, Vt.: Sereno Wright, 1805.

———— and Joel Foster. *A Literary Correspondence between Joel Foster, A. M., Minister of the Congregational Society in New-Salem, and Hosea Ballou, an Itinerant Preacher of the Sect Called Universalists.* Northampton, Mass.: Butler, 1799.

———— and Ebenezer Paine. *A Doctrinal Controversy, between the Hopkintonian and the Universalist; Begun on the Part of the Universalist by Brother Ebenezer Paine, of Washington, N.H., and Brother Hosea Ballou, of Barnard, Vt. To be Continued by the Rev. Reed Page, of Hancock, and the Rev. Isaac Robinson, of Stoddard, N.H., on the part of the Hopkintonian.* Randolph, Vt.: Sereno Wright, 1808.

———— Abner Kneeland, and Edward Turner. *Hymns Composed by Different Authors, at the Request of the General Convention of Universalists of the New England States and Others.* Walpole, N.H.: George W. Nichols, 1808.

Ballou, Silas, *New Hymns on Various Subjects, Viz.: On the Creation of the World; and the Formation of Man — the State Wherein He Was Created, and His Sad and Shameful Fall. On the Early and Extensive Promises of God — the Coming of Christ, and the Completion of the Father's Promises: Or the Eternal Redemption and Victorious Salvation of Mankind through Him.* Worcester, Mass.: S. Ballou, 1785.

Belknap, Jeremy. *The History of New-Hampshire,* vol. 2. Boston: Isaiah Thomas and Ebenezer T. Andrews, 1791.

———— *The History of New-Hampshire,* vol. 3. Boston: Belknap and Young, 1792.

Bellamy, Joseph. *An Essay on the Nature and Glory of the Gospel of Jesus Christ.* Boston: S. Kneeland, 1762.

Benedict, David. *A General History of the Baptist Denomination in America, and Other Parts of the World.* Boston: Lincoln and Edmands, 1813.

Bishop, Rufus and Seth Y. Wells, eds. *Testimonies of the Life, Character, Revelations, and Doctrine of Our Ever Blessed Mother Ann Lee, and the Elders with Her.* Hancock, Mass.: J. Tallcott and J. Deming, Jr., 1816.

Blood, Caleb. *A Concise View of the Principal Points of Difference between the Baptists and Pedobaptists, in a Familiar Dialogue . . . To Which Are Added, Remarks on the Atonement.* Boston: Lincoln and Edmands, 1815.

Bowdoinham Baptist Association. *Minutes of the Bowdoinham Association, held at . . . Livermore, August 28 and 29, 1799.* Portland, Me.: B. Titcomb, 1799.

———— *Minutes of the Bowdoinham Association . . . 1801.* Portland, Me.: B. Titcomb, 1801.

Brown, Thomas. *An Account of the People Called Shakers: Their Faith, Doctrines, and Practices, Exemplified in the Life, Conversation, and Experience of the Author during the Time He Belonged to the Society. To Which Is Affixed a History of Their Rise and Progress to the Present Day.* Troy, N.Y.: Parker and Bliss, 1812.

Bullard, William. *A Union, Prescribed and Recommended; Somewhat Similar to the Moravians . . . Instituted for the Honor of God, and for the Happiness of Mankind.* Windsor, Vt.: Nahum Mower, 1804.

Burton, Asa. *False Teachers Described: A Sermon Delivered at Thetford, Dec. 24th, 1809.* Montpelier, Vt.: Samuel Goss, 1810.

Buzzell, John. *The Life of Elder Benjamin Randel, Principally Taken from Documents Written by Himself.* Limerick, Me.: Hobbs, Woodman and Co., 1827.

———— *A Religious Magazine, Containing a Short History of the Church of Christ, Gathered at New-Durham, N.H., in the Year 1780 . . . Also, a Particular Account of Late Reformations and Revivals of Religion.* Portland, Me.: J. M.'Kown, 1811–12 and 1820–21.

_____ comp. *Psalms, Hymns and Spiritual Songs, Selected for the Use of the United Churches of Christ, Commonly Called Freewill Baptist, and for Saints of All Denominations.* Kennebunk, Me.: J. K. Remich, 1823.

Charette, Fr. Dan, ed. "A Historical Narrative of the Rise and Progress of the United Society of Shakers in Enfield, N.H." Library of the LaSalette Seminary, Enfield, N.H.

Chase, Ebenezer. *The Religious Informer and Freewill Baptist Register.* Andover, N.H., 1819–1821.

Colby, John. *The Life, Experience, and Travels of John Colby, Preacher of the Gospel.* Lowell, Mass.: N. Thurston and A. Watson, 1838.

Cram, Jacob. *Journal of a Missionary Tour in 1808 through the New Settlements of Northern New Hampshire and Vermont.* Rochester, Vt., 1909.

Davenport, James. *The Reverend Mr. James Davenport's Confession and Retractions.* Boston: S. Kneeland and T. Green, 1744.

Davis, Isaac. *What Love Jesus Christ Has for Sinners.* Somers, Conn., ca. 1820.

Delano, Stephen. *Miscellaneous Thoughts on the Doctrine of Limited Election and Reprobation.* Windsor, Vt.: Alden Spooner, 1799.

Dwight, Timothy. *The Dignity and Excellence of the Gospel, Illustrated in a Discourse.* New York: J. Seymour, 1812.

Edwards, Jonathan. *The Works of President Edwards.* Worcester, Mass.: Isaiah Thomas, 1808.

Elsworth, Samuel. *Solemn Predictions of Future Events . . . Together with a True Account of Appearances in the Heavens, Seen by the Inhabitants of New England.* Bennington, Vt.: Haswell and Russell, 1787.

Ferriss, Walter. *Five Sermons on the Following Subjects, Viz. I. The Love of God to His Creatures. II. The Christian's Evidence of His Having Passed from Death into Life. III. The Finite Nature of Things Unseen. IV. God's Love to Zion. V. The Lamb of God Which Taketh Away the Sin of the World. By the Late Rev. Walter Ferriss. To Which Is Subjoined a Festival Sermon by Brother Hosea Ballou, Delivered at Chester (Vt.) June 24, A. L. 5806.* Randolph, Vt.: Sereno Wright, 1807.

_____ "Walter Ferriss' Book," Universalist Historical Society, Andover-Harvard Theological Library, Cambridge, Mass.

Fessenden, Thomas. *A Theoretic Explanation of the Science of Sanctity.* Brattleboro, Vt.: W. Fessenden, 1804.

Freewill Baptist Connection. *The Centennial Record of the Freewill Baptists, 1780–1880, Revised Edition.* Dover, N.H.: Freewill Baptist Printing Establishment, 1881.

_____ "Elders Conference Records." New Hampshire Historical Society, Concord, N.H.

_____ *Minutes of the General Conference of the Freewill Baptist Connection.* Dover, N.H.: Freewill Baptist Printing Establishment, 1859.

Frothingham, Ebenezer. *The Articles of Faith and Practice, with the Covenant That Is Confessed by the Separate Churches of Christ in General in This Land.* Newport: J. Franklin, 1750.

General Association of Connecticut. *The Records of the General Association of ye Colony of Connecticut. Begun June 20th, 1738. Ending June 19th, 1799.* Hartford: Case, Lockwood, and Brainard, 1888.

Gill, John. *A Body of Doctrinal Divinity; Or, A System of Evangelical Truths, Deduced from the Sacred Scriptures.* London, 1769.

Gillies, John. *Memoirs of the Rev. George Whitefield.* Middletown, Conn.: Hunt and Noyes, 1829.

Green, Calvin. "Biographic Memoir of the Life and Experience of Calvin Green." Shaker Manuscripts, VI, B-28. Shaker Collection of the Western Reserve Historical Society, Cleveland, Ohio (also on microfilm: Microfilming Corporation of America, Glen Rock, N.J.).

———— "Biographic Memoir of the Life, Character, and Important Events in the Ministration of Mother Lucy Wright." Shaker Manuscripts, VI, B-27. Shaker Collection of the Western Reserve Historical Society, Cleveland, Ohio (also on microfilm: Microfilming Corporation of America).

———— "Biographical Account of the Life, Character, and Ministry of Father Joseph Meacham," ed. Theodore E. Johnson. *Shaker Quarterly*, 10 (Spring, Summer, and Fall, 1970), pp. 20–32, 51–68, 92–102.

———— "Biography of Elder Henry Clough." Shaker Manuscripts, VI, B-24-26. Shaker Collection of the Western Reserve Historical Society, Cleveland, Ohio (also on microfilm: Microfilming Corporation of America).

———— "A Treatise upon the Work of God in Different Ages." Library of the United Society of Shakers, Sabbathday Lake, Me.

———— and Seth Youngs Wells. *A Summary View of the Millennial Church, or United Society of Believers Commonly Called Shakers*, 2d ed. Albany: C. van Benthuysen, 1848.

Greenleaf, Jonathan. *Sketches of the Ecclesiastical History of the State of Maine*. Portsmouth, N.H.: Harrison Gray, 1821.

Grosvenor, Roxalana, comp. "Incidents Related by Jemima Blanchard of Her Experience and Intercourse with Mother Ann and Our First Parents." Berkshire Atheneum, Pittsfield, Mass.

Hall, Robert. *On the Terms of Communion: With a Particular View to the Case of Baptists and Paedobaptists*. Boston: Wells and Lilly, 1816.

Hart, Joseph. *Hymns, Composed on Various Subjects*. London, 1811.

"Harvard, Massachusetts, Shaker Church Record Book." American Antiquarian Society Library, Worcester, Mass.

Harvard, Massachusetts, Town Records. Massachusetts Archives, State House, Boston, Mass.

Haynes, Lemuel. *Universal Salvation, a Very Ancient Doctrine: With Some Account of the Life and Character of its Author. A Sermon Delivered at Rutland, West-Parish, in the Year 1805*. Brattleboro, Vt.: Wm. Fessenden, 1806.

Hopkins, Samuel. *The System of Doctrines, Contained in Divine Revelation, Explained and Defended. Showing their Consistence and Connection with Each Other. To Which is Added a Treatise on the Millennium*. Boston: Isaiah Thomas and Ebnezer T. Andrews, 1793.

Hudson, David. *History of Jemima Wilkinson*. Geneva, N.Y.: S. P. Hull, 1821.

Kendrick, Ariel. *A Brief Reply to a Pamphlet Lately Published by S. Delanoe . . . in Favour of Universalism*. Hanover, N.H.: Benjamin True, 1798.

Kneeland, Abner. *Five words Spoken with the Understanding, in Two Discourses Delivered at Langdon, New Hampshire, July 22d, 1805*. Walpole, N.H.: Charter and Hale, 1805.

———— *A Sermon Delivered Before the Northern Association of Universalists . . . upon the Two Covenants*. Walpole, N.H.: Nichols and Hale, 1807.

Langdon, New Hampshire, Town Records, New Hampshire State Library, Concord, N.H.

"Langdon, New Hampshire, Universalist Church Records." Universalist Historical Society, Andover-Harvard Theological Library, Cambridge, Mass.

Leland, John. *The Writings of John Leland*. New York: G. Wood, 1845.

Meacham, Joseph. "A Collection of the Writings of Father Joseph Meacham Concerning Church Order and Government; Evidently Intended for Waymarks, for All Who Are or Should Be Called in Spiritual or Temporal Care, in the Church," ed. Rufus Bishop. Shaker Manuscripts, VII, B-59. Shaker Collection of the Western Reserve Historical Society, Cleveland, Ohio (also on microfilm: Microfilming Corporation of America, Glen Rock, N.J.).

———— *A Concise Statement of the Principles of the Only True Church.* Bennington, Vt.: Haswell and Russell, 1790.

McClure, David and Elijah Parish, *Memoirs of the Rev. Eleazar Wheelock, D. D.* Newburyport, Mass., 1811.

McLoughlin, William G., ed. *Isaac Backus on Church, State, and Calvinism: Pamphlets, 1754–1789.* Cambridge, Mass.: Harvard University Press, 1968.

Minot, George Richards. *The History of the Insurrections, in Massachusetts, in the Year MDCCLXXXVI, and the Rebellion Consequent Thereon.* Worcester, Mass.: Isaiah Thomas, 1788.

Moore, Stitilia. "Hymnal." Library of the United Society of Shakers, Sabbathday, Lake, Me.

Murray, John. *Letters and Sketches of Sermons.* Boston: Joshua Belcher, 1813.

———— *Records of the Life of the Rev. John Murray, Written by Himself.* Boston: Munroe and Francis, 1816.

———— *Some Hints Relative to the Forming of a Christian Church — To the Right Understanding of the Scriptures . . . To the Rectifying of a Few Mistakes Respecting Some Doctrines Propagated under the Christian Name.* Boston: J. Bumstead, 1791.

New Durham, New Hampshire, Town Records, vol. 1, 1759–1803. Film, New Hampshire State Library, Concord, N.H.

The New Hampshire Gazette, 12 October 1770.

Norcott, John. *Baptism Discovered Plainly and Faithfully, Being a Clear and Distinct Investigation of the Important Doctrine of Believers' Baptism.* Bennington, Vt.: Haswell and Russell, 1785.

Oxford, Massachusetts, Universalist Society. "Minutes of the Oxford Universalist Society." Universalist Historical Society, Andover-Harvard Theological Library, Cambridge, Mass.

Peak, John. *The Memoirs of Elder John Peak.* Boston, 1832.

Peck, John. *A Poem, Containing a Descant on the Universal Plan.* Keene, N.H.: John Prentiss, 1801.

Perkins, Nathan. *A Narrative of a Tour through the State of Vermont, from April 27 to June 12, 1789.* Woodstock, Vt.: Elm Tree Press, 1920.

Pote, Dorothy. "Hymnal." Library of the United Society of Shakers, Sabbathday Lake, Me.

Pote, Elisha. "Letters to Tuftonboro." Library of the United Society of Shakers, Sabbathday Lake, Me.

Proud, Joseph. *Hymns and Spiritual Songs, for the Use of the Lord's New Church, Signified by the New Jerusalem in the Revelation,* 2d ed. London: R. Hindmarsh, 1791.

Randel, Benjamin, *A Sermon, Delivered at Farmington, New Hampshire, February 27th, 1803, at the Interment of Murmoth Fortune Herrick, Son of Hallibut and Sally Herrick.* Limerick, Me.: Star Office, 1827.

———— "A Summary of the Order and Disciplines of the Church of New Durham." William S. Babcock Papers, American Antiquarian Society, Worcster, Mass.

———— to Aaron Buzzell, 9 September 1793. American Baptist Historical Society, Rochester, New York.

———— to Aaron Buzzell, 19 November 1800. American Baptist Historical Society, Rochester, New York.

Rathbun, Reuben. *Reasons for Leaving the Shakers.* Pittsfield, Mass.: Chester Smith, 1800.

Rathbun, Valentine. *Some Brief Hints of a Religious Scheme, Taught and Propagated by a Number of Europeans, Living in a Place Called Nisquennia, in the State of New York.* Hartford, 1783.

"Record of Church in Loudon and Chichester, 1780–1782." New Hampshire Historical Society, Concord, N.H.

"Record of the First Monthly Meeting of Freewill Baptist Church of Christ in Edgecomb, Maine." American Baptist Historical Society, Rochester, N.Y.

"Record of the New Durham Monthly Meeting." New Durham, New Hampshire, Public Library.

"Record of the New Durham Quarterly Meeting." New Hampshire Historical Society, Concord, N.H.

"Record of the Parsonsfield Freewill Baptist Church." American Baptist Historical Society, Rochester, N.Y.

"Records of the General Convention of Universalists." Universalist Historical Society, Andover-Harvard Theological Library, Cambridge, Mass.

"Records of the Western Universalist Association." Universalist Historical Society, Andover-Harvard Theological Library, Cambridge, Mass.

Relly, James. *Union, Or a Treatise on the Consanguinity and Affinity between Christ and His Church.* Boston: Edes and Son, 1779.

Rich, Caleb. "A Narrative of Elder Caleb Rich." *Candid Examiner,* Montrose, Pa., 2 (April 30–June 18, 1827): 179–181, 185–189, 194–197, 201–202.

Ross, Robert. *A Plain Address to the Quakers, Moravians, Separatists, Rogerenes, and Other Enthusiasts; On Immediate Impulses and Revelations.* New Haven: Parker and Company, 1762.

Sands, David. *Journal of the Life and Gospel Labors of David Sands.* New York: Collins, 1848.

Sawyer, Otis, comp. "A Record of Appointments and Removals in Regular Succession of the Elders, Deacons, and Trustees of the Church and United Society of Believers in Gloucester and Portland, Cumberland County, State of Maine." Library of the United Society of Shakers, Sabbathday Lake, Me.

"Shaker Music," vol. 398. Shaker Manuscripts, Western Reserve Historical Society, Cleveland, Ohio.

Shepard, Samuel. *The Principle of Universal Salvation Examined and Tried.* Exeter, N.H., 1797.

Smith, Elias. *The Life, Conversion, Preaching, Travels, and Sufferings of Elias Smith.* Portsmouth, N.H.: Beck and Foster, 1816.

Stacy, Nathaniel. *Memoirs of the Life of Nathaniel Stacy.* Columbus, Pa.: Abner Vedder, 1850.

Stewart, I. D. *The History of the Freewill Baptists, for Half a Century.* Dover, N.H.: Freewill Baptist Printing Establishment, 1862.

Stiles, Ezra. *The Literary Diary of Ezra Stiles,* ed. Franklin Bowditch Dexter. New York: Charles Scribner's Sons, 1901.

———— *The United States Elevated to Glory and Honor.* New Haven: Thomas and Samuel Green, 1783.

Stillman, Samuel. *A Sermon Preached before the Honorable Council, and the Honorable House of Representatives of the State of Massachusetts-Bay, in New England, at Boston, May 26, 1779.* Boston: T. and J. Fleet and J. Gill, 1779.

Stinchfield, Ephraim. *Some Memoirs of the Life, Experience, and Labors of Elder Ephraim Stinchfield.* Portland, Me.: F. Douglas, 1819.

Stoddard, Solomon. *A Guide to Christ.* Boston: J. Allen, 1714.

Taylor, Amos. *A Narrative of the Strange Principles, Conduct and Character of the People Known by the Name of Shakers.* Worcester, Mass.: Isaiah Thomas, 1782.

Thompson, Zadok. *History of the State of Vermont.* Burlington, Vt., 1833.

Thornton, John Wingate, ed. *The Pulpit of the American Revolution: Or, the Political Sermons of the Period of 1776.* Boston: Gould and Lincoln, 1860.

Turner, Edward. "Notebook." Universalist Historical Society, Andover-Harvard Theological Library, Cambridge, Mass.

―――― "Records of the Proceedings of the Conference of Ministring Brethren Belonging to the Convention of the Four New England States and Others." Universalist Historical Society, Andover-Harvard Theological Library, Cambridge, Mass.

Walker, Jeremiah. *The Fourfold Foundation of Calvinism Examined and Shaken.* Richmond, Va.: John Dixon, 1791.

Warner, John. "Short Account of the Birth, Character and Administration of Father Eleazar and Mother Hannah." Shaker Manuscripts, VI, B-7, Western Reserve Historical Society, Cleveland, Ohio.

Warren Baptist Association. *Minutes of the Warren Association in Their Meeting at Attleborough, September 7th and 8th, 1779.* Boston?, 1779.

―――― *Minutes of the Warren Association in Their Meeting at Royalstown, September 12th and 13th, 1780.* N.p., 1780.

―――― *Minutes of the Warren Association in Their Meeting at South-Brimfield, the 11th and 12th of September, 1781.* Providence: John Carter, 1781.

―――― *Minutes of the Warren Association, Convened at Providence, the 10th of September, 1782.* Providence: John Carter, 1782.

―――― *Sentiments and Plan of the Warren Association.* Germantown, Pa.: C. Sower, 1769.

Watts, Isaac. *Hymns and Spiritual Songs, 1707–1748,* ed. Selma L. Bishop. London: Faith Press, 1962.

Wells, Seth Youngs, comp. *Millennial Praises, Containing a Collection of Gospel Hymns, in Four Parts; Adapted to the Day of Christ's Second Appearing, Composed for the Use of His People.* Hancock, Mass.: Josiah Talcott, 1813.

―――― , comp. "Unpublisht Testimonies of Mother's First-Born Children in America ." Shaker Manuscripts, VI, B-42 and 43. Shaker Collection of the Western Reserve Historical Society, Cleveland, Ohio (also on microfilm: Microfilming Corporation of America, Glen Rock, N.J.).

Wesley, John. *A Collection of Hymns for the Use of the People Called Methodists. With a Supplement.* London: John Mason, 1780.

Whitefield, George. *Eighteen Sermons Preached by the Late Rev. George Whitefield . . . Taken Verbatim in Short-Hand, and Faithfully Transcribed by Joseph Gurney. Revised by Andrew Gifford, D.D.* Newburyport, Mass.: Edmund M. Blunt, 1797.

―――― *George Whitefield's Journals, 1737–1741,* ed. William V. Davis. Gainesville: Scholars' Facsimiles and Reprints, 1969.

Whittaker, James. *The Shaker Shaken; Or, God's Warning to Josiah Talcott, as Denounced in a Letter from James Whittaker, One of the United Society of Believers in Christ's Second Appearing.* New Haven: Bibliographical Press, 1938.

Williams, Samuel. *The Natural and Civil History of New Hampshire.* Walpole, N.H.: Thomas and Carlisle, 1794.

Winchester, Elhanan. *A Course of Lectures on the Prophecies That Remain to Be Fulfilled.* Walpole, N.H.: Thomas and Thomas, 1800.

―――― *The Universal Restoration, Exhibited in Four Dialogues between a Minister and His Friend; Comprehending the Substance of Several Real Conversations Which the Author Had with Various Persons, both in America and Europe, on That Interesting Subject, Chiefly Designed Fully to State and Fairly to Answer the Most Common Objections That Are Brought Against It from the Scriptures.* Philadelphia: Th. Dobson, 1792.

Woodstock Baptist Association. *Minutes of the Woodstock Baptist Association.* Woodstock, Vt., 1810.

Worcester, Leonard. *The Doctrine of Atonement, and Others Connected with It, Stated and Vindicated.* Peacham, Vt.: Samuel Goss, 1802.

Wright, Stephen. *History of the Shaftesbury Baptist Association.* Troy, N.Y.: A. G. Johnson, 1853.

Youngs, Benjamin Seth. "Diary, 1794–1804." Emma B. King Memorial Library, Old Chatham, N.Y.

_____ "Journey to the East, September 14th, 1802–March 10, 1803." Emma B. King Memorial Library, Old Chatham, N.Y.

_____ "Journey to the North, June 30th–December 6th, 1802." Emma B. King Memorial Library, Old Chatham, N.Y.

_____ and Calvin Green. *The Testimony of Christ's Second Appearing,* 2d ed., corrected and improved. Albany: E. and E. Hosford, 1810.

SECONDARY SOURCES

Ahlstrom, Sydney E. *A Religious History of the American People.* New Haven: Yale University Press, 1972.

Allen, John Henry and Richard Eddy. *A History of the Unitarians and the Universalists in the United States.* New York: Christian Literature Co., 1894.

Andrews, Edward Deming. *The Gift to Be Simple: Songs, Dances and Rituals of the American Shakers.* New York: J. J. Augustin, 1940.

_____ *The People Called Shakers,* 2d ed. New York: Dover, 1963.

Armstrong, Anthony. *The Church of England, the Methodists, and Society, 1700–1850.* Totowa, N.J.: Rowman and Littlefield, 1974.

Armstrong, Maurice W. *The Great Awakening in Nova Scotia, 1776–1809.* Hartford, Conn.: American Society of Church History, 1948.

Bailyn, Bernard. *The Ideological Origins of the American Revolution.* Cambridge, Mass.: Harvard University Press, 1967.

Balch, W. S. "Caleb Rich." *Universalist Quarterly and General Review,* n.s. 9 (1872): 58–78.

Baldwin, Alice Mary. *The New England Clergy and the American Revolution.* Durham, N.C.: Duke University Press, 1928.

Ballou, Adin. *The Ballous in America.* Providence, 1888.

Banks, Ronald F. *Maine Becomes a State.* Middletown, Conn.: Wesleyan University Press, 1970.

Bassett, William. *History of the Town of Richmond, Cheshire County, New Hampshire, from Its First Settlement to 1882.* Boston: C. W. Watkins and Co., 1884.

Baxter, Norman Allen. *History of the Freewill Baptists.* Rochester, N.Y.: American Baptist Historical Society, 1957.

Benedict, David. *A General History of the Baptist Denomination in America.* Boston: Lincoln and Edmands, 1813. 2nd ed., New York: Lewis Colby and Co., 1848.

Beuchner, Alan. "Yankee Singing Schools and the Golden Age of Choral Music in New England, 1760–1800." Ph.D. dissertation, Harvard University, 1960.

Bowen, Clarence W. *The History of Woodstock, Connecticut.* Norwood, Mass.: Plimpton Press, 1926.

Bradley, Asa M. "Sketches of New Hampshire Churches." Universalist Historical Society, Andover-Harvard Theological Library, Cambridge, Mass.

_____ "Sketches of Vermont Churches." Universalist Historical Society, Andover-Harvard Theological Library, Cambridge, Mass.

_____ "Universalism in New Hampshire." Universalist Historical Society, Andover-Harvard Theological Library, Cambridge, Mass.

Brebner, John Bartlet. *The Neutral Yankees of Nova Scotia.* New York: Columbia University Press, 1937.

Brinton, Howard. *Meetinghouse and Farmhouse.* Pendle Hill, Pa.: Pendle Hill Publications, 1971.

Brown, Robert E. *Middle Class Democracy and the Revolution in Massachusetts, 1691–1780.* Ithaca: Cornell University Press, 1955.

Buck, Levisa. *Memoir of Thomas Barnes.* Portland, Me.: S. H. Colesworthy, 1856.

Bumsted, J. M. *Henry Alline, 1748-1784.* Toronto: University of Toronto Press, 1971.

Burgess, Gideon A. and John T. Ward. *Free Baptist Cyclopedia, Historical and Biographical.* N.p.: Free Baptist Cyclopedia Co., 1889.

Burrage, Henry S. *A History of the Baptists in New England.* Philadelphia: American Baptist Publication Board, 1894.

Bushman, Richard L. *From Puritan to Yankee: Character and the Social Order in Connecticut, 1690-1765.* Cambridge, Mass.: Harvard University Press, 1967.

Campion, Nardi Reeder. *Ann the Word: The Life of Mother Ann Lee, Founder of the Shakers.* Boston: Little, Brown, 1976.

Canfield, Mary Grace. "Universalism in Vermont and the Connecticut Valley." Universalist Historical Society, Andover-Harvard Theological Library, Cambridge, Mass.

Carter, N. F. *The Native Ministry of New Hampshire.* Concord, N.H.: Rumford Printing Co., 1906.

Cassara, Ernest. "Hosea Ballou and the Rise of American Religious Liberalism." *Universalist Leader,* 140 (April 1958): 83-95.

———. *Hosea Ballou: The Challenge to Orthodoxy.* Boston: Beacon Press, 1961.

———. *Universalism in America: A Documentary History.* Boston: Beacon Press, 1971.

Chase, Daryl. "The Early Shakers: An Experiment in Religious Communism." Ph.D. dissertation, University of Chicago, 1936.

Chessman, Daniel. *Memoir of Thomas Baldwin, D. D.* Boston: True and Green, 1826.

Chestnut, Peter I. "Universalism in America, 1770-1803." Ph.D. dissertation, Duke University, 1974.

Child, Hamilton. *Gazetteer of Grafton County, N.H., 1709-1886.* Syracuse, 1886.

Clark, Joseph S. *A Historical Sketch of the Congregational Churches in Massachusetts from 1620 to 1858.* Boston: Congregational Board of Publication, 1858.

Cole, Donald B. *Jacksonian Democracy in New Hampshire, 1800—1851.* Cambridge, Mass.: Harvard University Press, 1970.

Comstock, John M. *The Congregational Churches of Vermont and Their Ministry, 1762-1942,* rev. ed. St. Johnsbury, Vt.: Cowles Press, 1942.

Crocker, Henry. *History of the Baptists in Vermont.* Bellows Falls, Vt.: P. H. Gobie, 1913.

Daniell, Jere R. *Experiment in Republicanism: New Hampshire Politics and the American Revolution, 1741-1794.* Cambridge, Mass.: Harvard University Press, 1970.

Davidson, Philip. *Propaganda and the American Revolution, 1763-1783.* Chapel Hill: University of North Carolina Press, 1941.

Davies, Horton. *Worship and Theology in England from Watts to Maurice, 1690-1850.* Princeton: Princeton University Press, 1961.

Davis, Arthur Paul. *Isaac Watts, Life and Works.* New York: Dryden Press, 1943.

Desroche, Henri. *The American Shakers from Neo-christianity to Presocialism,* trans. and ed. John K. Savacool. Amherst, Mass.: University of Massachusetts Press, 1971.

Dexter, Franklin Bowditch. *Biographical Sketches of the Graduates of Yale College with Annals of the College History.* New York: H. Holt and Company, 1885-1912.

Downey, James. *The Eighteenth Century Pulpit.* Oxford: Clarendon Press, 1970.

Durnbaugh, Donald F. *The Believers' Church.* New York: Macmillan, 1968.

Eddy, Richard D. *Universalism in America: A History.* Boston: Universalist Publishing House, 1886-1894.

Emery, Edwin. *The History of Sanford, Maine.* Fall River, Mass.: Salem Press Co., 1901.

Escott, Harry. *Isaac Watts, Hymnographer: A Study of the Beginnings, Development, and Philosophy of the English Hymn.* London: Independent Press, Ltd., 1962.

Evans, Charles. *American Bibliography: A Chronological Dictionary of all Books, Pamphlets, and Periodical Publications Printed in the United States of America From the Genesis of Printing in 1639 Down To and Including the Year 1820.* New York: Peter Smith, 1941.

Foster, Frank Hugh. *A Genetic History of the New England Theology.* Chicago: University of Chicago Press, 1907.

Frisbee, James. *The History of Middletown, Vermont.* Rutland, Vt.: 1867.

Garret, Leo, ed. *The Concept of the Believers' Church.* Scottdale, Pa.: Herald Press, 1969.

Gaustad, Edwin Scott. *The Great Awakening in New England.* New York: Harper and Row, 1957.

Goen, Clarence C. *Revivalism and Separatism in New England, 1740-1800.* New Haven: Yale University Press, 1962.

Guild, Reuben Aldridge. *Chaplain Smith and the Baptists: Or Life, Journals, Letters and Addresses of the Rev. Hezekiah Smith, D. D., of Haverhill, Massachusetts, 1737-1805.* Philadelphia: American Baptist Publication Society, 1885.

Haroutunian, Joseph. *Piety Versus Moralism: The Passing of the New England Theology.* New York: H. Holt, 1932.

Hatch, Nathan O. *The Sacred Cause of Liberty: Republican Thought and the Millennium in Revolutionary New England.* New Haven: Yale University Press, 1977.

Hazen, Henry A. *The Congregational and Presbyterian Ministry and Churches of New Hampshire.* Boston: Alfred Mudge, 1875.

Heimert, Alan. *Religion and the American Mind, from the Great Awakening to the Revolution.* Cambridge, Mass.: Harvard University Press, 1966.

Henretta, James. *The Evolution of American Society, 1750-1815: An Interdisciplinary Analysis.* Lexington, Mass.: D.C. Heath, 1973.

———. "Families and Farms: Mentalité in Pre-Industrial America." *William and Mary Quarterly,* 3rd ser. 35 (January 1978): 3-38.

Henry, Stuart. *George Whitefield, Wayfaring Witness.* New York: Abingdon, 1957.

Hofstadter, Richard. *America at 1750: A Social Portrait.* New York: Knopf, 1971.

Hurlin, William O.C. Sargent, and W.W. Wakeman. *The Baptists of New Hampshire.* Manchester, N.H.: John B. Clarke, 1902.

Jackson, George Pullen. *Downeast Spirituals and Others.* New York: J.J. Augustin, 1943.

———. ed. *Spiritual Folk-Songs of Early America.* New York: J.J. Augustin, 1937.

———. *White Spirituals in the Southern Uplands.* Chapel Hill: University of North Carolina Press, 1933.

Jones, Matthew Bushnell. *Vermont in the Making.* Cambridge, Mass.: Harvard University Press, 1939.

Jones, Rufus M. *The Faith and Practice of the Quakers.* London: Methuen, 1927.

———. *Quakers in the American Colonies.* London: Macmillan, 1911.

Julian, John. *A Dictionary of Hymnology.* New York: Charles Scribner's Sons, 1892.

Kingsbury, Frank B. *Historical and Genealogical Register of the Town of Langdon, Sullivan County, New Hampshire.* White River Jct., Vt.: Right Printing Co., 1932.

Koch, G. Adolf. *Republican Religion: The American Revolution and the Cult of Reason.* York: Crowell, 1933.

Leach, Douglas E. *The Northern Colonial Frontier, 1607–1763.* New York: Holt, Rinehart and Winston, 1966.
Lee, John Parker. *Uncommon Vermont.* Rutland, Vt.: Vermont Historical Society, 1926.
Lovejoy, Mary E. W. *History of Royalton, Vermont.* Burlington, Vt.: Free Press Printing Co., 1911.
Lowens, Irving. *Music and Musicians in Early America.* New York: W. W. Norton, 1964.
Lumpkin, Timothy, ed. *Baptist Confessions of Faith.* Chicago: Judson Press, 1959.
Lyford, James Otis. *History of the Town of Canterbury, New Hampshire.* Concord, N.H.: Rumford Press, 1912.
Main, Jackson Turner. *The Social Structure of Revolutionary America.* Princeton: Princeton University Press, 1965.
McCorison, Marcus Allen. *Vermont Imprints, 1778–1820: A Checklist of Books, Pamphlets, and Broadsides.* Worcester, Mass.: American Antiquarian Society, 1963.
McLellan, Hugh D. *History of Gorham, Maine.* Portland, Me.: Smith and Sale, 1903.
McLoughlin, William G. *New England Dissent, 1630–1833.* Cambridge, Mass.: Harvard University Press, 1971.
Melcher, Marguerite F. *The Shaker Adventure.* Princeton: Princeton University Press, 1941.
Metcalf, Frank. *American Psalmody: Or Titles of Books, Containing Tunes Printed in America from 1721 to 1820.* New York: Charles F. Heartman, 1917.
Miller, Perry. *Errand into the Wilderness.* Cambridge, Mass.: Harvard University Press, 1956.
Morgan, Edmund S. *Visible Saints: The History of a Puritan Idea.* New York: New York University Press, 1963.
Newman, Albert Henry. *A History of the Baptist Churches in the United States.* New York: Christian Literature Co., 1894.
Niebuhr, H. Richard. *The Social Sources of Denominationalism.* New York: Holt, 1929.
Patterson, Daniel W. *The Shaker Spiritual.* Princeton: Princeton University Press, 1979.
Pettit, Norman. *The Heart Prepared: Grace and Conversion in Puritan Spiritual Life.* New Haven: Yale University Press, 1966.
Pike, Kermit J. *A Guide to Shaker Manuscripts in the Library of the Western Reserve Historical Society.* Cleveland: Western Reserve Historical Society, 1974.
Quinby, Hosea. "History of the Freewill Baptists." *Freewill Baptist Quarterly,* 2 (September 1840): 185–210.
Rawlyk, George A. *Nova Scotia's Massachusetts.* Montreal: McGill-Queens University Press, 1973.
Richmond, Mary. *Shaker Literature: A Bibliography.* Hancock, Mass.: Shaker Community, Inc., 1977.
Robinson, Elmo Arnold. *American Universalism: Its Origins, Organization, and Heritage.* New York: Exposition Press, 1970.
Sanborn, Jeremy Leavitt. *The History of the Congregational Church in Chichester, New Hampshire, 1727–1894.* Providence: Remington Printing Co., 1905.
Schaff, Philip, comp. *The Creeds of Christendom.* New York, 1818.
Sears, Clara Endicott. *Gleanings from Old Shaker Journals.* Boston: Houghton Mifflin, 1916.
Shea, Daniel. *Spiritual Autobiography in America.* Princeton: Princeton University Press, 1968.
Shy, John. *A People Numerous and Armed: Reflections on the Military Struggle for American Independence.* New York: Oxford University Press, 1976.
Smith, James W. and Leland Jamison, A. eds. *The Shaping of American Religion.* Princeton: Princeton University Press, 1961.

Sosin, Jack M. *The Northern Frontier, 1763–1783.* New York: Holt, Rinehart and Winston, 1967.

Sprague, William Buell. *Annals of the American Pulpit.* New York: R. Carter and Brothers, 1857–1869.

Starr, Edward C. *A Baptist Bibliography, Being a Register of Printed Material By and About Baptists, Including Works Written Against the Baptists.* Philadelphia: Judson Press, 1947.

Stephen, Leslie and Sidney Lee, eds. *The Dictionary of National Biography.* London: Oxford University Press, 1921–1922.

Stewart, Gordon and George Rawlyk. *A People Highly Favoured of God.* Hamden, Conn.: Shoe String Press, 1972.

Stone, Edwin Martin. *Biography of Elhanan Winchester.* Boston: H. B. Brewster, 1836.

Sweet, William Warren. *Religion in the Development of American Culture, 1765–1840.* New York: Charles Scribner's Sons, 1952.

Taylor, Robert J. *Western Massachusetts in the Revolution.* Providence: Brown University Press, 1954.

Thrift, Minton. *Memoir of the Rev. Jesse Lee with Extracts from His Journals.* New York: N. Bangs and T. Mason, 1823.

Titus, Anson. "Reminiscences of Early American Universalism. Second Paper. Universalism in Maine Prior to 1820." *Universalist Quarterly and General Review,* n.s. 22 (October 1885): 430-453.

Tucker, W. H. *History of Hartford, Vermont.* Burlington, Vt.: Free Press Printing Co., 1889.

United States Bureau of the Census. *A Century of Population Growth from the First Census of the United States to the Twelfth, 1790–1900.* Washington, D.C.: U.S. Government Printing Office, 1909.

Upton, Richard F. *Revolutionary New Hampshire.* Hanover, N.H.: Dartmouth College Publications, 1936.

Vermont Historical Society. *The Upper Connecticut: Volume One. Narratives of Its Settlement and Its Part in the American Revolution.* Montpelier: Vermont Historical Society, 1943.

Walker, Williston. *The Creeds and Platforms of Congregationalism.* New York: Charles Scribner's Sons, 1893.

———— *A History of the Congregational Churches in the United States.* New York: Christian Literature Co., 1894.

Watkins, Owen C. *The Puritan Experience: Studies in Spiritual Autobiography.* New York: Schocken, 1972.

White, Anna and Leila Taylor. *Shakerism: Its Meaning and Message.* Columbus, Ohio: F. J. Heer, 1905.

White, Eugene E. *Puritan Rhetoric: The Issue of Emotion in Religion.* Carbondale, Ill.: University of Southern Illinois Press, 1972.

Whittemore, Thomas. *Life of Hosea Ballou.* Boston: James M. Usher, 1854–1856.

Wiley, Frederick. *The Life and Influence of the Rev. Benjamin Randel, Founder of the Free Baptist Denomination.* Philadelphia: American Baptist Publication Society, 1915.

Williams, George Huntston. *Wilderness and Paradise in Christian Thought.* New York: Harper, 1962.

———— *American Universalism: A Bicentennial Essay.* Medford, Mass.: Universalist Historical Society, 1971.

Wilson, H. Fisher. *The Hill Country of Northern New England: Social and Economic History, 1790–1930.* New York: Columbia University Press, 1936.

Winslow, Ola Elizabeth. *Jonathan Edwards, 1703–1758: A Biography.* New York: Macmillan, 1940.

Wisbey, Harold. *Frontier Prophetess: The Life of Jemima Wilkinson.* Ithaca: Cornell

University Press, 1963.

Wood, Gordon S. *The Creation of the American Republic, 1776–1787.* Chapel Hill, N.C.: University of North Carolina Press, 1969.

Wright, Conrad. *The Beginnings of Unitarianism in America.* Boston: Starr King Press, 1955.

Zuckerman, Michael. *Peaceable Kingdoms: New England Towns in the Eighteenth Century.* New York: Knopf, 1970.

Index